# The Way We Were:
# Remembering Durham

*MENA WEBB*

HISTORIC PRESERVATION SOCIETY OF DURHAM ❋ DURHAM, NORTH CAROLINA

Portions of this book were previously
published as articles in *The Durham Sun* and
*The Durham Morning Herald*, Durham, NC
from May 1989 through May 1992


Published by

Historic Preservation Society of Durham

P. O. Box 25411

Durham, NC 27702-5411

Copyright © 2003 by Mena Webb

Managing Editor: Linda Scovill Knechtel, Durham, NC

Design and composition by Debra Oakley, Chapel Hill, NC

Printed in the United States of America by
Laser Image Corporate Printing, Durham, NC 27713

ISBN 0-9615577-3-7 (paperback ; alk. paper)


5 4 3 2 1

*For Carol and Marion*
*with my love*

# Contents

## Movers & Shakers

# *Acknowledgments*

I am deeply indebted to the Mary Duke Biddle Foundation for its willingness to fund this book; to the Historic Preservation Society of Durham for agreeing to sponsor it; and to Linda Scovill Knechtel, publisher of *Fifty Plus Lifestyle* magazine, for undertaking the gargantuan task of sorting through and editing my many revisions and additions to the original manuscript. In a process that neither of us thought would be as long or as demanding as it became, this confident, resourceful, classy lady helped me keep my sanity and became a treasured friend.

I would also like to thank Elizabeth Oliver, who did much of the typing; Debra Oakley, who designed the book; and Paula Siwek, who took the current photograph for the back cover.

Others who helped immeasurably by agreeing to interviews, supplying pictures, and giving me valuable information in interviews, over the phone or in letters are: Mary S. Andersen, the late Peggy Altvater, R. L. Baldwin, Jr., Louise Beasley, the late Jessie Blount, Eleanor S. Bolich, Yetta S. Brandt, Anita Caldwell, the late Mary Toms Cameron, E. M. Cameron, Jr., Austin Carr, Watts Carr, Jr., Louis Carver, Marian Chandler, Howard Clement, W. E. Cranford, Jr., Virginia P. Daughton, Margaret Davis, the late Kitty B. Griggs, the late B. W. Harris, Larry Harris, M. D. Harris, the late Watts Hill, Jr., the late Lucy Holland, Meriwether W. Hudson, Rosalie H. Kelley, Tina Land, W. B. Mack, Elizabeth D. Mallard, Ila Mangum, Steve Massengill, Gail S.

McLean, Dr. Linda McCurdy, Harold Moore, John Moorhead, Ned Newsom, Marion O'Malley, Martha Pate, Carol Pullen, the late George Pyne, Lynn Richardson, Mrs. Dan Roach, E. T. Rollins, Mrs. Richard Saunders, the late Maye D. Singletary, Mary W. Smith, Elna Spaulding, Sara Stauber, Allston Stubbs, Mildred Teer, Meriwether Walker, Barrie A. Wallace, John White, the late Alfred Williams, the late Julia M. Wily, and Martha Uzzle. My sincere thanks go to all of them, and to any I may have forgotten, I send my sincere apologies.

Finally, to my daughters, Carol Pullen and Marion O'Malley, and my grandchildren, Tom Krueger, Kirsten Krueger and Corey O'Malley, I send my heartfelt thanks for the support and encouragement they gave me that made this book possible.

M. F. W.

# *Preface*

This book is a collection of stories about Durham and some of the people who made it the way it was for me during the 20TH Century, when "more social change occurred and more technological advances were made than at any other time in human history," according to a recent news report.

For all but the first fifteen years of that fabulous time I have been living my long and mostly happy life here and writing about it, off and on, since 1960; and this compilation of previously published historical columns, feature stories and excerpts from a personal journal is one of the results of a life-long preoccupation with my hometown and its history.

The bi-monthly columns appeared first in *The Durham Sun* from May 22, 1989 through December 31, 1990; and in *The Durham Morning Herald* from March 31, 1991 through May 31, 1992. The features were assignments for special editions of both newspapers, and the journal pieces are part of an autobiographical work-in-progress that I fully intend to finish one of these days, if my remaining days are long enough.

MENA WEBB
Durham, N.C.
April 30, 2003

# Beginnings

*There were giants in the
earth in those days . . .
men of renown.*

FROM GENESIS 6:4
KING JAMES VERSION 1611

*. . . it would therefore be proper if someone who has the true history
of the community at heart would concern himself to gather up
all the facts and interesting stories of the bygone days . . .*

JOHN SPENCER BASSETT

# Peeler's Place, best-known shady house

Back in 1906, Trinity College history professor John Spencer Bassett wrote an article for *The Archive*, Trinity's student publication, in which he observed that those who could still remember Durham's beginnings would soon "pass out of the world," and that "it would therefore be proper if someone who has the true history of the community at heart would concern himself to gather up all the facts and interesting stories of the bygone days and put them in printed accessible form for the use and delectation of posterity."

To illustrate his point, and perhaps to generate interest in his proposal, Bassett recounted a story he had heard from an old-timer about some "shiftless characters" who, around 1830, established a settlement called Pinhook on a tract of land that today is known as Erwin Square. Spurned by other pioneers

because of its poor soil, the place did have a spring of fine, clear water that had been attracting travelers for some years, and that attribute appealed to a man named Ben Peeler, who knew from experience that making whiskey did not require soil of any kind, good or bad, but did require water.

So Peeler and his family, consisting of "two girls, who were very wild, and also two sons whose names were Pet Tich Eye and Red Wine," built a house near the spring and advertised it by word of mouth as an inn. Later they built a grog shop, and in due time their reputation began to spread across the state. Inevitably, students from the University of North Carolina gravitated to Pinhook whenever they decided to "go off on a lark." Craving excitement, they found it at Peeler's place, where the innkeeper and his sons provided the excitement of drinking, gambling and

3

fighting, and the two daughters enhanced their father's reputation as the owner of "the best known of the shady houses."

According to Professor Bassett, another Pinhook entrepreneur (who remains nameless) made enough money selling cold watermelons to Peeler's hungover patrons to start a more reputable business in Durham that eventually made him quite rich. Bassett further stated that Ben Peeler's so-called inn could be especially dangerous for travelers who arrived on horseback, as the proprietor had few scruples against committing murder in order to acquire a horse that he later could take to Raleigh and sell.

But the infamous Pinhook was destined for respectability and achieved that status when tobacco manufacturer Benjamin Newton Duke established a textile mill there. After the Erwin Cotton Mill was built, the surrounding territory was called West Durham, and the name Pinhook was relegated to the history books.

As for John Spencer Bassett, he unwittingly assured himself of a place in Durham's history in 1903, when he wrote and published in the *South Atlantic Quarterly* an article entitled, "Stirring Up the Fires of Racial Antipathy." He had intended to explore, in scholarly fashion, the race problem in the South, but when he wrote that with the exception of General Robert E. Lee, Booker T. Washington was the greatest man who had been born in the South in 100 years, he stirred up not merely a few fires, but a holocaust.

Josephus Daniels, editor of *The Raleigh News and Observer*, was the first to tear into Bassett, but other newspapermen across the state were quick to follow,

and soon many were demanding that he be fired from the faculty at Trinity College. Although he was a native of Tarboro, a son and grandson of slave owners, and a Trinity alumnus, he was also a liberal thinker. Bassett deplored the fact that an amendment to the North Carolina constitution had disenfranchised blacks in 1900; and he viewed with obvious distaste and some alarm those reactionaries who dominated the Southern press, the Southern pulpit and Southern politics.

The furor his article caused no doubt would have resulted in Bassett's dismissal by the trustees of Trinity College had it not been for Walter Hines Page, another alumnus, and Benjamin N. Duke, one of the school's chief benefactors. Page convinced Duke and John C. Kilgo, the college president, that the academic freedom that was vital to any institution of higher learning was being threatened at Trinity, and when Kilgo confronted the trustees with that premise they had the good sense to agree.

The controversy over academic freedom brought recognition to Trinity College and enhanced Bassett's reputation as a scholar; and in 1906, the same year he told readers of *The Archive* about the Peelers of Pinhook, he was invited to join the faculty at Smith College. Offered a higher salary, a lighter teaching load, and more time for research, he accepted immediately, apparently with no regrets at leaving the South, and continued to teach and write history successfully until his death in 1928.

In the spring of 1989, sixty-one years after he died, I came across Bassett's story about the Peelers of Pinhook at the Perkins Library on Duke University's West Campus, and reading it made me think of present-day West Durham, of the magnificent First Union Bank building that soars above its Erwin Square, of Ninth Street with its trendy shops and expensive gourmet restaurants, and I couldn't help but wonder if the ghosts of Ben Peeler and his wild children ever come back to haunt it, to grieve over having been born too soon, before all the good things began to happen in this place where, so long ago, they lived their brief and violent lives.

Some of those good things and the men and women who made them happen in Durham's "bygone days" is what this book is about.

# Bartlett Durham

$\mathcal{I}$n 1848, when Dr. Bartlett Leonidas Durham paid less than $100 for 100 acres of land in a rather unpromising section of Orange county, he undoubtedly hoped to attract patients from the adjoining settlements of Pinhook and Prattsburg, but he probably had no idea of establishing a town.

Nevertheless Durham, then twenty-four-years-old, became the founding father of the present-day city of Durham when he gave a four-acre strip of that land to the North Carolina Railroad for use as a right-of-way, and the railroad responded by naming its newly acquired whistle stop Durham's Station, which by popular usage became Durham's and, eventually, just Durham.

Officials of the railroad had first approached William Pratt, who lived less than a mile east of the station on what is now known as Ramseur Street; but Pratt, who owned a large general store, refused their request because he was afraid noisy trains would frighten his customer's horses and reduce his trade.

The doctor, however, had nothing to lose by handing over four of his 100 acres to the railroad, and so for a donation worth approximately $3.80, he saw the tracks laid and his name painted on the station house. He also became the company's agent and enjoyed the clamorous arrivals and departures of the amazing Iron Horse until his premature death from pneumonia in 1858.

Tall, heavy-set and weighing over 200 pounds, Bart Durham was a free-wheeling bachelor who loved to drink and sing with his cronies and enjoyed the company of women, but his deepest feelings were for his patients. According to recent history, whenever he lost one of them to death, he would invariably "disappear for a week or two and drown his sorrow in drink."

The lifestyle of the founder of Durham undoubtedly shortened his lifespan, but his brief stay on Planet Earth was colorful, at least. He also attained posthumous fame, of a sort, by having two funerals. Although they were seventy-six years apart, one mourner managed to attend both services.

In 1858, Durham was buried in an unmarked grave at the Snipes burying ground in Chatham

County, about eight miles from Chapel Hill. In December 1933, after a considerable search of the old graveyard, he was exhumed at the request of a group of historians and historically-minded Durham citizens who felt that his final resting place should be in the city that bears his name.

Mebane Edwards, the son of a slave belonging to Bart Durham's family, had been a wide-eyed boy of nine at the Chatham County rites, and at the age of eighty-four he was again a spectator at the more elaborate service on January 1, 1934 in Maplewood Cemetery. There Durham lies beneath a granite monument that states: "The merit belongs to the beginner, should his successors do even better."

Bartlett Durham had many successors who "did better" than he in a monetary sense, among them W. T. Blackwell, Julian S. Carr, Washington Duke and George W. Watts, to name a few. But both the city of Durham and Durham County exist today because of the railroad station, and the station existed— before urban renewal tore it down—because of the doctor's gift of $3.80 worth of land.

# THREE

# Riches to Rags—
# Owner of 'Bull' trademark lost his fortune

William Thomas "Colonel Buck" Blackwell was born on a farm in Person County, North Carolina, became a school teacher, ran a country store, peddled tobacco to soldiers during the Civil War, and afterwards operated a jobbing house in Kinston, North Carolina.

Hardly the stuff of which fame is made.

But in 1868, at the age of twenty-nine, when he became associated with tobacco manufacturer John Ruffin Green, whose product received much favorable notoriety after the war ended, Buck Blackwell's luck changed.

While William Tecumseh Sherman and Joseph E. Johnston sipped whiskey and negotiated the South's surrender at a farmhouse in Orange County, their troops camped out in nearby Durham, which had been classified neutral ground. Jubilant over the war's ending, many celebrated in the bar rooms and brothels that had given the little whistle stop an unsavory reputation; others, less sophisticated or less solvent, pleasured themselves by foraging, and one of their first victims was John Ruffin Green.

Green's small factory near the train station was locked against intruders, but locks proved no difficulty for men who had become adept at petty thievery, and in a matter of minutes they had the door open and were helping themselves to tobacco already shredded and packed for shipping. Finding it far superior to the tongue-biting rations of their respective armies, these soldiers, along with other "bummers" who straggled into Durham during the next few days, made off with every sack of Green's tobacco.

Back home after the surrender, they kept remembering the mild, sweet taste of that stolen leaf, and soon orders for "that good Durham tobacco" began to flood Durham's post office, and John Green, who had thought himself ruined, realized that what he had regarded as a tragedy was giving him a great deal of excellent advertising at absolutely no cost.

Green also realized that he would need more help

William Thomas Blackwell. ca. 1880.

W. T. Blackwell. Formal portrait. ca. 1920.

in order to meet the growing demand for his popular brand, and thus began his business relationship with Buck Blackwell and James R. Day, another Person County native who shared Blackwell's expertise in judging, buying and selling tobacco. Failing health prompted him to make partners of the two younger men, who shouldered most of the work that went into manufacturing Durham Smoking Tobacco; and when Green died of tuberculosis in 1869,

Blackwell bought the factory. More importantly, he also bought Green's trademark, the side view of a black short-horn bull.

It was destined to become one of the most famous trademarks in advertising history, and Buck Blackwell retained it exclusively for twenty-four years.

Incorporating under the name of W. T. Blackwell and Company, he added the word "Genuine" to Green's brand name, and in 1870 he took in a third partner, Julian Shakespeare Carr, of Chapel Hill, whose high-powered advertising techniques made what came to be known as "Bull Durham Tobacco" world famous.

Inevitably, the growing popularity of the brand inspired imitation in both Virginia and North Carolina, and widespread piracy of his trademark by unscrupulous rivals plunged Blackwell into fifteen years of expensive legal battles that were not completely resolved until four years after he retired from the business in 1883. But the company, which retained his name even after he left it, finally won the exclusive right to the Durham Bull, whose likeness circled the globe and, for a time, was seen on one of Egypt's pyramids.

Part of Blackwell's success can be attributed to his major role in breaking Virginia's monopoly of the tobacco markets. Fed up with increasingly uncomfortable trips by wagon to Danville, Lynchburg, Petersburg and Richmond, he and Henry A. Reams, another friend from Person County, built Durham's first tobacco warehouse next to Blackwell's factory and opened it for business on May 18, 1871.

Both agreed that there was no valid reason why Virginia should continue to hog all the markets in the Bright Belt, and they also believed North Carolina farmers felt the same way, but they were not prepared for the enthusiastic response their venture received.

That first sale in Durham was conducted by Edward James Parrish, whose jovial personality and talent for chanting won him an immediate following among both farmers and buyers.

By the end of the year, Parrish had "cried sales" of over 700,000 pounds of tobacco for Blackwell and Reams and when that figure jumped to two million pounds in 1872, Blackwell's decision to build a second, larger warehouse on Main Street encouraged other men to follow his lead. In less than ten years, Durham had become North Carolina's foremost tobacco market, with most of its nine warehouses offering overnight accommodations for farmers, wagons and horses.

As Blackwell grew more affluent, he invested in land and financed the construction of more than 300 houses for laborers who were coming to work in the factories and mills his own booming business was attracting to town. He also became an incorporator of both the Durham & Northern and the Durham & Roxboro railroads, which later became the Seaboard Coastline and Norfolk & Western, respectively.

Born and raised a Baptist, Blackwell contributed $1,000 to that denomination's first Durham church in 1878 and, a decade later, he established Blackwell Baptist Church in honor of his mother. Eventually, Eleanor Blackwell's memorial became Temple Baptist Church, which stands today on West Chapel Hill Street.

Education was of primary importance to the former teacher. He was a strong supporter of Durham's first graded school, which opened in 1882 despite fierce opposition from many people who balked at paying taxes to support it.

When those opponents succeeded in having it declared unconstitutional on the grounds of racial discrimination, Buck Blackwell thwarted the move. Saying "I would rather see the destruction of every factory in Durham, than the collapse of the graded school," he offered to underwrite it until a constitutionally acceptable law could be enacted by the General Assembly.

Other Durham residents, impressed by his stand, rallied to the cause and began a money-raising campaign so Blackwell would not have to carry the burden alone, but he did contribute the lion's share—$4,000 of his own money—to sustain the school until it could be established legally.

After leaving the tobacco business in 1883, Blackwell went into banking, but apparently was so lacking in judgment when it came to lending money, especially to friends, that his Bank of Durham failed on November 14, 1888, and he lost not only his fortune, but many fair-weather friends. He once said that while he was wealthy, people frequently stopped him on the street to chat and apparently found his company so delightful that it sometimes took him two hours to walk from his home to his business; but after his bank failed and "now my money is spent," he added, "I can walk downtown and hardly a person speaks to me."

Blackwell took his fall from wealth in dignified and philosophical fashion, however, and although he was forced to give up expensive tastes and to live a life of strict economy, one historian recorded that "he never lost his warm heart and his generous impulses and his regard for his fellows."

By serving as Durham's postmaster from 1894 to 1898, he was able to pay off some of the claims held against him, and he also held the position of city treasurer until his death in November 1903.

*I was present and participated in the first sale of*
*leaf tobacco ever held in this community . . .*

JULIAN S. CARR

# Tobacco pioneers alter Durham

Durham's tobacco pioneers, as colorful a lot of characters as any to be found in fiction, included Julian Shakespeare Carr, Washington Duke and George Washington Watts. They were not the first, by any means, nor were they the last to manufacture tobacco here, but they were the "Big Three," the outstanding businessmen of those early years after the Civil War when Durham was just emerging from obscurity. All of them came from other places and Carr, a native of Chapel Hill, was the first to appear, in 1870. Duke followed from his farm about four miles away in 1874, and Watts arrived from Baltimore in 1879.

In background, character and personality, the three were vastly different from each other, but one thing they had in common was tobacco. Tobacco brought them success and a great deal of money, and their money helped to change Durham from "a roaring old place" of grogshops and brothels into a respectable and prosperous city.

Tobacco money brought the textile industry to their adopted town because they needed bags to put tobacco in, and tobacco money created the machine industry because they needed more advanced methods of manufacturing tobacco than human hands could accomplish.

It was tobacco money that encouraged education, first by paying teachers in the public school system when the system threatened to collapse from lack of support; later by bringing Trinity College from Randolph County to Durham; and, ultimately, by establishing Duke University.

Tobacco money gave the city its first hospital, as well as one of the finest medical centers in the country; and by founding and supporting many local churches, both black and white, tobacco money influenced the moral and social values of the community.

So because these men and their concern with tobacco had a direct effect on our city as we know it today, their stories bear retelling. Julian Carr, Washington Duke and George Watts all had the touch of genius when it came to business, and Durham reaped the fruits of that genius through their philanthropies.

JULIAN SHAKESPEARE CARR'S birth on October 12, 1845 probably went unnoticed except in the village of Chapel Hill, where he was the fourth in a family of nine children born to John Wesley and Eliza Bullock Carr. He was a handsome lad, with a determined chin and steady blue eyes, and he kept his good looks throughout his long and vigorous life. At seventy, although a bit portly and by no means tall, he still turned heads wherever he went, for he had tremendous presence and was always impeccably groomed, the carnation in his lapel as much a part of him as his snow-white hair and mustache. Every day he looked as if he were dressed for a special occasion, usually wearing a swallow-tail coat and bat-wing collar, with a jeweled stickpin gleaming in his tie.

But for outstanding occasions, such as commencements, reunions, weddings and holidays, he was apt to deck himself out in a beautifully tailored Confederate general's uniform, something he loved to do. Just putting on that regalia, blazing with gold braid and often embellished with a scarlet sash, made him happy, and Jule Carr's happiness was contagious. People caught it even while they recalled

Julian S. Carr

that he was never a bonafide general, and that he really never got beyond the rank of private in the Confederate army. But they remembered, too, that after the Civil War he became a one-man veteran's administration for those with whom he had served by helping them financially, lobbying for them in the state legislature, and sending them to Confederate reunions by the train carload.

So because of that largesse, when the United Confederate Veterans organized in 1889, "Old Jule," as his fellow soldiers called him, advanced rapidly in its ranks and in less than ten years became a general, an honorary title that he took with complete seriousness for the rest of his life and one by which most people addressed him.

Occoneechee Farm. ca. 1920. In the foreground is the playhouse; background is the big house.

Carr never intended to live in Durham, a shoddy little hamlet halfway between two dreary and somewhat disreputable settlements known as Pinhook and Prattsburg, but when his father convinced him that there was money to be made in that unlikely place and offered to lend him $4,000 to buy an interest in one of its three small tobacco factories, Julian overcame whatever scruples he may have had, took Durham to his heart, and became one of its chief benefactors. At the age of twenty-five, full of bounce and energy and new ideas, he became a partner of W. T. Blackwell and James R. Day, two gentlemen who badly needed his borrowed money to continue manufacturing Bull Durham Smoking Tobacco. Thus began the career that would make Julian S. Carr the first man in America to launch a worldwide advertising campaign that would make him one of the wealthiest men in the South after the Civil War.

When he arrived in Durham in 1870, "we were 300 souls," he said, "and some of those kids, then small children, were real little princesses, for among them I had the good fortune to find my wife." (He married the mayor's daughter, Nannie Graham Parrish.) In addition to the railroad station, there was a post office, a blacksmith shop, several small stores and half a dozen barrooms; but within six years the population had jumped to over 2,000 and there were sixteen tobacco factories, twenty-two stores, six boarding houses, seven restaurants and bars, a hotel (which Carr built), two carriage shops, five lumber mills, a tin shop, a newspaper and a job printing office. This was progress in a high degree, and all of

The Hotel Carrolina, founded and built by Julian S. Carr, burned to the ground in 1907. ca. 1905.

it related, as John Wesley Carr had foreseen, to the manufacture and sale of tobacco, a business in which his son, Julian, was now an undisputed leader.

But leading came natural to Carr, who loved to be first and didn't mind saying so. "I witnessed the first brick placed that went into the first brick structure in Durham," he once told a local audience, "and I went to the laying of the cornerstone of the first church erected. I saw the commencement of the foundation of our first schoolhouse, and I stood by the first new-made grave in our cemetery and assisted in laying away the first body. I was present and participated in the first sale of leaf tobacco ever held in this community, May 18, 1871, conducted by H. A. Reams."

There were numerous "firsts" for this man whose energy and enthusiasm never seemed to diminish.

Any move to improve the status quo excited him and got his immediate support. He gave the land for Durham's first public library, also the first in the state open to the public without payment of dues or fees; and he built Durham's first hotels, the Claiborn (so-called for his father-in-law) in the early 1880s, and the Carrolina (emphasizing the family name) in the early 1890s. The Golden Belt Manufacturing Company, which made cloth bags for tobacco, was his creation, as was the Durham Cotton Manufacturing Company, predecessor of Durham Hosiery Mills, which in its time was the largest textile operation in the world.

Although few people other than historians are aware of it, Carr gave Trinity College, now Duke University, its first endowment of $10,000 in 1887; and he was the first man south of the Mason-Dixon line to make a donation to any educational institution north of the Potomac when he subscribed $10,000 to the American University in Washington. An ardent believer in education, he gave prodigiously to his beloved alma mater, the University of North Carolina, but his generosity by no means stopped there; it included the Methodist Female Seminary, Trinity, Wake Forest, Elon, Davidson, St. Mary's and Greensboro College, among others.

One of his first contributions to Methodism occurred when, as a new member of Trinity Church, he climbed on its roof and repaired several leaks. He continued to serve the church throughout his life, not only with large gifts of money, but also as superintendent of the Sunday School, chairman of the Board of Stewards, and teacher of a Bible class for over twenty years. He also gave a new Methodist church to the East Durham community, and contributed regularly to the support of the denomination's homes and orphanages. He often referred to himself as "an ordinary Methodist from hat to heel," but the love he evidenced for his fellow men was neither ordinary nor without frills, as his involvement with a young Chinese boy, Chiao-chun Soong, clearly shows.

Soong, a stowaway on the side-wheeler Colfax, was dumped in Wilmington, North Carolina where he was converted to Christianity and took the American name of Charles. A concerned Methodist in Wilmington sent him to Carr, who took him into his own home, dubbed him "Charlie," and often said, "He was like a son to me." With Carr's help, Charlie Soong went first to Trinity College and then to Vanderbilt

Charlie Soong

University; and years later, back in China, he founded one of the most influential families in the Orient. His sons were T. V. Soong, president of the Bank of China, T. L. Soong, director of the Manufacturer's Bank and the Whangpoo Conservancy Board; and T. A. Soong, a Treasury official in charge of collecting one-fourth of China's governmental revenues.

Soong's three daughters, Ai-ling, Mai-ling and Ching-ling, whose names have been compared to the sound of temple bells, became the wives of Dr. H. H.

Kung, Generalissimo Chiang Kai-shek and Dr. Sun Yat-sen, three of the most important men China ever produced. In 1914, Charlie Soong entertained his benefactor, whom he called "Father Carr," at a lavish round of receptions in Shanghai attended by top government and military officials of the Chinese Republic, who came to pay their respects to the man who had given the head of the great Soong family his start in life.

Carr's magnanimity went throughout his own life beyond the boundaries of race. He helped a black man, John Merrick, start a business in Durham that later became the largest Negro insurance company in the world; and he sent another black, W. G., Pearson, to Shaw University in Raleigh. Pearson later became superintendent of the Negro school system here, and he often said that Carr had meant more to Durham's black people than any other man in the city. North Carolina College for Negroes, now North Carolina Central University, once made him chairman of its board of trustees, and a former president of the institution, Dr. James Shepard, said: "I never knew a black man to go to General Carr for help who did not get it."

Around 1900, the general bought a house and 800 acres of land near Hillsborough. Originally the property of James Hogg, an early settler who called it "Poplar Hill," Carr changed the name to "Occoneechee" and established a model farm there. Named for the Occoneechee Indian Tribe, it became a showplace unequaled anywhere in the state, a rich man's dream farm where he raised horses, Holstein cows, hogs, many varieties of chickens, ducks, geese, turkeys, pigeons, guineas, peafowls, monkeys, parrots and birds of paradise. Crops included grain, clover, alfalfa, soybeans, hay, cotton, corn, and fruit. Every year, Occoneechee dominated exhibits at the State Fair, and there were even pictures of Jule Carr's fabulous farm in grammar school geography books.

There were, of course, people who did not like Julian Carr, and some Hillsborough aristocrats talked for years about the dreadful things he did to Poplar Hill, adding porches and gee-gaws and gingerbread fretwork to an authentic early American house and giving it an Indian name. While their own homes were falling into genteel disrepair, he had the effrontery to provide his stock with a slate-roofed, tile-floored barn, and his grandchildren with a "club house" designed solely for playing and parties. Such displays, it was whispered, were in questionable taste, but gossip did not bother the general.

Few men equaled his achievements, and twenty-five years after his death in 1924, the General Assembly of North Carolina recognized him by issuing a resolution in honor of his memory. It said, in part, that "measured by the past and those of his day, he was the state's greatest businessman," but Julian Carr was much more than a captain of industry with a genius for making money and a penchant for giving it away. Soldier, manufacturer, promoter, builder, politician, teacher, public speaker, writer, farmer, friend of the black man and the Confederate soldier, he was, above all, a loyal Southerner who viewed himself as the hero of an exciting drama, and he played the part with all the skill and timing of a born actor.

*Only by living a God-fearing, honest, sober*
*and industrious life can you be happy.*
WASHINGTON DUKE

# Washington Duke tied stern will to duty

The oldest of Durham's founding fathers, Washington Duke, was approaching his fiftieth birthday by the time he established W. Duke and Sons, forerunner of the giant American Tobacco Company that eventually swallowed up most of the tobacco manufacturing concerns in America, including Julian S. Carr's Blackwell's Durham Tobacco Company, makers of the famous Bull Durham brand.

Duke was, in many ways, the antithesis of Carr, but there were striking similarities, too. Both were born in Orange County and raised in the Methodist church. Both fought in the Civil War and survived it to go into the tobacco business, and both became millionaires and philanthropists. "Wash" Duke lived at the west end of Durham and "Jule" Carr at the east end, each near his own factory, his own church, his own relatives, and his own special friends. The town

of Durham, which lay between their costly Victorian mansions, waxed fat and prosperous as a result of their efforts to outdo each other in business and good works.

Five days before Christmas in 1820, Washington Duke was born on a farm about seven miles from the present city of Durham. His parents were sober, God-fearing, respectable people, but feeding and clothing ten children left nothing for them to give to a son to help him get started in the world. So Duke started with nothing but a strong will. He rented a patch of land, farmed it for four years and saved every penny he could spare to buy property for himself. When war broke out in 1861, he owned 300 acres.

Duty before pleasure was Duke's rule of life. He believed in hard work and no debt, and he stayed sober and didn't gamble. A constant church-goer who had been converted at the age of eleven, he never missed a service unless he was sick, and he often said that "only by living a God-fearing, honest, sober and industrious life can you be happy."

A big, deep-chested, grey-eyed man who walked with a long, deliberate stride and spoke in a calm, deliberate voice, Duke married twice, first in 1842. Mary Clinton, of Orange County, was his wife for five years and bore him two sons, Samuel and Brodie, before she died in 1847. In 1852, he married Artelia Roney of Alamance County and they had three children, Mary, Ben and James Buchanan, called Buck. Both Artelia and Duke's eldest son, Samuel, died of typhoid fever in 1858, so when Duke was drafted into the Confederate navy he was a forty-three-year-old widower with four children, a man who never believed in slavery or secession. He did duty on a ship that defended Charleston Harbor, later transferred to the artillery and was captured and confined to Libby Prison after Richmond fell. When war ended a few weeks later, he was sent to New Bern. From there he walked home — 135 miles.

With nothing but a fifty-cent piece, two blind mules and four capable children, Washington started over when he was forty-five years old. His daughter, Mary, took over the housekeeping duties, and his sons helped him farm. But when their first cotton crop brought only five cents a pound, Duke decided that tobacco was a better bet, since land around Durham produced a particularly good leaf that cured into the kind of smoke and chew men liked. He and his children, working in a sixteen-by-eighteen room, found they could process 500 pounds of tobacco a day by hand, and in 1866, they

Washington Duke

manufactured 15,000 pounds, sold it for sixty cents a pound, and paid a tax of twenty cents on each pound. To realize $6,000 so soon after the war was no small accomplishment.

In 1869, the eldest son, Brodie, decided to move into the little town of Durham and set up a factory. In 1874, the rest of the family followed and eventually joined forces with Brodie in a new building, forty-five by seventy-five feet and three stories high. It was the beginning of W. Duke and Sons, and a meager one, but in less than thirty-five years the company would cover ten acres of ground and manufacture more tobacco than any one plant in America.

Washington Duke believed God helps those who

J. W. Karnes on bicycle at "Fairview," home of Washington Duke at corner of Main and Duke Streets, Durham, 1910.

help themselves, and he advised anyone who asked him how he succeeded to work hard, avoid paying interest, spend less than they made and "support your churches and schools. Give to the support of the Gospel . . . because you know it is right". Duke organized a Sunday school in one room of that first Durham factory, and from it grew a church he would belong to and support the rest of his life, the Main Street Methodist Church, later named Duke Memorial Methodist Church. He also gave more than $2 million to Trinity College between 1890 and 1913,

and his sons, Ben and Buck, followed his lead. As a result, what began as a struggling Methodist school in Randolph County became Duke University, which today ranks as one of the nation's finest institutions of higher learning.

Washington Duke went literally from rags to riches. But in spite of his great wealth his tastes remained simple, and he rarely left Durham because he loved it and wanted to contribute to its progress. After all, it was in Durham that he got the second chance he needed after the Civil War left him penniless.

# SIX

*I want to make some tangible expression of what life
in Durham has meant to me and my family.*

GEORGE W. WATTS

# Durham development interest Watts

Unlike Washington Duke, George Watts did not "graduate at the plow-handles," nor did he have much in common with Horatio Alger heroes who invariably achieve success in spite of seemingly insurmountable stumbling blocks. As a matter of fact, Watts came closer to being "born with a silver spoon in his mouth" than any of Durham's pioneer tobacco manufacturers, including his senior partner, Duke, and his business rival, Julian S. Carr.

Julian Carr was a high-spirited six-year-old and Washington Duke was a solemn lad of eighteen when George Washington Watts, son of Gerard and Annie Wolvington Watts, was born on August 18, 1851. The early years of his life were spent at "Beverly," his parent's home in Cantonville, Maryland, near Baltimore; and because his father was a prosperous wholesale tobacco merchant, he had an excellent education

that began in Baltimore and ended with his graduation from the University of Virginia in 1871. Like most young men at Virginia during those hard days after the Civil War, Watts was a serious student and also a devout one. Outnumbered by Episcopalians and Presbyterians, he was one of only two Lutherans on campus, but he attended prayer meetings at the YMCA every Wednesday and Friday morning.

After graduating with degrees in both chemistry and engineering, he went to work for his father, selling tobacco "on the road" and, at the same time, learning all phases of the business. A few years later he was married to Laura Valinda Beall in a wedding described as "one of the highlights of the season," and they had one child, a daughter whom they named Annie Louise. (Annie Louise Watts married John Sprunt Hill in 1899; their children were George

Watts Hill and Mrs. Valinda H. DuBose of Chapel Hill and Mrs. Francis Hill Fox, of Durham.)

In 1878, when Gerard Watts learned by the business grapevine that the North Carolina firm of W. Duke and Sons was in need of financial help, he smelled opportunity and came down to Durham with a proposition. If they would take his son George as a partner, said Gerard Watts to Washington Duke and his sons, he would pay them $14,000 for a one-fifth interest in their business. After due consideration, Washington, Brodie, Ben and Buck Duke agreed, and thus began a long and profitable relationship between the young man from Baltimore and the Dukes of Durham.

W. Duke and Sons was changed to W. Duke Sons and Co., George Watts becoming the "Co." and also the secretary and treasurer. It was a lucky move on both sides. The new partner, with his training, education and native intelligence, became invaluable to the organization; and the organization, in less than a dozen years, made Watts a wealthy man with interests that went well beyond tobacco to include banks, railroads, chemicals, electric power and textiles.

In spite of such extensive involvement in business, however, Watts also managed to devote a great deal of time to religious activities. Finding no Lutheran congregation in Durham when he arrived, he joined the First Presbyterian Church on Main Street, where he soon became a deacon and, later, an elder. In 1885 he organized a Sunday school and was named superintendent, a position he held for thirty-six years. It was his habit to look in on various classes, appearing suddenly (and seemingly from out of nowhere) to stand quietly in the doorway, listening, a tall figure whose rimless spectacles caught the Sunday morning sunlight and whose smile, beneath a neat brown mustache, was gentle, almost benign. One small student, then in the Cradle Roll and now in her eighties, admits that "until I was seven years old I honestly believed Mr. Watts was God."

George Watts was a firm believer in church schools. After making the closing address at his own each Sunday morning, he went in the afternoon to the Pearl Cotton Mill, one of Brodie Duke's enterprises, and taught a class he had helped to organize for the workers; and he also led prayer services at the same mill on Friday nights. Like the Dukes and the Carrs, both staunch Methodists, Watts gave a considerable amount of money to the Presbyterian Church, especially for foreign missions and for the education of its ministers. For many years he was the sole support of Soonchun Station, a mission in Korea; and he also give liberally to missionaries in Brazil, Africa, Kentucky and North Carolina.

He became keenly interested in Union Theological Seminary, and gave $50,000 toward its removal from Hampden-Sidney to Richmond, Virginia. Further gifts to this institution made possible the building of a chapel and a dormitory, both of which are named for him; and he also established the Walter W. Moore Foundation, from which the seminary president's salary is paid. All in all, George Watts gave over $270,000 to Union Theological Seminary during his lifetime, a sum that compares favorably with the largess of Julian Carr and Washington Duke toward their own denomination. And, like them, he also gave to educational institutions, among which were Davidson, Lees-McCrae, Flora Macdonald, and the Stuart Robinson School.

But the urge to share his wealth was not satisfied.

Mrs. George W. Watts

George W. Watts

In his own words, he wanted "to make some tangible expression of what life in Durham has meant to me and my family," and so, in 1895, he offered to build a hospital for the city. Located on Main Street near Trinity College, it cost $30,000 to build and had an endowment of $20,000. At the time, there were only six general hospitals in North Carolina; this new one contained twenty beds, with only four of them designated for private patients. About thirteen years later, because of Durham's rapid growth and the increased need for medical facilities, Watts built a new 100-bed hospital on the outskirts of town at a cost of $535,000, plus an endowment of $300,000. He said he "hoped no patient would ever have to be denied admission because of lack of funds"; and that he wanted the hospital "not to be the largest, but large enough, and as good as the best." This wish was realized when Watts Hospital became the first general hospital in North Carolina to be on the Class A list of the American Medical Association.

Watts's wife, Annie, died in 1915, and two years later he married Sara V. Ecker, of Syracuse, New York. During the four years they spent together before his death in 1921, they traveled abroad whenever his health permitted; and during the last year of his life he attended the World Sunday School Convention in Tokyo, where he was elected a vice president of that body.

This engraving of the City Hospital—built at the corner of Main Street and Buchanan Blvd., shows three buildings: a center building with porch and main entrance, and two matching wings connected to main building by covered walkways. ca. 1890.

Although he was a quiet and rather modest man, he was extremely friendly, and enjoyed social life to such an extent that he joined eleven country clubs, from Maine to Florida, and often visited them to play golf, which was his favorite sport. His primary interest, however, was in the development of Durham, and to that end he contributed not only money but his time, as well.

Like Julian S. Carr, George Watts was often first. He served on the first school board, was one of the organizers of the Lyceum, a group dedicated solely to the promotion of culture in Durham; and led the first successful drive to establish a YMCA in his adopted city by giving $7,500 toward a proposed $20,000 building in which to house it. In addition to funding two banks, the Home Savings and the Durham Loan and Trust Company, he had a strong hand in the organization of three railroads. These were the Lynchburg and Durham, the Oxford and Durham, and the Durham and Northern.

Other businesses in which he had financial interests were the Durham Electric Light Company, Erwin Cotton Mill, Pearl Cotton Mill, Golden Belt Manufacturing Company, Durham Cotton Manufacturing Company., Mayo Cotton Mills and Cooleemee Mills. Some of these firms were controlled by Carr, and others were controlled by the Dukes; but Watts, with characteristic diplomacy, was able to work in both rival camps to the satisfaction and profit of all concerned.

While he may have lacked the strong charisma of Julian S. Carr, the "genial general," and the ruggedness of Washington Duke, the "old gentleman," it is certain that George Washington Watts possessed all the integrity and bearing of an aristocrat, which he was.

Durham owes much to its "Big Three," for each of them affected its growth from a town of factories to a center of education, science and research. None of them should be forgotten.

# SEVEN

# Merrick, Moore and Spaulding created largest black-owned business in the world

*D*urham's early history is full of rags-to-riches stories, most of them thanks to brightleaf tobacco, but not all of the town's successful entrepreneurs were the WASP tobacco manufacturers who made it "renowned the world around." Three of the most compelling characters in the story of Durham's rise to international prominence were black men who could not vote, were generally regarded as inferior to whites, and who had to live in Hayti, the "colored section" across the railroad tracks that ran parallel to Main Street. In spite of those obstacles and many others they encountered, John Merrick, Aaron McDuffie Moore and Charles Clinton Spaulding created and sustained a small insurance company that eventually became the largest black-owned business in the world, putting Durham on the international map a second time and thereby assuring themselves of a lasting place in the history of the New South.

On October 29, 1898, the North Carolina Mutual and Provident Association, later renamed North Carolina Mutual Life Insurance Company, was organized in a small room on a dirt street in Hayti by John Merrick, with six friends who were willing to invest $50 each in the venture present at that meeting. Today it is housed in an imposing ten-story concrete-and-glass skyscraper at the intersection of Chapel Hill and Duke Streets, where Ben Duke's mansion, Four Acres, once stood. Now called Mutual Plaza, the building was dedicated on April 2, 1966 by the Honorable Hubert H. Humphrey, Vice President of the United States, and is simply "The Mutual" to most people, so familiar is its presence in what used to be a stronghold of the Duke clan and one of Durham's most prestigious lily-white neighborhoods.

Less familiar to today's generation, however, is any knowledge of its founders. With the exception of Mutual officers, company employees and history buffs, not many Durham citizens know much, if anything, about John Merrick, Aaron Moore and C. C.

Left to right: Dr. A. M. Moore, C. C. Spaulding, and John Merrick

Spaulding, an ex-slave and two farmers' sons from eastern North Carolina who became the city's most prominent black businessmen and the progenitors of its first "black aristocracy."

John Merrick, born on a plantation near Clinton, North Carolina on September 7, 1859, was the son of a slave woman and a white man, a healthy, handsome child with a sunny disposition, a bright mind and a remarkable talent for getting along with "white folks," something he may have acquired during his early years on the plantation and later in Chapel Hill, where he moved with his mother in 1871. While she worked as a house servant, he worked as a hod carrier in the local brickyard and also learned, for the first time, how to read, write and "figure" at a Reconstruction school in the village.

In 1871 his mother married and moved to Washington, D.C., and Merrick, by that time a skilled brickmason, went to Raleigh and worked on the construction of Shaw University's first building. A second job as a bootblack in a popular barbershop introduced him to John Wright, an older barber who taught him the tonsorial art of shaving faces and cutting hair that boosted him from bootblack to barber and eventually brought him to the attention of Washington Duke and Julian Shakespeare Carr.

Unable to get satisfactory service in their own small town at that time, these rivals in Durham's burgeoning tobacco industry frequently combined business trips to the capitol city with the pleasure of a "decent" shave and haircut; and although they rarely saw eye to eye in many instances, they both viewed Wright and his young protoge as their favorite barbers. Merrick, especially, impressed them as the "ideal Negro," good looking, good natured, intelligent, ambitious and, above all, unfailingly courteous. Julian Carr called him "a Chesterfieldian Gentleman," and one historian credits Carr with finally persuading Wright and Merrick to "come to Durham and grace the New South City with the kind of tonsorial parlor that wealthy white men deserved."

When they arrived in 1880 and opened a barbershop on Main Street (possibly with a loan from Carr), Wright was the owner and Merrick his assistant, but within six months Merrick was a full partner and half owner of the establishment, which gave him not only a good living but a valuable education in business methods, as well. While he ministered to the successful whites who were his special customers, "the industrious young barber learned much," said one

Booker T. Washington, sixth from left in center row, met with a group of black leaders in Durham around 1910. To Washington's right is John Merrick and seated in front of them is C.C. Spaulding.

source, and "Only a deaf man could have escaped the profound influence of this indirect tutelage," said another; but an even more direct source of information and support came from Washington Duke.

Duke became increasingly fond of Merrick, dubbed him his personal barber and, on several occasions, took him to New York, showed him the wonders of the big city, and introduced him to some of the titans in the world of Big Business. Duke also encouraged him in his entrepreneurial ventures, which began after Wright retired in 1892 and sold Merrick his share of the business. As it continued to prosper, Merrick began to expand and soon owned a small chain of barbershops, three for whites and three for blacks.

With his profits he bought land in Hayti, and when Duke hired him to tear down and haul off an old barn, he used the lumber to build two houses, which rented immediately. Sensing another opportunity in the growth of the tobacco industry and a consequent need for housing in Hayti, he launched a construction company and also a real estate business. By 1898, at the age of thirty-nine, he was a man of considerable means, and it may have been then that he began to feel an obligation to "teach by example what the Negro could achieve in the world of finance."

John Merrick with daughters, Geneva, Mabel, and Martha. ca. 1909.

Merrick had long been a strong believer in the gospel according to Booker T. Washington, whose doctrine of self help and racial uplift through industrial education also appealed to Durham's white leaders. Washington preached that if blacks worked hard, saved part of what they made, started their own businesses, supported their own churches and schools, lived Christian lives and stayed out of politics, "the better class of whites would help them," and Durham's better class—those with the most money and therefore the most power—said *Amen,* knowing that a prosperous black community would lessen the fear and distrust that existed between the races.

So the climate into which the North Carolina Mutual and Provident Association was born in 1898 was a friendly one, due in part to Booker Washington's blueprint for the salvation of his race, but mainly to John Merrick's success in dealing with whites. Without it, the business never could have survived, but even with that valuable asset the infant company almost died from lack of customers during its second year and would have, if Aaron McDuffie Moore, Durham's first black doctor, had not rescued it.

Moore, a distant cousin of John Merrick, was born in Columbus county, North Carolina on September 6, 1863. Descended from a succession of free black land-owning farmers of mixed Negro-Indian-Caucasian blood, he was more interested in learning than in farming and attended the county schools for eight years before going on to normal schools in Lumberton and Fayetteville. In 1885 he went to Shaw University intending to be a teacher, but his own teachers convinced him to enter the university's Leonard School of Medicine, from which he graduated in three years instead of the usual four; and he also placed second in the state's medical board examinations.

When Moore came to Durham in 1888 and opened an office on Fayetteville Street, he stepped straight into Hayti's upper class and very soon into the good graces of the Dukes, their partner, George Watts, and Albert Gallatin Carr, Julian Carr's brother and Durham's first white doctor. These men later helped him to establish Lincoln Hospital, Durham's first black medical facility, but Moore made his first contribution to racial uplift as medical director and treasurer of the fledgling Mutual and Provident Association when he and Merrick reorganized it in 1899. Unable to give all of their time to nursing it back to health, however, they hired Moore's nephew, Charles Clinton Spaulding, to manage the office, take care of customers, and sell life insurance.

Spaulding, called "C.C.," had the ambition, energy and determination of a typical Horatio Alger hero. Before coming to Durham in 1889, he had lived and worked on his father's farm in Columbas County, where he was born on August 1, 1874; but he had no intention of following the family tradition. Like his Uncle Aaron, he attended the county schools, and in Durham he got the equivalent of a high school education at the Whitted School in Hayti before he took on a series of jobs—dishwasher, waiter, bellhop, office boy, butler and manager of a cooperative grocery store—that led him, finally, to the ailing Mutual and Provident Association.

While Merrick and Moore concentrated on their more important jobs, Spaulding kept the office clean, did the clerical work, and attempted to sell life insurance to anybody who would listen to him. Described as "a pioneer in saturation advertising," he displayed the company name on ads in barbershops, stores, offices and lodges; on matchbooks, calendars, pens and pencils—anywhere and everywhere he could. He recruited agents with such zeal that by the end of his first six months as manager, he had placed them in twenty-eight towns and cities across the state; and although setbacks during the next two years forced Merrick and Moore to pay claims out of their own pockets more than once, Spaulding never lost his optimism nor his propensity for hard work.

By the end of 1903, he had agents in over 50 towns, and with expenses no longer exceeding income, the Merrick-Moore-Spaudling team, which became known as "The Triumverate," was able to rent more office space, hire three fulltime clerks, and buy a typewriter and a safe. C.C. Spaulding had pumped fresh young blood into the dying Mutual and Provident's veins, and his senior partners agreed that he well deserved the first salary ever paid by the company, a princely sum of $15 per week.

Thus began the century-long journey of the North Carolina Mutual Life Insurance Company from Hayti to Mutual Plaza. The whole story of that phenomenal journey has been told again and again in books, magazines, newspapers, dissertations, term papers and company archives, and it's one of the most fascinating and inspiring reads I've ever encountered.

Unfortunately, there's just not enough space here to tell all of it again.

# Growing Pains

*It was a good neighborhood, one of the best, but it's long gone. If I went back now to where it used to be, I would walk among ghosts, and through the mists of a thousand old memories.*

# EIGHT

# Trip down memory lane leads to old Fuller School

*Durham Illustrated*, a promotional tract put out by the Durham Merchants Association back in 1921, is a little gold mine of information about the city's past, just twenty-three pages in all; and for me, exploring it for the first time was like taking a rocket ship down memory lane to my own past. For instance:

Reading that Durham's population grew from less than 200 in 1869, the year the town was incorporated, to more than 33,000 in 1921, I remembered that 1921 was the year I was finally able to go to Fuller School, which was directly across from our house on Cleveland Street, where the First Baptist Church now stands. The year before, watching my brother Bacon and my sister Carolyn and every other child in the neighborhood climb the granite steps and disappear through the double front door of that ivy-streaked red brick building, I stood on the sidewalk and bawled, overcome by envy, self-pity, and the shame of being only five years old.

My mother, who did not approve of public displays of emotion, came down the front porch steps and down the walk to take me by the hand and drag me,

still wailing, back into the dining room and my unfinished breakfast. Pulling a chair away from the table, she sat down and took me in her lap. "Shhh," she whispered, hugging me close and patting me on the back. "Shhh, now. You'll be able to go to school, too, next year."

Next year might as well have been never, as far as I was concerned. But it did come, eventually. And I went to school.

Fuller School was named for my grandfather, Bartholomew Fuller, a lawyer who, back in 1882, was one of three members of Durham's first Board of Education and Learning. His picture hung on the wall opposite the principal's office, and because he already had a beard and a mustache, the children who ordinarily would have drawn hair on his face resorted, instead, to drawing horns on his head and sticking postage stamps over his eyes.

Miss Maggie Holloway, the principal, used an art-gum eraser on the horns, but she had to scrape the stamps off with a penknife. Then she would spit on her finger and rub it over the glass, right over Grandpa's eyes. I know, because I watched her do

Built in the 1930s, the Fuller School was a massive two-story brick double-winged building, typical of public school construction during the 30s and 40s. ca. 1950.

that one day while I was waiting in her office to be punished for some now-forgotten infraction of the many rules designed to prevent chaos at Fuller School. Talking out loud, probably. Or succumbing to a fit of giggling.

Fortunately, I did not get a switching from Miss Maggie, which would have precipitated another one at home, once the news leaked back. But I got a tongue-lashing that left me feeling like a criminal. "Your grandfather would be mortally ashamed to own you," she said, just before sending me back to the classroom, and I reckon she was right. I wished, then, that the stamps were still over his eyes, so he couldn't see me.

Maybe Fuller School was where I got most of my hang-ups, from being teased at recess on the playground when I was in first grade. Being chubby and tow-headed and freckle-faced and big-mouthed was bad enough, but being named Fuller was a definite handicap. If I hadn't been a fast runner and a mean scratcher, I might never have survived the pecking order.

In 1921, Durham had ten schools, 4,970 pupils, and 154 teachers, mostly women. Those I remember best, in addition to Miss Maggie, were Miss Nell Umstead, the assistant principal, who was nobody to mess with, believe me; Miss Madeliene and Miss Mary Knight, sisters who were experts in arithmetic

Durham's Union Station, trackside with trains. ca. 1910.

and music, respectively; and Miss Alice Marrow, guardian of the third grade, the most beautiful lady I had ever seen, and the object of my first schoolgirl crush. Miss Alice, who came to Durham from Henderson, was gentle, kind and velvet-voiced, and I adored her.

According to *Durham Illustrated*, in 1921 five railway lines radiated out of Durham in seven directions, and twenty-six passenger trains steamed in and out of Union Station every twenty-four hours. That bit of information takes me back to my first train ride, and the wonder of a swaying dining car where, miraculously, the water glasses and plates of food and silverware did not slide off the table, and the white-coated

steward staggering down the aisle did not slosh a single drop of soup from the shallow bowls he carried on a tray balanced high above his head on one hand.

On that magic journey I had the unforgettable experience of sleeping in a narrow berth behind a billowing green curtain, with my clothes swinging in a little hammock above my head. Next morning I knew the ultimate thrill of being suddenly snatched from bright daylight and plunged into five minutes of noisy, rocking, total darkness while the train was hurtling along a tunnel that had been dug, I was told, straight through the side of a mountain.

At that time, Durham was being billed as "the educational center of North Carolina," because of its public schools, Trinity College, Southgate Memorial College for Women (now Duke University's Southgate Dormitory), the University of North Carolina "only twelve miles away and easily reached by an eighteen-foot hard surface road," the Conservatory of Music, the Durham Business School, and the brand new Durham Public Library, in part a product of Andrew Carnegie's largesse.

Everything about the "liberry" fascinated me—the tall, golden oak desk that I could barely see over (the top coincided exactly with the end of my nose); the matching long-legged chair that swiveled completely around, like a piano stool; the pencils that stamped the day, the month and the year on the book cards; and, best of all, the books. Packed on shelves that reached from floor to ceiling, they glowed like jewels whenever dust-moted beams of sunlight, slanting through the tall, uncurtained windows, touched their spines. When I discovered that I could walk into that beautiful building, choose any book I wanted, and take it home, I came as close to heaven as I had ever been in my short life.

I knew about heaven and also about hell (a word I was not allowed to say) as a result of going to Sunday school at First Presbyterian, one of the twenty-five white churches that dotted the city in 1921. Mr. George Watts was superintendent of the Sunday school, a round brick building directly back of the church, with pie-shaped classrooms and an assembly hall, also round, in the middle. Mr. Watts was tall and thin and had a flourishing mustache, and I remember his spectacles flashing in the sun as he stood in the doorway and watched us children troop up the walk on Sunday mornings. I also remember the minister then, Dr. D. H. Scanlon, a sturdy, bespectacled gentleman who wore gray pinstriped trousers and a cutaway coat when he preached, and who mispronounced my name when he officiated at my wedding fifteen years later. Wilhelma, he called me, instead of Wilhelmena, my Scottish grandmother's name.

It was an understandable mistake, as neither he nor anybody else ever called me by my rightful name, but it was one my husband immediately pounced on and never forgot. From time to time during the half-century of our cohabitation he would tell me that our marriage was illegal because of Dr. Scanlon's error; and those pronouncements, I can see now, were calculated to add a slightly racy component to our fifty-year liaison, one I would not have been without. And for which I am still indebted to an upright Presbyterian preacher.

Other facts about Durham, and the effects they invariably have on this fact-finder, are waiting in the wings, so to speak. Assembled over the years by succeeding chambers of commerce, they can open doors to the past that have been closed for decades, and childhood revisited can be a real trip—especially when most of its landscape has been obliterated, in the name of progress, by urban renewal.

# NINE

# Rules were a fact of life, like night and day . . .

Changing fashions in houses, lawns, cars, clothes, furniture, food, drink, hairstyles, music literature, sex, education, religion, parenting—the list goes on and on, makes us wonder who's controlling our lives today and who'll be doing it ten years from now.

Who, actually, determines how long or short a lady's skirt or a gentleman's hair should be? Who changes the eating and drinking habits of a nation? Who makes people drag themselves out of bed at dawn and jog four miles before breakfast? And who, pray tell, decides how today's children should be raised?

I don't know the answers to any of those questions, but I do know that Queen Victoria of England decided how I, and millions of other children, should be brought up. That rotund, grim-faced little monarch whose philosophy spread across the Atlantic and seeped into a large part of America, including Durham, had a great deal to do with shaping my psyche back in the 1920s.

To say that the shadow of Victorianism lay across our neighborhood, which encompassed Cleveland,

Liberty, Dillard and Main streets, is to put it mildly; and if switchings, confinement to quarters, and loss of privileges constitute child abuse, as some would have us believe, then everybody I grew up with was abused from time to time, and probably with good reason.

In our neighborhood, four churches—Baptist, Methodist, Presbyterian, Episcopalian—and the jail on top of the courthouse proclaimed that this was a God-fearing, law-abiding community. The Durham Public Library and Fuller School also underlined that fact with the mute but nevertheless powerful statement that learning and culture were of extreme importance, too.

On those quiet streets, where iron picket fences or privet hedges separated the yards, and walkways leading to doorways were bordered with ivy or boxwood, some of the houses were imposing and some were modest. Many had turrets and gables and gingerbread frescoes, others were boxy and unadorned. But almost all had porches with banisters, where men and boys could prop their feet.

On summer evenings, old folks and babies filled

Caro Bacon Fuller, "Mama"

Ralph Bell Fuller, "Papa"

the swings and high-backed rocking chairs on the porches, while bigger children romped and hollered through the long twilights, playing Hide and Seek, and Slinging Statue, and No Bears Out Tonight.

When the lamplighter came at dusk, signifying his approach by the rusty creak of chains as he let down the lights and lit them and then drew them back up, the children's voices grew high and shrill, and bugs and bats appeared suddenly from nowhere, it seemed, swooping down out of the darkening sky and sometimes smacking into the round glass globes. As the lamplighter moved along each street and the chains creaked down and up, light flowed to the ground to form pale circles at the base of each iron pole, and little by little the games stopped and the players went inside, because that was the rule.

Rules were a fact of life, like night and day, hot and cold, wet and dry, and so forth, and we didn't question them. If you broke a rule and got caught, which was almost always, you paid for it one way or another, because long before you were born the Queen of England decreed that children should not be coddled.

Disobedience, disrespect and shows of temper brought swift punishment, because parents were not as concerned about their children's psyches as they were about the ultimate salvation of their children's souls, and rules were the road marks to salvation.

There were plenty of rules at our house, especially at mealtime, when children were to be seen and not heard unless invited to join the conversation. Babbling at the table was not encouraged, but good manners were. Good manners not only were encouraged, they were enforced. That meant no chewing with your mouth open, no talking with your mouth full, no slouching in your seat, no elbows on the table, no reaching for anything like salt, sugar, butter, et cetera. And no slurping (soup), crunching (celery, nuts), or gobbling (good stuff like turkey, chocolate pudding, apple pie, home-made ice cream, devil's food cake).

If we erred, we were reprimanded quietly, either with a look from Papa (that's all it took) or a whisper from Mama. If we erred a second time, we were sent away from the table, banished until the next meal. And banishment could be excruciating if the meal was supper (dinner at night had not yet come into fashion) and we knew our favorite dessert was upcoming.

There was definitely a generation gap in the 1920s, but it didn't have a name. Nor had the word *togetherness* been coined. Nobody catered to you merely because you were a child, nor did anybody care whether or not you were entertained. There were games for both indoors and outdoors, and there were books to read, and if you didn't feel like playing or reading, you ran the risk of being put to work around the house, or in the yard. Nobody wondered if you were unhappy until you cried, and if you did cry, the source of your pain was soon rooted out.

A skinned knee or a bumped head got you iodine or witch hazel, a conciliatory pat, and a brisk order to "run on out and play"; and a mean, hateful, teasing brother or sister got you a lecture: it takes two to make a quarrel, and you shouldn't be a baby, and so forth.

Nightmares, thought to be caused by overeating, did bring parental reassurance of a sort, but usually it was accompanied by a teaspoon of baking soda in a glass of water and a whispered warning not to wake up the whole house.

At our house, Papa was the Law, Mama was his Deputy, and "spare the rod and spoil the child" was the dictum. There was a switch bush in the yard (spirea) and an ivory-backed hairbrush on Mama's bureau, and we learned to respect them. We learned, too, that the quiet, tree-shaded neighborhood was full of watchful, benevolent eyes; that our parents invariably backed each other up; and that it behooved us, therefore, to behave.

We need more neighborhoods like that, especially now.

So should we say, "Long live the queen?"

# TEN

*Durham was a small town then. A little
place. But it was a good place to live.*

MARY CAMERON

# Mrs. Cameron recalls . . .

*I*n 1989, when I began writing *The Way We
Were* for *The Durham Sun*, my first interview
was with a long-time friend and many-times neigh-
bor, Mary Toms Cameron. When I was a child, our
families lived four doors apart on Main Street; and
later, when I was a pre-teen and she a young-married,
we were across the golf course from each other in
Hope Valley. Finally, on the day we talked throughout one long summer afternoon, we had come full
circle and were again living just a few doors apart, in
a most happy place called Dunbarton. When we finished our talk, it took me three minutes to walk
home, and the next day I wrote what follows:

Mrs. E. M. Cameron, formerly Mrs. J. H. Erwin Jr.
and originally Miss Mary Newby Toms, is a Durham
native who not only remembers a great deal about
the way we were in the early part of this century, but
also recalls who some of us were, where we lived,
and what we did as youngsters.

A pretty woman with sparkling blue eyes, a strong,
husky voice, and a bright smile that eighty-six years
of living has not dimmed, Mary Cameron is forceful,
intelligent and sure of herself. She is a woman who,
for more than half a century, has tackled and completed many daunting jobs, regarding obstacles as
challenges, rather than stumbling blocks, and carry-
ing others along on the waves of her own enthusiasm. Because detailed accounts of what she has contributed to her hometown have appeared periodically
in Durham's newspapers for the past sixty years, only
a brief outline of Mary Cameron's accomplishments
is needed here.

Suffice it to say that in 1928 she organized the Red
Cross Motor Corps, which evolved into the Charity

League of Durham, which became the Junior League of Durham, which founded the Durham Babies Milk Fund, which became the Durham Family Service Association. Also, she was an early president and trustee of the Calvert Method School, which became Durham Academy.

During World War II she headed the Gray Ladies at Camp Butner and, at the same time, worked as a volunteer at both Duke Hospital and the Veterans Administration Hospital. Twice chairman of the Durham Debutante Ball Society, she has served on its board of trustees since 1955. Other boards that have benefited from her executive expertise include the Council of Social Agencies, the Salvation Army Maternity Home, the Junior League, Durham Academy and North Carolina Central University.

Long before she became a mover and shaker, Mary Toms was a little girl growing up in a big house on Main Street with her parents, Clinton White and Mary Newby Toms; her sister, Mattie; and her brothers, Clinton Jr., Edgar, Zack and George. Her father was superintendent of the Durham schools and such an effective administrator that he caught the attention of James B. Duke, who lured him to New York in 1914 to become the second president of Liggett and Myers Tobacco Company.

Asked to talk about the neighborhood that was home to her before the move to New York, Mary Cameron's blue eyes narrow, as if looking back in time. After a minute she begins to speak in the firm, positive tone that is typical of her, and with what appears to be almost total recall.

"We lived on the corner of Main and Dillard, where the bus station used to be, and cater-cornered

Mary Cameron

across the street from us was General [Julian S.] Carr, and directly across from us was his brother, Dr. A. G. Carr. Next to the Doctor Carrs were the Julian Carrs—Julian Carr Jr., that is—and next to them the Smiths, who had a daughter named Livvie, Miss Livvie Smith. Then around the corner and down

Queen Street were the Wahabs. They lived on the corner of Queen and Pettigrew, and their son, Charlie, was one of the best looking boys I have ever seen. And not only good looking, but intelligent. Very, very intelligent."

Queried as to what became of this handsome near-genius, Mary Cameron says Charlie Wahab went to Des Moines and "did very well out there, and I hear from him every Christmas." Then, after a short, thoughtful pause, she continues:

"Next to our house was the Episcopal church, St. Philip's, and then the W. A. Guthries, and across Queen Street from the Guthries were the Thomas Gormans—he was General Carr's secretary, you know—and then (she points a finger at me) next to the Gormans were your cousins, the Southgates, Tom and Loula, and next to the Southgates were you all, the Fullers, and next to the Fullers was the public library, and next to the library was the Presbyterian church, and that was the end of that block.

"Now, if you want to know about the other side of Main Street I can tell you that the I. F. Hills were across from the Gormans, and next to them were Frank and Gertrude Webb, and next to the Webbs were the Days. Lillian Day married your cousin, Frank Fuller, and they lived there for a while, across the street from where you lived. But of course you know all that, so let's get on, now, up to Dillard Street. Right back of us, on Dillard, were the Lambes, and then the Griswolds, and up a little farther were the Yearbys, and next to them were the Fannings. You must remember Devoe Fanning, because he was as good looking as Charlie Wahab, only taller. But so good looking."

Devoe Fanning's looks warrant a pause while we remember that he taught, briefly, at Durham High School and set female hearts to fluttering both in and out of the classroom. But we have not finished with Dillard Street, and so:

"The McPhersons, Dr. Sam and Miss Katie Lee, were next to the Fannings, and across the street were Dr. [John] Manning and the Thomases and the Markhams and Captain Peay—his daughters were such good friends of your mother—and next to the Peays were the N. E. Greens, just before the Wrights. Mr. Richard Wright—Uncle Dick, we called him—and his brother Tom's widow, Miss Bettie and all her children—Tom, Dick, Lila, Lucy, Nannie Bet, Cora and Mary Ruth, all the children of Mr. Tom Wright lived there before they moved out to the country, out to Bonnie Brae."

And where did all the children in the neighborhood go to school?

"We all went to Fuller School, where Mr. W. A. Bryan was the principal, and I remember so many of the teachers—Mrs. J. A. Robinson taught first grade, and Miss Sudie Whitmore second grade, and Miss Nell Umstead fifth grade, and oh, she was strict, very strict. We were all scared of Miss Nell. My sixth-grade teacher, Miss Maggie Holloway, was strict, too, but she was so kind, and very fair. I think she meant more to me than anybody else while I was at Fuller School. I really think that was the reason I looked up to her and admired her so much. She was strict, but she was kind, too."

After school, in the afternoon, what did you do?

"Almost every afternoon I'd go with Margaret Louise Carr* to her grandfather's house across the

* Eldest granddaughter of Julian S. Carr.

street, to Somerset Villa, and ride the ponies. Tom Charleston was the name of the coachman there, and he took care of the horses and the ponies and he would saddle the ponies for Margaret Louise and me and we'd ride them all around the grounds. You see, I practically lived over there because Margaret Louise and I were the same age and best friends, and sometimes we'd get on the streetcar—but you had to have a grownup or a nurse with you—and go way out to the reservoir, to the end of the line and back.

"And when we were a little older and everybody got crazy on the subject of baseball, we'd catch the streetcar at the corner of Main and Dillard and go to the baseball field down in East Durham—down past the William Rowlands and across the Dry Bridge, and that was the end of the line that way. Then, of course, we rode the streetcar to Lakewood Park to go swimming and skating, and when we were old enough we went to dances out there. They had a pavilion and an orchestra—there were no jukeboxes then, and I remember Gerald Bryan, Rose Elwood Bryan's younger brother, got up a little orchestra, and he played the violin, played beautifully.

"But when you weren't doing something special, you went downtown. Everybody went downtown almost every day, because it was where everybody was. My sister Mattie and I used to go to Main Street Pharmacy, right across from the court house, to get ice cream, and then we'd go up to the old Fidelity Bank, there on the corner of Main and Corcoran and stand there until John Buchanan came to the window. We both thought he was divine, and he began to look for us in the afternoon, after school, and sometimes we'd take him an ice cream cone or a box of popcorn. I was the one who introduced him to Mattie, and then, later on, they got married, as of course you know.

"But getting back to Margaret Louise and me, when we got old enough, Pa Pa—that's what all the children called General Carr—would take the two of us with him when he went on trips, and oh, that was wonderful!"

Mary Cameron smiles, and her eyes sparkle. Her face mirrors the enjoyment she obviously is experiencing as she remembers:

"There was a time when Pa Pa very seldom went on a trip that he didn't take us with him. We went to so many places it's hard to remember them all, but there was a World Exposition, or something like that, in California, and we went with Pa Pa. We were about fourteen years old then, just beginning to get boy crazy, and we had the time of our lives. Of course, every time we went, we had the time of our lives, but this was just the most divine time because our mothers and fathers let us go with him way out there, knowing he would take care of us, and of course Pa Pa just let us do what we pleased.

"He was such a sweet man, such a kind man, a real old timey grandfather, the most lovable creature, and just wonderful, he really was a wonderful person. He took us on trips to New York, and to Philadelphia and Richmond, so many places I can't remember all of them, and of course we always went by train.

"At that time, every place you went out of town you went on the train, and every place you went in Durham you went by horse and buggy. We had a horse and buggy and a stable right there on the cor-

Julian S. Carr and two servants watch the children with their dog in a goat cart at Occoneechee Farm. ca. early 1920s.

ner of Main and Dillard, and of course Pa Pa had a huge stable and a lot of horses and ponies, but more of course, at Occoneechee.[*]

Did you spend a lot of time in Occoneechee?

"I guess almost every time Margaret Louise went to Occoneechee, I went with her. What a wonderful place it was! We couldn't wait to be with the horses and ponies and goats and sheep, and we couldn't wait to jump in the haystacks. Such a big farm, with the Eno River running right down through it, and we could wade in it, and it was so exciting, just terribly exciting to us. And in those days, if the weather got bad and we couldn't play outside, we'd get on the train and come home. When the train coming from

[*] General Julian S. Carr's model farm in Hillsborough, NC

Greensboro stopped at Hillsborough, Pa Pa would get word to the conductor somehow, and the conductor would stop the train at Occoneechee and pick us up and bring us down to Durham."

General Carr had a special arrangement with the railroad?

"He certainly did. If he wanted the train to stop, it would stop."

And what about his wife, Miss Nannie? Do you remember her well?

"Indeed I do. And she was so lovely, so sweet, so good to us children. The two of them were Ma Ma and Pa Pa to me, because Margaret Louise and I were like sisters, and so I guess I was like another grandchild to them. Margaret Louise and I practically lived together, and after we were old enough to go with boys, we'd drive the horse and buggy out to Trinity College sometimes, and if we saw any boys we knew, we'd ride them around town and back."

How far did the town extend at that time?

"Well, if you went down Main Street from our house, everything ended at Trinity College; and if you went north from there, the reservoir was where everything stopped. And if you went out Chapel Hill Road, Lakewood Park was the end, and Morehead Hill was the last place toward the end of it. There was nothing but woods on what we call University Drive today. No Forest Hills, no Rockwood, none of that.

"You see, Durham was a small town then. A little place. But it was a good place to live. Looking back, I realize that I had a lot of advantages, but most people had a good life then. There were a few wealthy people, of course, but all the rest were about equal, as I remember it, and I don't believe we had many poverty-stricken people because everybody worked. There was no loafing in Durham. Folks worked for what they got, and they seemed to have a good time, too, and I just don't believe people in other towns had the pleasure we had, especially growing up."

So even though you lived in New York for a while, Durham was always home?

"Oh, yes, because you see, we never gave up our house here. We always came back in the summer, and Father would come down on weekends. So Durham has always been my home, and looking back and considering everything, I know that I would rather have lived here than any other place in the world, because of the people. People are friendly here, and they've always been friendly."

Remembering that Durham once was "The Friendly City," instead of "Tobaccoland, USA," or "The City of Medicine," I find that a good note on which to end a profitable afternoon with one of Durham's outstanding citizens who has never forgotten the way it was when she was growing up.

Of such conversations, history is made.

# ELEVEN

*We cannot flatter ourselves that we approach the
full measure of what we ought to be as a Christian
community until we can boast of a public library.*

JULIAN SHAKESPEARE CARR

# Durham County Library's founding spawned varying tales

*I*t was once alleged by a Durham County commissioner that "most Americans don't read one complete book a year." But we don't think that statement applies here because from June 1911 to June 2003, the Durham County Library, with its seven branches and its bookmobile, circulated a total of 35,175,611 materials, including not only books but non-print materials, such as videos and CDs, as well. That's a fact to be proud of and one due in part to a chance remark made ninety-four years ago by a Trinity College professor named Edwin Mims, according to local history. But history being exactly what the word implies—his story (or hers, as the case may be)—multiple versions of the same happening often exist, and readers sometimes are hard put to know which, if any, is gospel.

With regard to the first Durham Public Library, for instance, several accounts of how it began are housed in the same room of the present Durham County Library, and any reader can plainly see that although each contains the same kernel of truth, each one is biased, too, depending on who wrote it. One version credits Trinity College history professor Edwin C. Mims with originating the idea and Miss Lalla Ruth Carr, daughter of tobacco and textile mogul Julian Shakespeare Carr, with promoting it. Another, contained in carefully preserved library records, states unequivocally that it was Lalla Ruth Carr who first conceived the idea of a free public library. Edwin Mims, who went along with it, presented it to "the Men's and Women's Clubs of that day," and endorsed it at a public town meeting. Still another version incorporates those facts into a story, of sorts, and goes this way:

Julian Shakespeare Carr, one of Durham's five pioneer tobacco manufacturers, was at one time the wealthiest man in North Carolina, and he enjoyed a spectacular career as an entrepreneur. Starting new ventures was second nature to him, and rarely, if ever, did he back away from a challenge. He also was a "pussycat," in today's vernacular, when it came to his daughters, Lida and Lalla Ruth. In fact, Carr found it well nigh impossible to refuse either of them anything they asked for, within reason, and what could possibly be more reasonable than Lalla Ruth's wish to raise the cultural and intellectual climate of Durham?

Carr's second daughter was a striking girl with intense blue eyes, his own square, determined jaw, and an easily-triggered, infectious giggle. Friendly, outgoing, and endowed with a keen sense of humor, she quickly became a popular member of Durham's younger set following her graduation from Miss Summer's School in Washington, DC, but the pursuit of pleasure did not top her list of priorities, by any means. In 1896 she acquired a budding sense of social consciousness through membership in the town's first literary organization, the Canterbury Club, which included a number of Trinity College professors on its roster, among them Edwin Mims.

When Mims suggested that the Canterbury Club might be able to inject a much-needed dose of culture into the community by starting a movement to establish a public library, Lalla Ruth transmitted her enthusiasm for the idea to her father, who shared her love of reading and also resented the fact that Durham was generally regarded by neighboring cities, Raleigh in particular, as "lacking in refine-

Lalla Ruth Carr

ment and unfit for young women in their formative years."

So Carr decided that if a library would help to erase that image of the place he called home, he would lend his support to the effort, and he lost no time in doing so by enlisting the aid of other influential citizens. By the time a town meeting was called to broach the subject to the general public, a number of civic leaders already were solidly behind it. They were, in addition to Carr and Edwin Mims, George W. Watts, E. J. Parrish, Thomas B. Fuller,

R. W. Winston, L. B. Turnbull, James H. Southgate. C. W. Toms, J. F. Wily, H. A. Foushee and H. H. Markham, and they became the Durham Public Library's first board of trustees when it was incorporated on March 5, 1897.

Carr, with the bit firmly in his teeth at that town meeting on April 30, 1896, told the assembled company: "We cannot flatter ourselves that we approach the full measure of what we ought to be as a Christian community until we can boast of a public library." Then, in the name of his daughter, Lalla Ruth, he donated a building site valued at $2,500 and located at the western end of Main Street, in a section known as Five Points. When someone suggested that because the lot was pie-shaped, it might not be wide enough for a building designed to house a great many books and also provide space for readers, a prosperous tobacco broker by the name of Thomas H. Martin, who owned the adjacent lot, agreed to donate the necessary footage. These two initial offerings sparked individual subscriptions of over $1,300.

Because the sum fell far short of the estimated $4,000 needed to build an adequate library, a group of Durham women, including Lalla Ruth Carr, formed themselves into a Board of Lady Managers and staged a house-to-house campaign to solicit funds. Mrs. Brodie Duke was chairman of that board, Lalla Ruth was secretary, and Mrs. James A. Robinson, whose husband was editor of *The Durham Daily Sun* (and could therefore supply much-needed publicity), was treasurer. Volunteering to help them organize and direct the drive were Julian Carr's brother-in-law E. J. Parrish; his sister-in-law, Mrs. Albert G. Carr; and the president of his bag factory

(Golden Belt Manufacturing company), Thomas B. Fuller.

Happily, the fund-raising drive was successful enough for construction of the Durham Public Library to begin in 1897, and when it opened on February 11, 1898 it had the distinction of being the first library in the southeast to make books available to the public without payment of dues or fees. Furthermore, because it had been given a stipend of $50 a month by the town council, it also became the first library in North Carolina to receive municipal support. Perhaps naturally, Julian Carr was chairman of the first board of trustees, and he figured prominently on that board for the next twenty-six years.

He also had a large hand in selecting what went into the cornerstone box when it was laid on September 4, 1897. Among the contents, which were notable for the number of documents obviously donated by, and attesting to, the prominence of Julian Shakespeare Carr as a citizen of Durham, was a photograph of Lalla Ruth, "the lady who fostered and promoted the building of the Durham Public Library." And there were copies of *The Durham Morning Herald*, *The Durham Daily Sun*, *The News and Observer*, the *North Carolina Presbyterian*, the *Biblical Recorder*, the *Christian Educator*, the *Durham Almanac* and the Trinity College *Archive*.

The rest of the contents consisted of a signed copy of the deed to the land donated as a library site by Carr and his friend Thomas Martin; a copy of the charter and by-laws of Blackwell's Durham Tobacco Company, of which Carr was president; a catalogue of the thoroughbred and trottingbred horses Carr owned, and a bulletin of the exotic chickens he raised at Occoneechee, his model farm near Hillsborough; minutes of a meeting of the Grand Chapter of the Royal Arch Masons, of which he was a staunch member; and a copy of Confederate President Jefferson Davis's "last paper of a public nature written from a sick bed just five days before his death." Davis was second only to General Robert E. Lee in Carr's estimation, and he made no secret of his abiding loyalty to the Confederacy.

Carr also was extremely loyal to the library, which flourished during its early years and then, gradually, began to decline as public enthusiasm deteriorated into near apathy. But in 1908, a movement to reorganize it "on a business basis" resulted in the formation of the Durham Library Association. The minutes of its first meting on May 11, 1908, state that "attendance was not all that could have been desired but many who were prevented from coming by other engagements . . . sent their pledges and gave their willingness to sign the cards for support of the association." Its first officers were: Mrs. W. L. Wall, president; John Sprunt Hill, vice president; Lila Markham, secretary; and John F. Wily, treasurer. Dues were set at $3 a year—a lifetime membership cost $100—and pledges amounting to $1,000 were signed at the initial gathering of those "friends" of the library.

The board of trustees was chaired by Carr and included C. W. Toms, John Sprunt Hill, John F. Wily, Thomas B. Fuller, H. A. Foushee, James H. Southgate, W. J. Brogden, C. W. Massey, Edwin Mims, W. D. Carmichael and the Reverend Sidney Bost. They decided to renovate, remodel and modernize the small frame building at Five Points that sheltered 3,700 books, and within six months the deed was done.

On November 12, 1908, the newly-painted library was the scene of a reception given by the trustees "to stimulate interest in the library movement and to attract people to it who will aid the board in making the reading room even more popular than it has ever been." While guests browsed through the refurbished facility, a chorus of Durham's best singers, listed as "Mesdames T. D. Jones, J. M. Manning, A. G. Carr, N. F. Yancy, C. W. Bryant and Messrs, R. E. Piper, A. E. Lloyd, F. E. Ogburn, A. G. Carr, Sligo and Rosemond" furnished entertainment, while association members "talked up" the library to prospective members and plied them with refreshments.

Persuading people that they should support free access to books and encourage reading was not always easy, but an especially heartening statistic, and one that may have been used by recruiters that night, was the fact that each of the Durham Library's 3,700 volumes had been read eleven times, "three times as much as the [Olivia] Raney Library of Raleigh and four times as much as any Carnegie Library."

A Carnegie Library was, of course, what a few of the most dedicated trustees had been dreaming of ever since the Scottish steel baron began to give away millions for the purpose of financing them. The easing of Andrew Carnegie's conscience was making public libraries possible in cities throughout America, so why not get one for Durham? It was an idea whose time had not quite come, but unbeknown to those who enjoyed the library association's gala in the fall of 1908, it was on its way.

Within three years, a graduate of the Carnegie Library School of Atlanta would arrive in Durham

Durham's first library.

Durham's main library today.

and take over the reins of the library, and under her guidance, it would expand and grow far beyond the expectations of its founders. Lillian Baker Griggs, a South Carolina native, would bring added prestige to Durham by being the first professionally-trained librarian in North Carolina, and she would add yet another "first" to the city's growing list by initiating "the first bookmobile in North Carolina and one of the first in the country."

Lillian Griggs, of Anderson, South Carolina, was widowed at the age of thirty-two and faced with supporting herself and a nine-year-old son. That was a challenge in the early part of the twentieth century, especially in a male-dominated society that did not look kindly on career women. But Mrs. Alfred Flournoy Griggs took it as she would take so many more challenges during her lifetime—with determination and the saving grace of humor.

Arriving in Durham on June 29, 1911, Lillian and Alfred Griggs, Jr. were met at Union Station by Mrs. W. L. Wall, president of the Durham Library Association. After observing the amenities and, no doubt, sizing each other up, they proceeded "to the R. L. Baldwin home at 606 Chapel Hill Street, where a room had been rented for the new librarian." Proof of Lillian Griggs' charm and her ability to make lasting friendships is documented by the fact that she and Alfred became virtually a "part of the Baldwin family" and stayed with them for twenty years. They even accompanied their landlords "to New York in 1914 to help choose furnishings for the new Baldwin home at 904 Vickers Avenue," according to a Duke University historian, and by that time the new librarian had been accepted by the entire community as a woman who got things done with dispatch without ruffling bureaucratic feathers.

This diminutive lady, who said she never weighed more than ninety pounds, had charmed the library's board of trustees at their first encounter. Toward the end of that meeting, Thomas B. Fuller, a member whose dedication to books and reading matched Lillian Griggs's, moved that they turn the library over to her "and that all we ask for is results." Relieved that she was free to go ahead with her ideas, she began by cataloging and classifying over 4,000 books, and then she went to the board of aldermen, persuaded them to double the monthly appropriation so she could establish a workable budget, and began to keep meticulous records that later would appear in annual reports.

"Haphazard" no longer applied to the way the library began to be run under Lillian Griggs's leadership, but there was nothing of the martinet in her. Gentle with children, gracious with adults, and invariably kind to adolescents, she made the library attractive to patrons of all ages and encouraged reading in a variety of ways. Those ways included a rental collection of the latest fiction for people so eager to read it that they willingly paid a dime for the privilege of borrowing a bestseller for seven days; and placing books at favorable locations in other parts of the city, such as West Durham, East Durham, Edgemont and Lowe's Grove. Her latter effort met with such favorable response that branch libraries in each of these districts eventually were established, thus proving Mrs. Griggs's theory that if people could

Lillian Baker Griggs

only see and touch and look between the covers of books, they would want to read them.

She proved that again by helping to establish a library in Durham High School, and yet again by providing books for young readers at the county schools. With the cooperation of teachers who came into town to select them, she either wrapped and mailed their choices, or prevailed upon friends who owned cars to deliver the packages to their various destinations. Of the twenty-six schools in the county, twenty-one participated in this popular program which eventually led to the creation of the "bookmobile," specially made from a Ford truck "by adding shelving behind exterior doors on each side."

The device was financed by the local Kiwanis Club, of which Lillian Griggs's good friend, R. L. Baldwin, was president, and it raised the money for this library-on-wheels by putting on a local talent show called, *The Jollies of 1923*. The production ran for two nights at the Academy of Music and was staged and directed by Freeman Gosden and Charles Correll, who would later become famous as "Amos 'n Andy," the best-known radio stars of that era.

Probably one of the most satisfying experiences of her career was Lillian Griggs's success, with the help of trustee Thomas B. Fuller, in obtaining a Carnegie grant for a new library building in 1917. It was a difficult task fraught with interruptions and opposition, and it was further delayed by World War I and her assignment by the American Library Association to the Army of Occupation in Germany. She spent the year 1919 stationed in Coblentz and traveling "into villages up and down the rivers," supplying hospitals with books and magazines for ill and wounded servicemen.

Back home in 1920, she resumed negotiations with architects and contractors and a lengthy correspondence with the Carnegie Foundation, which agreed to give $32,000 toward constructing a building at a site on Main Street between the First Presbyterian Church and the residence of Thomas B. Fuller. When the beautiful new library "in the Colonial style of architecture" was presented to the city by Fuller on July 6, 1921, it was the "last word," with ample space for 8,000 volumes, ranging from nursery books to reference books, and plenty of windows and skylights, so that "even on the darkest days the natural light was sufficient for reading purposes." There was a children's corner, a reading room, a reference room, a librarian's desk and Mrs. Griggs's office on the main floor. The basement housed a storage room, a bindery, a rest room, and a clubroom "to be open at all times for meetings of any of the women's clubs in the city or the county."

For Lillian Griggs, it was a dream come true, but only one of many, for her career was by no means over. Other accomplishments awaited her, and as the years passed she became more active in library associations throughout the South and was well-known as an articulate and persuasive speaker. In 1924 she left Durham to live and work in Raleigh, as director of the North Carolina Library Commission. Six years later, in 1930, she returned to become the librarian of the Women's College at Duke University, another challenge that she took eagerly and "with the same dedication to high standards in librarianship" she had demonstrated since her first day at the little library at Five Points, in the summer of 1911.

*Steel Magnolias*, the catchy title of a popular movie, is an especially apt term for gutsy Southern females who, confronted with adversity, grab it by the throat and quietly choke it to death. Without sacrificing their femininity, their integrity or their lady-like demeanor, they prevail, and sometimes their impact on a community affects the course of history.

Such a lady was Lillian Baker Griggs.

# TWELVE

# The Durham Sun: Conceived through contention

For over 100 years *The Durham Sun* exhibited a feisty instinct for survival in spite of periodic setbacks and many changes in management and personnel.

Conceived in an atmosphere of bitter contention between Washington Duke and Julian Shakespeare Carr, two of Durham's leading tobacco manufacturers, the paper came into the world with strings attached: either it would pay its way from the beginning or it would be allowed to die quickly, before its progenitors could lose money on it. But from the day of its birth, on February 26, 1889, *The Durham Sun* was destined for a long life, and until it died on December 31, 1990, just two months short of its 102nd birthday, it was the city's oldest existing newspaper.

*The Durham Sun* was established for one reason and one reason only: to persuade the general public and a majority of the town's board of aldermen that the newly franchised Durham and Northern Railroad should be allowed to extend its tracks approximately one mile from the depot on Dillard Street to the tobacco factory of W. Duke Sons and Company. The Durham and Clarksville Railroad, chartered

two years earlier by Julian Carr and two of his friends, Caleb Green and Peter M. Wilson, already had lines running to the Duke factory, but the Durham and Clarksville refused to allow the Durham and Northern to use its tracks or infringe on its right-of-way.

Understandably, Washington Duke, president of W. Duke Sons and Company, was extremely unhappy about that fact. It bothered Duke that the tobacco factory owned by Julian Shakespeare Carr, his arch rival in business, stood almost adjacent to the depot, and that Carr would benefit immediately from the new railway connection while he, Duke, would not. It also bothered Duke that Carr, who had for some years owned Durham's leading newspaper, *The Tobacco Plant*, had recently jumped the gun on him and bought *The Durham Recorder*, the only other local newspaper of any consequence. That left Duke with no voice in the press, as Carr, naturally, would not allow either of his publications to give editorial support to his biggest competitor.

Washington Duke was determined to get those tracks laid to his loading docks so that he, as well as

Edward Tyler Rollins

garnering public support for a cause that, they assured him, would ultimately benefit the whole town.

Robinson, who came to be known as "Old Hurrygraph," may have earned his nickname during his first month as editor of *The Durham Sun*, for about four weeks after the paper's first edition, his initial mission was accomplished: the board of alderman authorized the Durham and Northern Railroad to extend its tracks, alongside those of the Durham and Clarksville, to Duke's factory.

As historians have recorded, however, "authorization was one thing and laying the tracks was another." Everybody knew that the Durham and Clarksville would fight for its right-of-way, especially as Jule Carr was one of that railroad's founders, but nobody knew how long and bitter the fight would be.

It began exactly two weeks after the Durham and Northern had steamed and whistled its way into the station on Dillard Street for the first time on March 26, 1889. Two weeks later, a group of Durham citizens who were in sympathy with Washington Duke took matters in their own hands, and under the supervision of Northern engineers, they began laying tracks to W. Duke Sons and Company around midnight. By daylight on Tuesday they had reached Corcoran Street, about half the distance to their destination.

By noon, they were all under arrest for trespassing on the Durham and Clarksville's right-of-way; but by sunset they were free again, courtesy of three hastily assembled Durham justices, who dismissed the warrants against them.

Work resumed that night, and Wednesday morning saw the job finished, but Washington Duke's sat-

Jule Carr, could increase shipments of tobacco, and Duke was not an easy man to stop. Discussing his grievance with some of his friends on the board of aldermen, of which he also was a member, he convinced them that what Durham needed was a third paper and an experienced newsman to run it.

These aldermen (with the exception of Duke, they remain nameless) then contacted James Algernon Robinson, already working for Jule Carr on *The Durham Recorder*, and persuaded him to leave his job for what could be a better one, if he succeeded in

isfaction was brief. Within a few hours, the Durham and Clarksville had its work crews busily tearing up the tracks, and they managed to demolish about 100 feet of steel before they were arrested, by Durham police, for vandalism.

Then, presumably, the invisible wheels of power began to turn even more rapidly. Before the day was over a restraining order against the Durham and Clarksville Railroad had been issued by a federal judge in Greensboro, and the disgruntled citizens who had set out to bring a second railroad to Duke's factory were able to complete the job, this time under armed protection.

Nevertheless, the battle continued to rage in the North Carolina courts for fourteen years, and by the time it was finally resolved in 1903, the Durham and Clarksville had been taken over by the Southern Railway, and the Durham and Northern was owned by the Seaboard Air Line. The Seaboard, incidentally, lost the case and had to begin renting the track it had been using for over a decade from the Southern.

So the cause that "Old Hurrygraph" Robinson espoused at the beginning of his career as editor of *The Durham Sun* finally was lost, but by then nobody remembered that the paper had been spawned by a power struggle between two of Durham's leading citizens, or that it had been expected to outlast its chief competitor, *The Tobacco Plant*. (A few months after the *Sun*'s advent in 1889, the *Plant* was sold, became *The Globe*, and eventually went out of business, but Robinson continued to publish the *Sun* for twenty years.)

In 1910, J.A. Robinson sold the *Sun* to Julian S. Carr, the man who had been the main cause of its in-

ception, and R. O. Everett, a Durham lawyer. Their ownership was brief and unsuccessful, however, and from then until the summer of 1929, *The Durham Sun* had thirteen different owners and eleven different editors. They came from such diverse locations as Raleigh, Tarboro and Burlington; Springfield, Hamilton and Columbus, Ohio; Goshen and Marion, Indiana.; St. Louis, Missouri; Columbia, South Carolina, and Columbus, Georgia. Somehow it was able to withstand those often traumatic changes in management, however, and became such a formidable rival of *The Durham Morning Herald* that the *Herald*'s owner, Edward Tyler Rollins, decided it would be better to buy the *Sun* than try to compete with it.

A few months before the stock market crash of 1929, Rollins bought *The Durham Sun* and continued to publish it. Operating under the same roof with *The Durham Morning Herald*, it became an even more dedicated rival, continuing to try and "out scoop" the *Herald* for the next seventy years.

When E. T. Rollins died in 1931, Carl C. Council, who had served as advertising manager, circulation manager, and business manager, assumed overall management of both papers. Under his guidance, The Durham Herald Company, sometimes called the Herald-Sun Papers, continued to expand, and its acquisition of radio station WDNC, in 1936, made it more than ever a force in the community.

C. C. Council died in 1964, and E. T. Rollins' eldest son, Steed Rollins, who had moved up by degrees from a sweeper in the composing room to executive editor of both the *Herald* and the *Sun*, became president of the Durham Herald Company.

His brother, E. T. Rollins, Jr., who had also learned the business from the ground up, was named vice president, and H. B. "Mack" Webb became executive editor.

Further changes in management began to occur in 1981, when Steed Rollins became chairman of the board. E. T. Rollins, Jr. took over as president and publisher of the company and served in that capacity until 1987, when Richard J. Kaspar, of Columbus, Georgia, became president and W. E. N. Hawkins, of Baltimore, Maryland, was hired as executive editor.

Like most of the nation's afternoon dailies, *The Durham Sun* eventually fell victim to television's evening news and its charismatic anchormen, Brokaw, Jennings, and Rather. On New Year's Day, 1991, the two old rivals merged again to become one under yet a new banner, *The Herald-Sun.*

So far, it seems to be a happy marriage.

# THIRTEEN

# Durham's churches have a rich history

Anyone attempting to put an in-depth history of Durham's churches between the covers of one book had better be completely dedicated to the project, devoted to hard labor, and possessed of great stamina. Not that there is any lack of source material; on the contrary, the material is so voluminous that getting it together and sorting it out would be like trying to beach a whale with bare hands. But columnists, unlike historians, seldom fish for whales. Columnists fish for minnows, and what follows is merely one small, variegated catch seined from an ocean of ecclesiastical information.

In the beginning were the Baptists. As early as 1805, long before the little hamlet of Durham even existed, enterprising Baptists built a church near a stream called Cedar Fork, about twelve miles southeast of the present city of Durham. Forty years later, the Rose of Sharon Baptist Church came into being and, according to an early historian, was the first denomination to establish itself in the immediate vicinity. Baptists were here not only to stay, but also to expand, and a little over 100 years after their Rose of Sharon came on the scene, they had thirty-two churches here.

By that time, Durham also had Methodists, Episcopalians, Presbyterians, Unitarians, Christian Scientists, Latter-Day Saints, Hebrews, Seventh-Day Adventists, Friends, Greeks, Catholics, Lutherans, Jehovah's Witnesses and Christians, and most were attending their own houses of worship.

Among the city's "first families," the Dukes were Methodists and went to Duke Chapel, which was named for Washington Duke's brother, William. "Uncle Billie," as William Duke was called, was a renowned circuit rider, and it was he who persuaded his little brother, Wash, to join the church. Converted at the age of eleven, Wash Duke was a staunch believer all of his life and never missed a Sunday service, unless he was too sick to get out of bed. In contrast, his youngest son, Buck, founder of American Tobacco Company, Duke Power Company and Duke University, was far from devout and rarely went to church. Nevertheless, Buck Duke once said the Methodist circuit riders of his boyhood were "the greatest human influence in my whole life, save that of my own father."

Incidentally, his own father once said that three things he had never been able to understand were "electricity, the Holy Ghost and my son Buck."

But back to Durham's first churches: In 1878, a young deacon at Chapel Hill's Chapel of the Cross, upon hearing there were Episcopalians living in Durham who had no minister and no church, decided that something should be done about the situation, and that he was the one to do it. Joseph Blount Cheshire, fired with youthful missionary zeal, walked the twelve rough, dusty and sometimes muddy miles from Chapel Hill to Durham as often as he could, in order to tend that small flock and help them organize.

Two years later, after holding sporadic services in various places, the communicants of St. Philip's acquired their first church; and in 1912, thirty-four years after his first long walk to Durham, Joseph Blount Cheshire, by that time a bishop, came back to dedicate the stone edifice that now stands on Main Street, between Queen and Dillard.

As for Presbyterians, none settled here until 1860, when Dr. Richard Blacknall came with his wife, two daughters and three sons. For several years the Blacknalls, being the only Presbyterians in town, attended church in Chapel Hill; but it was a long, bone-bruising ride, and when they couldn't make it they met, instead, in the Rose of Sharon Baptist Church.

As the town began to grow after the Civil War and a few more Scots arrived, Mrs. Blacknall began to hold Sunday school classes in her home, and occasionally a visiting minister would preach to the small congregation in either the Baptist or the Methodist church. Then, in 1871, Durham Presbyterians decided the time had come to organize. Meeting at Durham Academy, the public school on Cleveland Street, eleven charter members elected two

The First Presbyterian Church sits at the corner of Main Street and Roxboro Road. ca. 1890.

ruling elders and one deacon, and for the next two years they worshipped at Trinity Methodist, on Church Street. Later they moved to a rented hall on Mangum, but they were tired of having no home of their own, and in 1876 they bought a lot on the corner of Main and Mangum.

There they put a small, box-like wooden structure that served them until 1889, when they could afford a brick-and-masonry building with a Sunday school in the rear.

Twenty-six years later, on April 26, 1915, work began on a third First Presbyterian Church and a connecting school building that was, for some reason, as round as a biscuit. All the classrooms were pie-

An imposing snowy shot of Duke University's Duke Chapel during the winter in 1940. Note the old car with a rumble seat, parked at the steps.

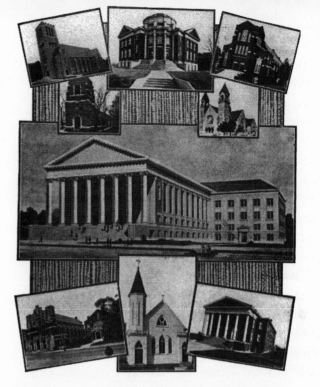

Nine religious institutions—Top row, left to right: Trinity Methodist, Branson Methodist, Trinity Avenue Presbyterian. Second row, left: St. Philip's Episcopal; right: Duke Memorial Methodist. Center: First Baptist. Bottom row, left to right: First Presbyterian, Church of the Immaculate Conception (Catholic), East Durham Baptist. ca. 1928.

shaped, and there was an assembly room in the middle with a dais for Mr. George Watts, the superintendent, to stand on while he told us children what to do in order to stay out of the "Bad Place"—grown-ups avoided saying "hell" in those days, especially in front of small fry.

This writer, born Presbyterian, still remembers with vivid clarity the tall, spare figure and benign face of Mr. Watts, and the way the Sunday morning sun flashed on his pince-nez, and highlighted the whiteness of his starched shirt collar and cuffs as he spoke of salvation and how to earn it.

One last bit of incidental information about Durham churches: There are over a million pieces of glass in the stained-glass windows of present-day Duke Chapel, and they are worth going to see. Looking at their multi-colored brilliance, set in cool gray stone, one thinks not of the labor and the cost that went into creating them, but of the glory of God.

Which is as it should be.

# FOURTEEN

# An old neighborhood stirs old memories

*L*iving with the smell of tobacco in my nose and the sound of the Bull Factory whistle in my ears—it blew noontime and quitting time every day but Sunday—I grew up in a neighborhood of quiet streets shaded by big trees and lined with good, solid houses. Some were small, some were large and rambling, and some were downright imposing, but none could match the towering magnificence of General Julian Carr's Victorian mansion, which he called Somerset Villa.

Sitting square in the middle of an entire city block at the eastern end of Main Street, it looked like a castle straight out of fairyland to me, with its turrets, its gables and its many windows. Balconies and upstairs porches were festooned in lacy gingerbread trim, and soaring high above the roofline was an ornate copper weather vane that gleamed like pure gold in the sunlight and was visible for half a mile in all directions.

An architectural journal published in Richmond, Virginia in 1888 reported that Carr's house had cost $125,000, a mind-boggling sum in those days, and that over half of that amount was spent on the interior of "one of the most beautiful and complete private houses in the world."

Wealthy individuals today no doubt will shrug off the fact that Carr spent $1,800 on the fireplace mantel in his reception hall, and $500 each for the newel posts at the bottom of the main stairway; but Durham folks, in the 1880s, gasped in astonishment at the very idea of such prices.

As for investing $40,000 in carpets and furniture, $6,000 in stained glass windows, and $5,000 in chandeliers, why nobody ever heard of such a thing!

Even though Carr was reputed to be the richest man in North Carolina in 1888, nobody in Durham ever heard of building a house with all those rooms, either—a massive reception hall, two parlors, a smoking room, a dining room big enough for a banquet table, a kitchen big enough for a hotel-size range, oven and broiler, five bedrooms with connecting dressing rooms and baths, quarters for two live-in servants, and a billiard room. Each bathroom had a tub and a shower, and the children's bathroom—

Somerset Villa, house of Julian Carr. ca. 1888.

who in the world ever heard of a special bathroom for children—had picture-book tiles decorated with reeds, cattails, pond lilies, frogs, turtles and storks.

By the time I became acquainted with it in 1921, Somerset Villa had been a beloved landmark for more than three decades, and Carr's grandchildren were using that fancy bathroom. They also were enjoying some very special playground equipment Carr had installed in the backyard, and as a friend of one of those highly privileged youngsters, I was enjoying it too on many long summer mornings.

Unlike any other house in town, Somerset was not made of just wood or brick or stone. Timber, brownstone, granite, marble, stucco, pressed brick, slate, terra cotta and bronze went into its construction, and it seemed to glow with the muted colors of those materials. Two wide stairways curved down from the broad front piazza to the rolling green lawn, where formal flowerbeds were always blooming with whatever was in season.

Considerably impressed with all of this opulence, I was never happier than when I was playing at Somerset, where the swings were bigger and went higher than the swings at Fuller School, and the clang of metal as we flung ourselves around the "giant stride" had the resonance of church bells on Sunday morning. I have not forgotten the fearsome thrill of going down the long, steep sliding board on my belly, with the wind in my face and another body, far too close for a safe landing, right behind me. That was never my choice of ways to slide, but all Carrs were notorious "dee-double-dog" darers who would hound any "scaredy-cat" right out of their yard, and I would rather have died than suffer such ignominy.

Yes, playing with the Carrs could build character and also, on occasion, draw blood. Knees, noses and elbows were especially vulnerable, but all of us wore our bandages and scabs like medals of honor in that neighborhood. It was a good neighborhood, one of the best, but it's long gone. If I went back now to where it used to be, I would walk among ghosts, and through the mists of a thousand old memories. I might even get mugged.

So I don't believe I'll go, except in my mind.

# FIFTEEN

# What's really behind the history in history books?

*P*eople, of course. And if you choose to write about real people, living or dead, there's always an unknown quantity that eludes you, something just beyond your mental grasp even though you sense it strongly, you know it's there, you can almost reach out and touch it with your mind.

What you learn from direct confrontation with a living person is still only an infinitesimal fragment of that person's story (history), for who can reveal himself, or herself, to another human being with complete candor? All of us mask the truth about ourselves, even to ourselves; our egos are too fragile to view it naked, defenseless.

On the other hand, what you're able to discover about the dead is even more tantalizing. Half truths caged in printed words between the covers of books, or on the brittle, yellowing pages of old newspapers. Search out the facts about a long-gone citizen of your hometown and you may read that "he was a champion of the poor, an ardent defender of the rights of every human being, a God-fearing man who never missed a service at his church, a devoted husband and father."

But then you begin to wonder. You wonder if this paragon ever cheated anybody, or lied about his income tax, or slept through a dull sermon at one of those church services he supposedly never missed. You wonder if he ever took his wife for granted, demanding his "rights" as a husband, and complaining about the food on the table, the fingerprints on the woodwork, the children's noise, their crying, their bad manners, their outlandish clothes, et cetera, et cetera. And then you think: Well, he was human. And so you imagine him doing the human, imperfect things that were left out of the books and newspapers, and little by little he becomes real, you like him better.

But the best way to write about people is to know them while they're living, and then read about them after they're dead. Put behind-the-scenes with what's on paper. What you sometimes come up with, when you do that, is often far more real, infinitely more satisfying. And it's safer. For instance:

Edwin Wexler Kennedy—my Uncle Ed—was Durham's first school superintendent. A native of Tennessee, he moved to Goldsboro to teach in the public school there, and after Durham voted to establish a similar institution here in 1881, the first board of education, comprised of Eugene Morehead, J. B. Whitaker and Bartholomew Fuller, hired Kennedy to run it. An early Durham history book has this to say about him: "As the success of a school depends very largely on the capability of the Superintendent, the committee was very fortunate in securing the services of Professor E. W. Kennedy for this most important position. A fine scholar experienced in the graded system of instruction, with superior executive ability and without equal in the State as a disciplinarian, he has given abundant evidence by his conduct of the school that he is the right man in the right place. Devoted to his work, with a determination to succeed, and moreover, a close student, the increasing brilliancy of his reputation attests that the highest success awaits him. During the vacation of 1884, he proposes to visit Germany and Italy and other European countries, and while absent will apply himself to special studies . . ."

Reading the above, all I could think was: *Can this really be Uncle Ed?*

Marion Fuller, my father's sister, was a member of the grade school's first graduating class in 1884. She subsequently married Mr. Kennedy, and he became our Uncle Ed, a small, dapper, handsome fellow, very much like those little men you used to see on top of wedding cakes, except that his hair and moustache were snow-white. Always meticulously groomed, he smelled of Bay Rum and clean, starched linen, and his skin was as pink and clear as a baby's.

If, indeed, he had executive ability and was without equal as a disciplinarian, he confined these qual-

Marion "Mannie" Fuller Kennedy

ities entirely to the schoolroom, for at home he was completely henpecked by my Aunt Marion, whom we called Mannie.

Mannie was tall, beautiful, slow-moving and dignified, and she treated her husband like a child, probably the child she never had. When she said "Mr. Kennedy"—she never called him anything but Mr. Kennedy—he came to attention like a bird dog. No matter what she told him to do, he always said "Yes, Ma'am!" and then he went and did it, no questions asked, no arguments, and no sulking.

He had a cheerful disposition, and he adored Mannie. Nothing she did, or said, seemed to faze him, not even being given cold oatmeal, left over from breakfast, to eat for supper. I discovered this when I went to visit them in Johnson City, Tennessee, where they eventually moved, and I have never forgotten the sight of that pale, gray, gelatinous blob of cereal, with nothing on it, that he ate so cheerfully, every bite of it.

One summer afternoon when Mannie and Uncle Ed were visiting my parents, other aunts and uncles, plus a few cousins, came to call on them. While they were gathered on the front porch, rocking and talking, Uncle Ed rocked back too far in his tall-backed, cane bottomed chair and tipped over backward, bringing shrieks from the women and children and causing the men to rush to his aid, to heave him back up on his feet, to brush off his coat and pat him on the back and peer into his face and ask, "You all right, Ed? You sure you all right?" Apparently, he was, and he said so; but Mannie, standing tall and quiet, her hands clasped together and her face pale and stern, spoke into the general hubbub.

"Go upstairs and get into your bed, Mr. Kennedy," she ordered; and in the silence that followed, Uncle Ed brushed at first one sleeve and then the other, gave a little nod of his head, and turned and went into the house. Mannie sat down. The rest of us sat down. Pretty soon everybody was rocking and talking again and when it was time for supper, Uncle Ed's place at the table was empty, but nobody mentioned it.

We didn't see him again until next morning at breakfast and then he was his usual affable self, eyes twinkling, cheeks pink, hair and moustache whiter than snow. We asked him how he felt, and he answered, "Fine! Wonderful! Couldn't be better!" Then, looking across the table at Mannie and pointing a finger in her direction, he said, "That woman, that woman" here the finger wagged and he shook his head, as if in disbelief—"that woman is a fine woman!"

Mannie, gazing back at him serenely, spoke quietly. "That will do, Mr. Kennedy," she said. "Eat your breakfast."

"Yes, Ma'am!" came the enthusiastic reply, and Uncle Ed started on his oatmeal—hot this time, and drenched in butter, thick cream, and brown sugar.

That's history, too.

# CHAPTER SIXTEEN

# Tom Thumb weddings:
# Who dreamed them up? And why?

Neither the Durham County Library on Roxboro Street nor the Perkins Library at Duke University was able to come up with a shred of information about "Tom Thumb" weddings when I inquired about their origins, but the photograph owned by the late Helen Dickson McKee, of Durham, is irrefutable proof that at least one such phenomenon did occur here in Durham around 1918 and may have attracted an audience of considerable size.

The fact that these mock weddings also occurred elsewhere became evident when several librarians with roots in such diverse locations as Kansas, Texas, West Virginia and Alabama admitted they knew all about Tom Thumb weddings. Audrey Evans, a former custodian of the Durham County Library's Shannon Road branch, remembers taking part in one at Lowe's Grove Baptist Church around 1949, but neither she nor anybody else I questioned could unearth any documentation as to when, where or why these Lilliputian nuptials originated.

It was suggested that they probably were connected to fund-raising of one sort or another, and although various encyclopedias, indices, dictionaries and histories failed to corroborate that premise, I tend to agree with it. Why else would otherwise sensible and caring mothers dress their defenseless children in formal adult garb and put them through the anxiety-producing ordeal of a marriage ceremony, except for a worthy cause? I know that stage fright can make grown men and women faint at their own weddings, because I saw a bride sag to the floor of an Episcopal Church sanctuary; and I saw a groom collapse, not once, but twice, in the Duke Chapel. So it is entirely within the realm of possibility that extreme tension accounts for the fact that there were no smiles on the faces of the Tom Thumb wedding that took place three quarters of a century ago somewhere in Durham.

Participants were the sons and daughters of a number of representative citizens, and with the exception of two who could not be identified, they were, from left to right: Frances Mason (Mrs. Donald

*Caption from The Durham Sun, 1939*: The "Lilliputians" taking part in this wedding have reached mature womanhood and manhood, and many cases parenthood. This miniature wedding was one of the ways the Civic Association had of raising funds. The late Mrs. I. F. Hill, who was active in the arrangements, thought the picture was made about 1915.

As far as it was possible to identify these children of 24 years ago, they are reading from left to right: Francis Mason (Mrs. Donald Clement), Agnes Lee Shackleford (Mrs. John G. Parks), Katherine Yancey, Alex Foushee, Helen Eubanks, Nelson McGary, Helen Dickson (Mrs. Louis McKee), Mary Lucy Green (Mrs. Henry Bost), Bill Farthing, Frances Foushee, William Pace Fuller, Kate Graham (Mrs. Charles Murphy of Washinton, D.C.), Julia Dewey Bryant (Mrs. Henry Van Stratton), E. B. Lyon, Rawles Cobb, Bobby Carmichael, Virginia Felts (Mrs. Palmer Pickard), Marion Lyon (Mrs. John Sessums), Egbert Haywood, Rececca Piatt (Mrs. Leonard Carey), Edward Beall, Bill Wannamaker, Emmett Shackleford, Sophronia Webb, Mary Elizabeth Boyd (Mrs. William Hamilton), Patsy Mason (Mrs. Allen Murdock), Francis Hill (Mrs. H. J. Fox).

Clement), Agnes Lee Shackleford (Mrs. John G. Parks), Katherine Yancey, Alex Foushee, Helen Eubanks, Nelson McGary, Helen Dickson (Mrs. Lewis McKee), Mary Lucy Green (Mrs. Henry Bost), William P. Farthing, Frances Foushee (Mrs. Hunter Sweaney), William Pace Fuller, Kate Graham (Mrs. Charles Murphey), Julia Dewey Bryant (Mrs. Harry Van Straaten), Edwin Buchanan Lyon, Rawles Cobb, Robert Carmichael, Virginia Felts (Mrs. Palmer Rickard), Marian Lyon (Mrs. John Sessums), Egbert Haywood, Rebecca Piatt (Mrs. Leonard Carey), Edward Beall, William Wannamaker, Emmet Shackleford, Sophronia Webb, Mary Elizabeth Boyd (Mrs. William Hamilton), Patsy Mason (Mrs. Allen Murdock) and Frances Hill (Mrs. Herbert J. Fox). Less than half of the group still survives, and three who have remained in Durham are Mrs. Parks, Mrs. Van Straaten and Mrs. Fox.

The bride and groom were Virginia "Gince" Felts, youngest daughter of Dr. R. L. Felts, a much-loved general practitioner, and E. B. "Buck" Lyon, grandson of Washington Duke, nephew of J. B. "Buck" Duke, and brother of Marian Lyon, the cherubic ring bearer who preferred to gaze at the ceiling rather than smile for the photographer. The minister, in white surplice and clerical spectacles, was Rawles Cobb, whose father, Alphonsus Cobb, managed two of Durham's finest hotels, the Carolina, which burned in the early 1900s, and the Washington Duke, imploded in 1975. The maid of honor, distinguishable by the basket of flowers on her right arm and the lacy scallops that edge the skirt of her dress, was Julia Dewey, youngest daughter of one of Durham's first attorneys, Victor Silas Bryant.

When this picture was made, Woodrow Wilson was president, Theda Bara was a popular "vamp" in silent movies, Jess Willard was the heavyweight boxing champion of the world, and the song that was all the rage was "When You Wore a Tulip." Incidental information of that nature was easy to uncover, but I'm still looking for the first Tom Thumb wedding and the individual who dreamed it up.

Bound to have been somebody's mama.

# SEVENTEEN

*During those seven days our house on
Main Street shed it's familiar persona and
became a place of mystery and expectency . . .*

# Christmas at our house

Once upon a very long time ago, when I was a true believer, the week before Christmas was the best time of the whole year. During those seven days, our house on Main Street shed its familiar persona and became a place of mystery and expectancy, where a great deal of whispering went on and Mama kept the door to the spare room closed and dared us to open it.

"I dare you to open that door," she would say to me if she caught me anywhere near it as she trotted up and down the stairs and in and out of the kitchen where Rose Murray, the cook, was queen and Mama, the lady of the house, was, nevertheless, her underling. Mama conferred with Rose every morning about what we would eat that day, and what groceries she would have to order from Mr. Charlie Atkins's store on Parrish Street; and during Christmas week she would call Mr. Charlie two or three

or even four times a day, sometimes, especially if she was worn out and distracted. "I'm so worn out and distracted I forgot to order the butter, Mr. Atkins," she might say about three minutes after she'd hung up the phone the first time; and then about twenty minutes later she'd trot back down the hall to the phone again and jiggle the hook to get Central's attention; and then she'd tell Mr. Charlie she must be losing her mind because she didn't know why she forgot ten pounds of sugar and a quart of whipping cream, and would he please add them to her order and get it out right away. "We need the cream for the eggnog, Mr. Atkins," she'd explain, "but I'm so distracted I can't seem to remember a single thing."

When the groceries came, packed in a paper box and deposited with a huge groaning sigh by the delivery boy, who had to wait while Mama took each thing out and checked it by her list, and then

69

checked her list by the grocery ticket, nine times out of ten something was missing, either because she'd been too distracted to remember it or Mr. Atkins had deliberately left it out, she would say to Rose and me as soon as the delivery boy had left. And then she would say what she always said when she was good and mad: "This life and one more, and then the blooming fireworks!" she would shout at the ceiling of the warm, fragrant kitchen, and Rose, standing at the sink, would shake her head and go, "Mmm, mmm, Miss Caro. You better go lie down and rest," and I would back out the door and get as far away from Mama as I could.

Every day or so the postman would bring big packages that Mama had to sign for, from my Aunt Nellie in Philadelphia, and my Aunt Mannie in Johnson City, Tennessee, and my Cousin Lillian Fuller, who lived in New York City, and Mama's baby sister, Aunt Lucy, who lived with Grandma Bacon in Atlanta, Georgia. Those bulky, brown-wrapped, string- tied bundles went straight upstairs to the spare room until Christmas Eve, when Papa brought them down for Mama to open after everybody else was in bed. Until then, they reposed on the embossed white counterpane that covered Mama's best monogrammed sheets and pillowcases that hid the rustling horsehair mattress on the big mahogany bed reserved for visiting relatives, and whenever I thought I could get away with it, dare or no dare, I sneaked into the forbidden spare room and looked at those mysterious boxes.

I would stand there looking and trying to guess what was inside, and praying that maybe one of them held a doll for me, a real doll with a soft body and a hard china head, a head with real hair, and blue eyes that opened and shut, and two little pearly teeth in the center of a rosebud mouth. But I couldn't spend a long time praying because the spare room was too cold, with the radiator shut off and no fire in the grate. Besides, the kitchen was the best room in the house during Christmas week.

That large, plain room, with its huge wood stove on one side and a long enamel sink opposite, underneath a window, and the scrubbed wooden work table in the middle, was my favorite place, anyway, and it got even better when strange exotic foods suddenly appeared there, as if by magic. Citron and mangoes and glazed cherries and pineapple, and dried figs and crystallized ginger and long, thin paper-shell pecans and strange, bumpy, hard-to-crack nuts from Brazil.

And always a coconut, dark and hairy and hard as a brickbat, a nut the size of a grapefruit that first had to be stabbed with an ice pick in two places, so the milk could run out of the holes into a waiting bowl, and then it had to be broken open with a hammer. Finally reduced to pieces, the tough white meat had to be pried away from the shell and grated, and I wondered why Mama ad Rose went to all that trouble for something that wasn't, to me, all that good. But Rose said, "You got to have coconut for the ambrosia. Your Grandma Fuller had it, along with the fruitcake, and now your Mama has it. And when you grow up to be a lady, if that sweet day ever come, you goan have it, too."

I didn't think so, but I knew better than to argue with Rose Murray.

Rosa Bumpass Linyear Murray, who had been our cook long before I was born, was one of the most important people in my life. Short and stout and shiny brown, she had white, even teeth that some-times got stained from the snuff she poked inside her bottom lip at least once a day, usually when she was resting her bunions. Her black, crinkly hair was divided into small, neat squares and then twisted into short, spiky plaits, and except for Sundays and holidays, most days she wore a dust cap that framed her round, benign face.

Her aprons, white and voluminous, covered all but the sleeves and neck and hem of the calico dres-ses she wore on weekdays, and on Sunday, as soon as dinner was ready to be served, she'd go to her room off the back porch and put on a black dress with a short, starched, small-bibbed white apron, and re-place the habitual dust cap with a white organdy band beaded with a black ribbon.

Once a day, Rose moved through the downstairs rooms of our house with the slow, stately tread of a monarch, dusting, sweeping, polishing and straight-ening, but her real domain was the kitchen, and I was allowed in it only so long as it pleased her. If she was what she called "low in my mind," she would have none of me; and if she was really busy she was apt to say, "Don't you set your foot in here 'til I tell you so," and I never did.

Rose didn't fuss at me, or nag, or complain about my behavior. If I came to her hungry, she always found something for me to eat—sometimes a tea-cake, scalloped around the edge, with a hole in the middle and a light dusting of sugar; or a cold biscuit with something in between, a piece of sausage or bacon saved from breakfast, or a dribble of molasses.

"Sit down yonder," she would say, nodding toward the kitchen table, and then she would hand me a thick white plate threaded with tiny cracks and

Rosa Bumpass
Linyear Murray

chipped in places on its edge. A warming plate, a kitchen plate, the kind of plate she ate from, and the kind I liked better than the gold-rimmed china that came to our dining-room table. That was china you had to be careful not to break or you would get *what for*, and *what for* was either a long lecture from Mama, if she wasn't too busy to put her mind to it, or banishment to your room for who knew how long. Eating in the kitchen, I was safe.

When I had something to say, Rose listened, or seemed to listen, anyway, nodding her head in agree-ment, or sympathy, occasionally murmuring, "Do tell," or "You don't say," or just "Mmm, mmm," and she never answered my questions with long, boring opinions of her own.

Besides emotional support, she gave me physical comfort when I needed it most. If I fell and skinned a knee or elbow, or raised a bump on my forehead, I usually ran, bawling, to Rose, and she never said "I told you not to climb up there!" Instead, she would pull me against her big, soft body and rub my back and say, "Hush, now, you goan be all right." If that didn't cure me, she'd lift me into her lap and rock us both back and forth, and sometimes she'd sing "Wash me and I shall be whiter than snow, Lord, whiter than snow, whiter than snow." Or maybe she'd sing, "Blind man sat on the road and cried," a song that was only that one refrain, and when I asked her what was the rest, she said "Ain't no rest, that's all it is to it."

But Rose was more of a hummer than a singer, and the tuneless sound that came from deep within her as she created her special desserts was one I loved to hear, a peaceful sound augmented by mouth-watering smells from pies all buttery-crunchy outside, and inside the sugary sweetness of apple and cinnamon, or dark, rich chocolate, or tangy lemon, or creamy custard crowned with two inches of feathery meringue.

And then there were puddings, everyday desserts like brown betty, or grated sweet potato pudding that Mama said took hours to make, or rice pudding served with a dollop of red currant jelly, or fig pudding topped with brandy hard sauce, not to mentioned gingerbread with lemon sauce, and muffin cakes with chocolate pour-over.

No doubt about it, we ate well all year long, and especially on Christmas, with the huge golden-brown turkey dominating the table, and Papa carving it and swearing that if he wasn't so hungry he could put all the slices back on the bones so nobody could tell it had ever been cut. Proud of his skill, and of Mama flushed and pretty down at the opposite end of the table, and us children on either side, Brother Ralph, Brother Bacon, Sister Carolyn and me, the littlest child who always, except on Christmas Day,

was served last because of "Age before beauty," something Papa always said when one of us complained about starving to death.

On Christmas Day, I always got the first helping of turkey and stuffing, a mixed blessing, because it was cold by the time everybody else got theirs and Papa said grace. But I didn't mind cold Christmas turkey because, for one brief moment, I had been special, on the most beautiful day of the year.

NOW, CHRISTMAS IS MY least favorite day in the year and I no longer apologize for that fact. Instead, I agree with the late E. B. White, long-time writer for *The New Yorker*, who said: "The only date I would like to see shifted is December 25, which I would like to see shifted to February 29, so that it occurs only once in every four years. This would have a profoundly beneficial effect on the nation and would set me back on an even course again." White also said that he enjoyed Christmas best when he could "just sit back and drink and let somebody else work it out," and although his remark is bound to create outrage in some circles, when you stop to think about it, there's no telling how many folks feel the same way and just won't admit it.

Here's how it usually is with me: Sandwiched between the faint exhilaration I sometimes manage to dredge up on December 24, and the sweet relief I experience on December 26, December 25 leaves me downright lethargic as soon as the packages under the tree are stripped of their bright wrappings, and the torn paper and useless ribbon relegated to the trash can, and the traditional feast is consumed.

By then the accumulated fatigue, engendered by everything I've done for the past two weeks, sweeps over me—all that brass cleaning and silver polishing and buying and wrapping, all that decorating and baking and freezing, all that addressing and licking and stamping and mailing and delivering—every last bit of it sweeps over me like a flood, and I realize I am in the state my mother used to call "worked to a boneyard finish."

Nor can I fall into bed as soon as my extended family departs after clearing the table and putting dishes into the dishwasher and collecting their assorted plunder and locating their many coats and jackets and scarves and gloves. Because of Mama's training, I simply cannot leave the house in a shambles. Instead, I must find space in the refrigerator for what's left of the turkey I will later convert into hash, and then soup. I must locate enough small bowls and plastic containers to hold what's left of the rice, the gravy, the candied yams, the creamed cauliflower, the green beans with almonds, and, yes, the ambrosia.

And I must put the fruit cake away in its special tin box, and transfer the last of the eggnog from Grandma Bacon's punchbowl to a glass jar for future imbibing, probably not later than tomorrow. Tomorrow is when I will carry my own gifts from the living room to my bedroom, and wonder how I'm going to incorporate them into my life, and how I'm going to find the strength to write thank-you notes for each one, which is what my mother raised me to do so long ago that it's a habit I cannot seem to break.

Now I think of the only present for which I never wrote any thanks at all, one of my favorites for the past twenty-five years and still in mint condition. It's a letter to Santa Claus from my father, Ralph Bell Fuller, dated December 23, 1876, and I gave it to myself 100 years later, in 1976, when I was doing

Wilhelmina Bell Fuller
"Grandma Fuller"

research in the Southern Historical Collection at the University of North Carolina. I found it, serendipitously, while I was collecting information for a biographical sketch of my great-grandfather, William Bell, and I treasure it because it gave me a glimpse of Bell's daughter, Wilhelmina, who became the grandmother for whom I was named, a lady who died before I was born.

All I knew about Wilhelmina Haldane Bell Fuller was that she was renowned for her sense of humor, and for the fortitude with which she lived through the Civil War, Reconstruction and twenty-three years of widowhood. During those years she never came out of mourning, but she never lost her sense of humor, either, according to my father and his three sisters. I like to think that it tickled her to persuade her three-year-old Ralph to ask for what he was going to get anyway on Christmas morning in 1876, and to write that letter to Santa Claus for him, and then help him send it up the chimney.

Now when I read it, so long after Papa's death, I am able to see him not as the benevolent tyrant he was, but as a little boy growing up in a terrible, bleak time in the South's history, making wishes at Christmas, just as I did once, and hoping that most of them, at least, would come true. Now, reading the copy I made of that scrap of paper, I relish it as one of my most favorite Christmas presents, and here's how it goes:

*Dear Uncle Santa Claus:*

*I wish you would send me for Christmas a nice wheelbarrow, large enough to bring Mama some chips.*

*A right large bank to put my money in. I have more than a dollar, and expect to get more before long.*

*A box of blocks with letters on them, so that I can build houses, and learn to spell.*

*A book with nice pictures.*

*A squeaking ball that will bounce well, and not make too much noise.*

*A knife and fork to eat my buckwheat cakes and sausage with.*

*Candy and oranges to fill up a good large stocking.*

*I am a good boy, and hope you will remember this when you come. Don't come down the chimney when the fire is burning, as you might get the wheelbarrow burnt.*

*Your affectionate little boy,*
*Ralph Fuller*

I keep that letter with my treasures, and clipped to it is another one, my Grandmother Fuller's recipe for eggnog. Papa made it every Christmas morning, ostensibly for a select group of kinsmen and friends but also, I suspect, to help him survive the holiday blues that seem to run, like premature baldness, in the Fuller family.

The recipe calls for 12 fresh eggs, 12 tablespoons fine granulated sugar, 1 teaspoon ground cinnamon, 1 bottle good apply brandy, 1 cup Jamaica rum, 1 pint whipping cream, 1 pint ordinary cream, 1 pint milk, and grated nutmeg to shake over bowl and each cup.

One by one, as we children grew old enough to help with all the beating, Papa recruited us, and under his strict supervision I learned, with a wire whisk, to beat cream into froth and egg whites into peaks, and how to grate nutmeg and cinnamon. But only Papa was allowed to touch the spirits, and once he'd dribbled them in, almost drop by drop, my interest in eggnog faded.

Nothing that looked and smelled so good should taste so bad, I decided after my first sip, and it was years before I changed my mind about the elixir Grandmother may have concocted to get her own self through a succession of Yuletide celebrations.

Now I imagine that the wit that was her hallmark became more scintillating as she sipped her own special remedy for the Christmas blues, and I wish I could have seen her presiding at the punchbowl in her elegant "widow's weeds" and dispensing gifts of laughter on Christmas Day.

# EIGHTEEN

# Associated charities helped Durham's homeless

According to Holy Scripture (Matthew 26:11), the poor have always been with us and they always will be. If you don't read the Bible, history will tell you the same thing, and if you don't read history—or just don't read, period—merely walking around town and keeping your eyes open will acquaint you with that irrefutable truth. Better still, and a lot safer these days, just close your eyes and remember how it was . . .

If you can recall a time when Durham seemed to be almost devoid of vagrants, you'll have to have a little age on you, as they say. You'll have to have been around during the decade that preceded the Great Depression; and if you were, and you lived on Main Street when its eastern end was part of a solid, church-studded neighborhood, it was only occasionally that you saw a tramp. That's what they called indigents in those days, before the word took on another connotation.

If you did see a tramp, you immediately experienced the spasm of fear your parents had carefully taught you to experience, and then you moved as far away as possible from something that made you feel bad inside until you managed to forget it.

Two highly noticeable and apparently harmless tramps whom you would never forget appeared on the downtown Durham scene around 1925 and were allowed, by police chief Walter Doby and his five sergeants—C. R. Marcom, B. W. Sharpe, G. W. Proctor, S. L. Woods and W. E. Burgess—to roam free long enough to become familiar sights.

First there was Crazy Charlie—nobody ever spoke of him as just plain Charlie—who appeared coatless, hatless and barefooted when it was freezing cold, who wore a long brown overcoat and a battered felt hat when it was blazing hot, and who always carried seven or eight silver dollars that he continually tossed from one cupped palm to the other. Mumbling to himself, shaking his head, and jingling the bright coins back and forth with a kind of effortless rhythm, he seemed intent on nothing more than walking his usual beat, which was from the Malbourne Hotel, on the corner of Main and Roxboro, down to Five Points and back, over and over until he got tired, or bored, maybe. Then he disappeared. But while he walked, apparently oblivious to everything about him, he looked straight ahead, never spoke, and nobody, including the one or two policeman who were always visible on Main Street, seemed to mind him. Crazy Charlie was simply there, an occasional part of the landscape, like the flags that lined the street on the Fourth of July, or the Christmas wreaths that hung on the lamp posts for a few weeks in December, and we children were told never to say one word to him, not one.

That dictum also applied to another tall, skinny, cross-eyed man known as "Four Thousand Dollars." Allegedly the victim of a long-ago bank failure, he had lost his mind, as the saying went, when he lost the $4,000 that constituted everything he had owned in the world. From then on he babbled, endlessly and audibly, about his dilemma. "Four thousand dollars, yeah, forty hundred. Four thousand, forty hundred dollars, buried on top of the First National Bank Building underneath the flagpole, yeah," he would say. And then he would add, for reasons known only to himself, something that sounded like "Skiddo! Scammo!"

Walking with a steady gait and addressing nobody in particular, this man wearing ragged clothes and a dark, sweat-stained baseball cap shared, over and over, in conversational tones and with no histrionics, his terrible loss with pedestrians on Main Street, and if those who heard him responded at all, it was with a suppressed smile, or a shake of the head, or a rueful glance at a companion. But mostly, people just pretended not to hear.

Sometimes, in the safety of our own backyards and with the gleeful cruelty common to all young children, we would mimic these men. Substituting pebbles for Crazy Charlie's silver dollars—where did he get all that money? we wondered—and flinging them, with far less dexterity, from hand to hand, we would lope about the yard muttering and wagging our heads. Or, crossing our eyes and altering our gait to signify a change in character, we would chant, "Four thousand dollars, yeah, four thousand, forty hundred, yeah, buried on top of the First National Bank Building underneath the flagpole, yeah!" And then, our voices rising, we would shriek the magic mumbo-jumbo that always doubled us over with laughter: "Skiddo! Scammo!"

Unhappily for me, my mother overheard enough of one of these impromptu performances to explode out of the back door on a wave of righteous indignation and snatch me, literally, inside the house and upstairs to the swift application of an ivory-backed hairbrush to my backside.

But the pain of that punishment was nothing compared to the shame and misery I felt during a long lecture, in which my mother informed me that my Uncle Tom was probably rolling in his grave and surely would have disowned me, had he been there to do it. Uncle Tom, she said, had been a humanitarian, but I—and here the wagging finger that still haunts me, on occasion, sliced the air in front of my nose—I was nothing but a mean little barbarian!

Much later I discovered that it was true about Uncle Tom being a humanitarian. Boyd's *Story of Durham* says that in 1900, W. L. Cunninggim, a Methodist minister, and Thomas B. Fuller, a Presbyterian layman, decided it was time for the city to do something about its poor people, and the result of their combined efforts in that direction was the Associated Charities of Durham. In addition to Cun-

T. B. Fuller
"Uncle Tom"
and great niece
Eleanor Southgate
(Bolich) around
1920.

T. B. Fuller as a young man.

ninggim and Fuller, the board of directors included Dr. E. R. Leyburn, the Reverend Thaddeus Troy, R. O. Blackburn, J. F. Wily, Julian S. Carr and George W. Watts; and because history records that the success of the Associated Charities "was due very largely to the untiring perseverance of Mr. Fuller, whose interest in individuals was as deep as his love for good causes," I do hope my Uncle Tom sleeps peacefully in Maplewood Cemetery now, and has forgiven the family barbarian.

# NINETEEN

# Tobacco-era boom sparked women's literary clubs

$\mathcal{M}$rs. Brodie Leonidas Duke, who was Miss Minnie Woodward of Gadsden, Alabama before she married Washington Duke's oldest son in 1890, is credited with founding both of Durham's oldest literary clubs for women, and both are still flourishing. The first, called the Up To Date Club, was 100 years old in 1996, and the Tourist Club, founded four years after the Up To Dates appeared on the Durham scene, celebrated its centennial in October of the year 2000. Indicative of an appreciation for tradition and continuity is the fact that each group lists several family connections—daughters, granddaughters, granddaughters-in-law, grandnieces, and a smattering of great-granddaughters—on its current roster.

Charter members of the Up To Date Club, in addition to Mrs. Duke, were: Mrs. W. A. Erwin, Mrs. T. D. Jones, Mrs. Leo D. Heartt, Mrs. W. L. Wall, Mrs. E. J. Parrish, Mrs. J. M. Manning, Mrs. Ed Heartt, Mrs. R. C. Stanard, Mrs. Julian S. Carr, Mrs. Eugene Morehead, and Mrs. Samuel Finley Tomlinson. Their husbands' prosperity, stemming either directly or indirectly from Durham's tobacco industry, had

ensured that they no longer needed to devote every waking moment to the care and feeding of their families and the maintenance of their handsome Victorian homes. For some time they had been able to hire cooks, nursemaids, laundresses (called washwomen), and gardeners (called yard men) to do many of the household chores that formerly had been theirs, so by 1896 they were well acquainted with that most sought after by-product of affluence, leisure time. But Victorian morality demanded that they put such time to good use, rather than frittering it away, and because only so many hours in the week could be spent on religion and good works, a social club with a high purpose seemed to have been an idea whose time had come.

It came first to Mrs. Thomas Decatur Jones and Mrs. Leo D. Heartt during a conversation over teacups that led to an agreement that they, as well as their friends, needed to improve their minds, and that the study of modern thought, new inventions, and current literature would be extremely beneficial to all of them. Inspired by the prospect of intellectual growth, Mrs. Jones and Mrs. Heartt shared their idea with Mrs. Duke, who was immediately intrigued by it and suggested that Mrs. W. L. Wall would be a great help in organizing such a club and deciding who should be asked to join. All of this communication eventually resulted in an organizational meeting at the Brodie Duke home, with the hostess "in the chair," according to the minutes, and eleven friends gathered around her, eager to begin the new venture.

When they parted a few hours later, it had been decided that they would call themselves "The Up To Date Club," and that they would meet twice a month, on Thursdays. Each member would answer the roll call with a current topic of interest, and each would contribute one new book a year, to circulate among the membership and provide source material for the papers each participant would write, and later read, at a designated meeting. Probably because of her leadership qualities, and perhaps because of her status as a member of one of Durham's first tobacco families, (and just possibly because of the size of her dining room), Mrs. Brodie Duke, nee Minnie Woodward, of Gadsden, Alabama, was elected club president.

The next meeting saw members responding to roll call with current events culled from newspapers, magazines, and the ever-reliable grapevine. They also presented their first books, which were: *Kate Carnegie*, by Ian McLaurin; *Quo Vadis*, by Quinkiewicz; *Cinderella*, by R. H. Davis; *Rodney Stone*, by Conan Doyle; *A Singular Life*, by Elizabeth Phelps; *Kentucky Cardinal* and *Choir Invisible*, both by J. L. Allen; *Louisiana*, by F. H. Barrett; *Madam* and *Sir*

*Rob's Fortune*, both by Mrs. Oliphant; *Sarquesara*, by Marion Crawford; *Gray Man*, by S. R. Crockett; and *Continental Tommy*, by J. M. Barrie.

Within a few years, this apparent preference for biography and fiction had given way to an interest in America's new territories, and in 1900 the program of study included Alaska, New Mexico, Iceland, the Philippines, Yellowstone Park, and Indian customs and relics.

As time passed, it became more and more evident that Up To Date members were dead serious about expanding their mental horizons. They studied England, Scotland and Wales; Ladies of the White House; Men and Women of Today; History of the Drama; Great Writers; Current Magazines; Ethnology; Historical Romance; Our Own Country; and, for an entire year, Woman. Under that general heading, papers were read, and animated discussion followed on such subheads as: How Primitive Woman Solved the Problems Before Her; Woman in Creative Art; Woman and Her Relation to Character; Woman as Ruler and World Builder; Woman the Spender; Woman and the Law; Woman and the Labor Problem; Woman's Duty to Woman; et cetera. Obviously, the topic was riveting, and the Up To Dates pursued it exhaustively. Woman in the making of America, on the frontier, in relation to commerce, in science, in medical and hospital work, in the evolution of home life, in prison reform—the list went on and on, and only the "sumptuous refreshments" that followed each program diverted the members' attention from the marvelous accomplishments of their own sex.

It had been decided, in the beginning, that each

hostess could entertain as simply or as lavishly as she chose, but most leaned toward lavish. Four and five-course luncheons or high teas, both featuring elaborate flower arrangements and displays of paper-thin china, sparkling crystal, gleaming silver and snowy table linen, were the order of the day. The bosomy, wasp-waisted, bustled ladies in their sweeping skirts and large, elegant hats made quite a picture as they gathered, twice a month, around what was described in the minutes as a "beautifully appointed table" and partook of a "delicious repast."

The stimulation of their minds sometimes revealed hidden talents among the members, as was the case when Mrs. Benjamin N. Duke, entertaining on April 2, 1902, surprised her guests with personalized place cards that she herself had made. Although both of the scheduled speakers were absent that day and there was no formal program, the club secretary reported that: "We thoroughly enjoyed ourselves with animated conversation which was very pleasant indeed but perhaps not quite as profitable as the papers would have been. When we were told to find our places in the dining room [we] did so amid peals of laughter. In our search we found our hostess had in a very clever manner so perfectly portrayed each lady on her card it was scarcely necessary to have the names at all. For once, we saw ourselves as others see us . . ."

A few years later, Mrs. S. W. Venable established herself as a master of doggerel when she recorded the minutes of a meeting held at the home of Mrs. A. G. Carr during the Christmas season of 1909. At some length, and with understandable literary license, the wife of the president of Venable Tobacco Company wrote:

"Last time we met with our president
Mrs. A. G. Carr, as you know,
The members were dressed up in their
    Sunday best,
All went, fifteen or so.

"Our hostess opened the meeting
With her usual grace and style,
She called our names in due order,
We answered, each with a smile.

"The Up To Date news was of interest,
The subjects racy and rare,
From Leopold's Baroness Vaughan
To the ships that fly through the air.

"No business came up for discussion.
The program was next taken up,
Mesdames Erwin and Duke were the ladies,
To pass up the special cup.

"The subject was of special interest,
Student life at Smith, Vassar, Bryn Mawr,
And a new way of learning by doing
Held us spellbound for over an hour.

"Mrs. Duke did the schools up in grand style,
Her lorgnette she managed with ease,
And though it was extemporaneous,
Mrs. Erwin spoke nice as you please.

"Mrs. Jones claimed the Christmas meeting,
She's had it for years and years,
A smile lit up each lady's features,
As the invitation fell on our ears.

"The dining room next was thrown open,
Such a vision as greeted our sight!
Red carnations and holly and popcorn,
Christmas trees, each with candles alight.

*"A toast for each lady was ready,*
*All apropos, jolly and bright,*
*We read them aloud to each other,*
*And our hearts were happy and light.*

*"And then came the good things, in courses,*
*Oysters, turkey, and cranberry sauce,*
*We thought of Mrs. Watts and Mrs. Parrish,* *
*And knew that our gain was their loss.*

*"The salad was cool and delicious,*
*With crackers so crispy and nice,*
*The ice cream and cake went like magic,*
*Bon-bons disappeared in a trice.*

*"And each heaved a sigh of contentment*
*As the coffee appeared on the scene,*
*And I for one felt too full for utterance,*
*Of the pleasures the evening had been.*

*"I wanted to toast our dear hostess,*
*But my brain was too addled to rhyme,*
*So here goes three cheers, and another,*
*For Mrs. Carr and the meeting last time!"*

Not all of the club's early minutes are as original as this particular offering by Mrs. Venable, but each is a window through which one reader, decades later, caught a glimpse of some of the women who helped to shape Durham "society" around the turn of the century.

EXACTLY WHY MRS. BRODIE DUKE resigned from the Up to Date Club in 1900 in order to organize the Tourist Club is not known, but it has been suggested that she may have needed a new interest to absorb

her mind and divert her attention from problems at home. It was common knowledge, though never talked about in public, that Mrs. Duke definitely had problems, the main one being her husband. Admittedly, Brodie was the best-looking and most personable male member of the Duke clan, but he also had an unfortunate weakness for strong drink and a tendency to speculate in stocks and real estate, sometimes with disastrous results. It was a combination of traits that did nothing to promote his wife's peace of mind, and because she sometimes "turned to sympathetic women friends (for) distraction from personal worries," it is possible that some of those friends felt that founding another literary group would be a kind of therapy for her at that particular time in the fall of 1900.

As had been the case with the Up to Date Club, the idea of a second group of women bent on improving their minds and enhancing their social lives sprang from a conversation. This time the dialogue was between Mrs. L. A. Carr and Mrs. J. E. Stagg, a granddaughter of Washington Duke and also a half-niece of the controversial Brodie. Mrs. Carr, who was known to her friends as "Jess," and Mrs. Stagg, whose intimates called her "Mamie," were members of Durham's younger married set, ladies with small children who apparently yearned for the kind of camaraderie the Up to Date members enjoyed; and one day, while sipping tea before an open fire in the Carr living room, they spoke of their desire for a club of their own.

Written testimony by a charter member of the

* Mrs. George W. Watts and Mrs. E. J. Parrish were absent from the meeting.

Tourist Club states that Jess Carr, noting the fact that the world had recently entered a brand new century, inquired of Mamie Stagg if she did not think it would be a good thing to start a brand new literary club in Durham. Mamie, without hesitation, said she thought it was a fine idea, especially as the Up to Date Club was "composed of older married women and we are not eligible."

Jess Carr then said she thought the group ought to be small, congenial and interested in subjects that would "stimulate our minds and take us away from babies and bottles for an hour or so every fortnight," whereupon Mamie Stagg agreed wholeheartedly. "I think you are just right in suggesting a club for young women like you and me," she said, and it may have been then that the two friends decided that Mamie's Aunt Minnie, having successfully organized one club for women, might be willing to organize another one.

But however it happened, Minnie Woodward Duke did, indeed, hold a second organizational meeting at her Duke Street home on October 19, 1900. Once again she was elected president, this time of an aggregation of young matrons who secretly may have wanted to get away from babies and bottles, but openly stated that their purpose was "to stimulate and promote mental culture; to collect and diffuse information concerning travel; and to advance the social enjoyment of the members."

Contemplating what to call themselves, they agreed that wanting to travel the globe qualified them as Tourists, a decision they reached only after considering, and discarding Travelers, Wanderers, and Tramps. Other business successfully concluded that day was the selection of a motto, "Step By Step We Go A Long Way," and a club flower, described by a later member as "that great botanical traveler, the goldenrod."

In addition to Mrs. Duke, Mrs. Peter Arrington, Mrs. W. D. Carmichael, Mrs. L. A. Carr, Mrs. F. L. Fuller, Mrs. I. F. Hill, Mrs. M. H. Jones, Mrs. W. A. Erwin, Mrs. Bessie Leak, Mrs. George Lyon, Mrs. J. E. McDowell, Mrs. E. K. Powe, Mrs. J. E. Stagg and Mrs. R. W. Winston were charter members of the new club, which met every two weeks, from October through May, to study faraway places that all of them hoped one day to see.

Between meetings, they read prodigiously, scribbled furiously between bouts of pencil chewing and narrow-eyed thought, and eventually produced papers that then had to be committed to memory, so that when they were presented to the club, they would appear to spring full-blown from the speaker's mind and, figuratively, off the top of her head.

This custom of memorizing papers prevailed well into the second quarter of the twentieth century and had a profound effect on the families of certain club members who needed to practice their presentations many times before the actual recitation took place. Husbands and children who became captive audiences also were expected to follow each written page and correct any lapse of memory or slip of the tongue the speaker might make; so it is not surprising that they sometimes learned more than they really wanted to know about the climate, customs and inhabitants of a number of foreign countries. One daughter of a dedicated Tourist discovered, at least fifty years after the fact, that she need not have

Ladies at a Tourist Club meeting hosted by Mrs. George Lyon. ca. 1907.

watched *The Last Emperor*, an award-winning film then being shown on television, because she not only knew the story of Henry Pu-Yi, the last sovereign ruler of China, but knew it almost by heart, thanks to her mother.

The Tourists were nothing if not thorough. When they studied Austria-Hungary, which they did for a year, they studied its government and religion; its armies and navies; its churches and universities; its composers, writers and artists; its royalty and its peasants; and its famous river, the Danube. And at each meeting, no matter what country they were "touring," a reading "pertinent to the program" preceded the recitation of at least one carefully memorized original paper and sometimes two, after which the members engaged in "lively discussion of selected topics of interest."

In 1901 and 1902, they pondered: "Which is more harmful in a family, scolding or bad cooking?" and "Do college girls make the best mothers?" and "Do large salaries afford assurance of honesty in employees?" and "Do we make Christmas a burden?"

Unfortunately, none of their conclusions were recorded for posterity.

During the first decade of its existence, the Tourist Club "traveled" to Ireland, Scotland, Wales, London, Paris, Italy, Russia, Holland, Spain, Portugal, Austria-Hungary, China, South America, Greece, Turkey and India. Whenever a member actually did go abroad, she gave the club a first-hand account of her adventures and occasionally wore a "costume" from one of the countries she had visited. Some even went so far as to serve the cuisine indigenous to that country, but as a rule the ladies enjoyed "tea with rich accompaniments," or elaborate seated banquets, especially during the Christmas and Thanksgiving seasons. In the beginning, they had opted for simple refreshments, but when one member took that resolve seriously and served tea accompanied by nothing richer than Nabisco wafers, nobody followed her lead and nobody ever mentioned the unfortunate incident until the club celebrated its fiftieth anniversary.

On that gala occasion, held at Hope Valley Country Club in the fall of 1950, an elderly charter member who had been asked to recall some amusing happenings from the past generated hoots of laughter by recalling, in some detail, the "Nabisco meeting."

Another recollection that elicited amazement among some of the younger matrons at that meeting concerned a Duke University faculty member, Dr. Rudolfo Rivera, who was invited to become an honorary member of the Tourist Club and accepted, without hesitation. Possessed of Latin good looks —coal-black hair, dark, heavy-lidded eyes, and a sensuous mouth beneath a small mustache—the professor taught history, held positions at both the Perkins Library and the Duke University Press, played golf, and spoke to the Tourist Club over and over, sometimes twice a year and, in all, for eight years running.

During those memorable years he kept the Tourists informed about what was going on in Central and South America (his specialty), and each time he appeared they fell more and more under the spell of what one Club secretary called his "Latin charm, [his] musical voice, and his evident enjoyment of tea party food and chitchat." There were other speakers before, during and after Dr. Rivera's time, but it is safe to say that none of them—including Dr. W. P. Few, Robert W. Winston, Dr. David Scanlon, R. D. W. Connor and John Sprunt Hill, to name only a few—ever surpassed the charismatic Rudolfo, who could have read for thirty minutes from the telephone book and still held his fellow-Tourists spellbound.

Like the Up to Date Club, the Tourist Club nurtured a few would-be poets among its membership, and one of these, Mrs. Thomas Fuller Hill, surprised the group on its fortieth anniversary with a rhymed profile that seems to be as good a way as any to end this saga. And so it goes:

*"The past to you now is no longer a mystery,*
*For you've both heard and seen an account*
*of our history,*
*How the very first Tourists did gather*
*together,*
*In bustle and train and gay ostrich feather,*
*To hear one of the members her speech*
*to declaim,*
*About tours she had taken to places of fame.*
*No matter how trembly or weak-kneed*
*she'd feel,*
*To read from her paper—well, that wasn't*
*genteel!*
*But for this ordeal she had quite a boost,*
*We've just heard of those banquets of turkey*
*and goose.*
*The Tourists of yore must have grown*
*plumper and bigger,*
*But oh my! What bliss not to consider*
*the figger.*
*Well, those days are gone, and I'm here*
*to relate,*
*How the Tourist club members have come*
*up to date.*
*Though our customs have changed —*
*And they have, quite a bit, for*
*Sometimes we smoke, and for soldiers*
*we knit, —*
*Tradition is strong and our standards*
*the same*
*As it was long ago, when the club was*
*first named,*
*For always the Tourists have stood for*
*the best,*

*In war time, and peace time, and time*
*of unrest.*
*They've tried through the years to*
*contribute their part*
*To culture in literature, music and art.*
*And I predict in the future*
*When we are white-haired dames,*
*Quite hard of hearing and hobbling*
*on canes,*
*Our grandchildren will gather and each*
*do her part,*
*In declaiming literature, music and art.*
*And though customs may change—they*
*may smoke cigars*
*And knit for the soldiers inhabiting Mars—*
*They'll still hold our standard aloft just*
*the same,*
*And be proud of their `Grannies' and the*
*Tourist Club name!"*

In 1904, the same year the Tourist Club adopted a constitution and bylaws, Mrs. Brodie Duke, once described as "this lovely, energetic girl from Gadsden, Alabama," left her husband, whom she subsequently divorced, and moved with her son, Woodard Duke, to California.

AUTHOR'S NOTE: *One of the things I remember vividly about my mother was her love for the Tourist Club, which she joined in 1902 after coming to Durham as a bride the year before. By the time I was five years old I knew that something called "Tourist Club" was extremely important to Mama; that it took her away from home at certain regular inter-*

vals; and that twice a year it radically changed her personality. That happened when she was what she called "having the program," and again when she was what she called "having the Tourists."

Only illness kept Mama away from Tourist Club meetings, and she was rarely ill. "I never have time to be sick," she sometimes said. "I'm always too busy taking care of you all to be sick myself."

You all, of course, meant Papa, who had what in those days was called a "delicate constitution;" and us, the four Fuller children who, over the years, had brought home measles, mumps, whooping cough, chicken pox, bad colds, influenza, cuts, bruises, sprains and sometimes broken bones for her to deal with until we were well again.

But unless our childhood illnesses and accidents put us in mortal danger, Mama left home eagerly, and obviously with immense relief, on Tourist day. That night, at suppertime, she would tell us all about the meeting—where it was, who gave the program, what it was about, what kind of refreshments the hostess served, what kind of flowers were on the table, what some of the ladies had worn, what some of them had said, who had poured tea, and so on and so forth.

I don't know how Papa, my two brothers and my sister reacted to Mama's monologues, but while we ate our evening meal and she picked at hers, having already stated that she was "too full for utterance," I listened avidly. All of it was fascinating to me, the littlest child who existed within the confines of the house and yard and, whenever Mama was gone, under the supervision of either our cook, Rose Murray, or a black teenager with a gold front

tooth, whose name was Ethel. My life, in other words, was totally without glamor, but when my mother spoke of what went on at Tourist Club meetings, I sensed that something big and exciting might come my way, too, once I grew up.

When Mama said "I've got to have the program at Tourist Club next month," it was fair warning that we were not to disturb her if she was reading or writing or talking to herself. Having the program sent her next door, to the public library for an armload of books and stationed her at her desk every afternoon for weeks, it seemed to me. If I was allowed to be anywhere near her during that time, I had to be absolutely quiet while she alternately read, chewed on a pencil, and scribbled in a lined notebook she had bought at Woolworth's five and ten cent store.

Eventually, the notebook became what she called "my paper," and it was time for her to begin learning it by heart. This was not a good time. Mama was high-strung, and as the days wore on toward the third Thursday of the month she became even more so. Putting her paper to memory, a must for all Tourist Club members, caused her to frown a lot, and shriek at sudden noises, and talk to herself almost constantly as she went about her household duties. After a while it was time for her to stand before mirrors and speak seriously to her own image, and because our house had mirrored mantels in every room but the kitchen, all of those rooms contained, for brief spells, the sound of Mama's high, sweet voice reciting her paper.

Finally, usually on the day before the meeting where she would perform, Mama rehearsed before Papa, who held the Woolworth notebook and checked her for accuracy and almost always said, as soon as she'd finished, "I declare, Caro, that was fine." But she was never reassured until the deed was done and her fellow Tourist members put their verbal seal of approval on what she had worked so hard to produce. Then my mother began to sing again, instead of muttering to herself, and the house returned to normal.

When it was Mama's turn to entertain the Tourists, the world once again shifted slightly on its axis as windows were washed, floors were waxed, silver and brass were polished, the Madeira tablecloth and matching napkins were washed and ironed again in spite of the fact that they were clean to begin with, and the yard man trimmed the shrubs and mowed the grass. Rose Murray's usually placid brown face became stern and her kitchen was off limits to children during the Monday, Tuesday and Wednesday before the third Thursday of that fateful month. Those were the days of preparation for the elaborate tea party that would follow the pro-gram at Mama's meeting—the chicken salad sandwiches, the cream cheese and olive sandwiches, the ham biscuits, the cheese straws, the salted nuts, the crystallized ginger, and the absolutely necessary snowballs that were Mama's specialty.

These confections, consisting of marshmallows dipped in boiled white icing and then rolled in freshly grated coconut were not easy to make, nor to eat with the fingers, but they were good. Delicious, Mama's fellow Tourists always told her, so, naturally, she felt she had to serve them whenever she entertained the club.

And when she did—when the big day finally came—we children were relegated to the homes of our best friends after school. Even Papa, the lord of the manor around whom the entire household usually revolved, was banished after breakfast and told not to come back until dark. It was Tourist day. It was Mama's day. But if we were lucky, if the ladies didn't eat up all the refreshments, we would get some mighty tasty leavings at suppertime, when Mama told us all about the meeting.

# TWENTY

*Ignoring the possibility of luck, either good or bad, Richard H. Wright
believed that "purpose should be behind every endeavor."*

# Public transportation had a bumpy start here

*N*ow that we are well into the twenty-first century, are there any bus riders in Durham today who ever wonder how DATA got its start?

According to one version of local history, it began on a spring day in 1885, when Julian S. Carr, W. T. Blackwell and Richard Blacknall introduced the novel idea of public transportation to their fellow citizens, and *The Tobacco Plant*, then the town's leading newspaper, put out a special edition covering the event. In a colorful ceremony involving sixteen young men and women, sixteen picks and/or shovels tied with red-white-and-blue ribbons, four horses and a bandwagon draped in red-white-and-blue bunting, ground was broken for the Durham Street Railway and speeches were made praising the vision of Carr, a tobacco manufacturer, Blackwell, his partner, and Blacknall, a local druggist.

According to the paper (whose publisher, incidentally, was Julian Carr), these three entrepreneurs were bound to succeed because "they always mean business when they take hold of anything," and all three had "the pluck and cash necessary." Had they known on March 10, 1885, exactly how much pluck and cash the Durham Street Railway was going to exact from them, they might have had second thoughts about the whole thing, but on that bright, breezy day they were not looking into the future.

They were looking, instead, at the gussied-up bandwagon with its load of stylishly-dressed, attractive young people; and at the large crowd gathered at "the foot of Redmond's Hill," near present-day Ramseur Street, to watch the proceedings. First, as always, a local minister offered up a prayer, because nobody dreamed in those days of launching a new venture without publicly petitioning the Almighty for assistance. Then the girls, no doubt giggling, and the boys, no doubt grinning with embarrassment, attacked the ground with their picks and shovels (too bad no photographers were on hand) and after a sufficient amount of earth had been turned, the orations began.

Among the speakers was Williamson Whitehead Fuller, an attorney widely known for his eloquence in the courtroom. He heaped a considerable quantity of fulsome praise on the founders of the new transportation system before announcing that reduced fares during certain hours of the day would enable all working people, "however slender their means, to use the cars," and that special rates for schoolchildren already had been established. There was much applause, especially when Fuller added that the incorporators intended to utilize their new system for transporting tobacco and other freight to the railway depot, and that they were planning to substitute electricity for horses as soon as that was feasible.

But by the time the Durham Street Railway was ready to operate, in 1887, the public's enthusiasm for it had soured. Laying the tracks had littered Main Street with rocks and clumps of clay, much of which nobody had bothered to remove; and the tracks themselves, fully six to eight inches above ground level, were an added hazard to both pedestrians and vehicles. Crossing Main Street had never been easy, especially in bad weather, but now it actually was dangerous, even during dry spells. Disgruntled citizens complained to the town authorities and they, in turn, complained variously to Buck Blackwell, president of the company, to Jule Carr, vice president, and to Richard Blacknall, secretary and treasurer of an organization that was already having enough trou-

ble simply staying afloat. Carr, who with Eugene Morehead and George Watts had been instrumental in bringing electricity to Durham in 1896, was impatient to electrify the street railway, but the electric light company, of which he was president, also was squabbling with city officials.

The Board of Aldermen contended that the purveyors of electricity were charging too much rent for their light poles ($10 per month per pole) and providing far less light than they had promised. As these altercations showed no sign of abating, Carr, Morehead and Watts periodically offered the Durham Electric Lighting Company for sale to the city, but the offer was always refused. Because their franchise did not expire until 1900, they were forced to put up with sporadic ill will from the public and accusations from city hall for almost fifteen years.

Julian Carr and his partners in the Durham Street Railway, however, did not have to suffer as long, because they were not the only Durham men interested in mass transportation as an investment. In 1891, just four years after their grand inaugural ceremony, they sold out to the Consolidated Land and Improvement Company, which was planning to develop a large tract in West Durham just beyond Trinity College and would need to make it more accessible. Electric trolley cars would do that for the developers, one of whom, interestingly enough, happened to be Julian Carr. Another one, equally aggressive, was Richard H. Wright.

And thereby hangs another tale.

THE CAST OF CHARACTERS in Durham's century-old drama of mass transportation and public utilities has been changing for over one hundred years, but in the beginning all of the actors were businessmen dedicated to making a profit. If at the same time they could earn a place in history as benefactors of their fellow men, so much the better, but profit was the name of the game then as it is now (and ever shall be, amen).

Long before much profit could be realized from either the Durham Street Railway or the Durham Electric Lighting Company, considerable feuding, fighting and fussing ensued between these two entities and the Durham Board of Aldermen. Echoing the sentiments of the public, the city fathers complained regularly and sometimes bitterly about the poor quality of service being supplied by both utilities, but whenever executives offered to sell the companies to the city (at a profit, no doubt) the fathers backed away. So Julian Carr, W. T. Blackwell and Richard Blacknall, organizers of the street railway, and Julian Carr, Eugene Morehead and George Watts, founders of the electric light company, were none too happy about their new ventures, which were neither fattening their bank accounts appreciably nor enhancing their public images.

Carr, however, could not be budged from his conviction that electricity, still a rarity in North Carolina, would one day be as commonplace as the gaslight that had all but replaced candles and kerosene lamps. Eventually, he knew, electric power would illuminate Durham's homes and streets, would pull Durham's trolley cars, would run Durham's factory machinery, and would do the Good Lord only knew what else. In the meantime he was going to hang on to what was bound to be a good investment in the long run.

Sharing Carr's views was forty-year-old Richard Harvey Wright, a former partner in the firm of W. Duke Sons and Company, who had since become the Dukes' competitor both in the manufacture of tobacco machinery and the acquisition of land in and around Durham. A native of Franklin County, Wright had moved here from Oxford in 1877 and begun to manufacture Wright's Orange of Durham smoking tobacco, and his talent for salesmanship soon caught the attention and the admiration of Washington Duke, who always kept a sharp eye on competition. No doubt, Wright had his eye on Duke, as well, because when the "old gentleman" decided to take life a little easier and devote himself to Methodism and Republican politics, he sold his share of the firm to Dick Wright, who was then twenty-nine years old.

Wright's first job at W. Duke Sons and Company was heading its branch office in Chicago, and from that base he pushed the sale of Pro Bono Publico and other Duke products in most of the western states. Two years later he set out to acquaint the entire world with those products, and his globe-circling tour through Europe, South Africa, India, the East Indies, Australia and New Zealand was the first of eight such junkets.

Seeing the world and achieving success may have pumped additional iron into Dick Wright's naturally strong will, for when he and Buck Duke disagreed on company policy in 1885 he decided to leave and offered his interest for sale at a specified price, which the Dukes and George Watts promptly declined. They then made Wright an offer that he declined, and so it went, back and forth and with increasing acrimony.

Law suits were threatened by both parties, but

R. H. Wright

Julian S. Carr

finally, in September of 1885, the issue was resolved out of court and Wright, with a sizable return on his original investment, bought into the Lone Jack Cigarette Company of Lynchburg, Virginia and became its managing director. While he was connected with that firm, he also bought the rights to sell the Bonsack cigarette machine in South Africa, Egypt and Asia, and with that move he became an even sharper thorn in the side of his former partner, Buck Duke.

Perhaps it was a shared resentment of Duke's "tobacco trust" that made business associates of Jule Carr and Dick Wright, first in the Consolidated Land and Improvement Company (Wright was president, Carr vice president), which bought the street railway in 1891; and later, with the same titles, in the Dur-

ham Traction Company, which took over the franchise of the Durham Electric Lighting Company in 1901.

Although two decades were to pass before Jule Carr's dream of seeing public transportation and the production of electric light and power combined into one public utility, that dream did come true in 1920, thanks to the vision and determination of Richard Harvey Wright.

TO SOME DEGREE, Dick Wright and Jule Carr were birds of a feather, sharing a talent for salesmanship that bordered on genius and the insatiable desire for success that typifies so many entrepreneurs. They also shared the Methodist faith and the same neighborhood—Carr lived on the southeast corner of Main and Dillard Streets and Wright lived opposite him, on the northeast corner—and in the decade following the Civil War they both went into the tobacco business. Both were forced out of extremely lucrative careers in that business when James Buchanan "Buck" Duke's giant American Tobacco Company took over the entire tobacco industry, so having no great affection for Duke may have forged a bond between them.

At any rate, the two neighbors decided to collaborate, first in 1891 under the aegis of the Durham Consolidated Land and Improvement Company, and later, in 1901, in the Durham Traction Company, the "granddaddy," so to speak, of the present Durham Area Transit Authority (DATA). As president and vice president, respectively, of both the land company and the traction company, Wright and Carr pioneered in suburban development and also managed to maintain the struggling street railway that Carr had been instrumental in founding in 1885. But most of the credit properly goes to Wright, as Carr then was primarily involved in building up the Durham Hosiery Mill, which he had established in 1898 after being forced to sell his Blackwell's Durham Tobacco Company to northern financiers, who later sold it to Duke.

Six years younger than Carr and, like him, deeply affected by the devastating aftermath of the Civil War, Dick Wright's need to make a living took him from his home near Louisburg to the mercantile business in Oxford. A few years later, when that business was destroyed by fire, he decided to go to Durham and get into manufacturing and selling tobacco, as so many young men in need of money had done. He set up shop next door to W. Duke Sons and Company, and his dedication to hard work so impressed Washington Duke that Duke offered him a partnership, which lasted approximately five years.

Selling for W. Duke Sons and Company gave Wright an opportunity for world travel that relatively few tobacco salesmen were privileged to enjoy, and as a result he acquired a degree of sophistication that went far beyond the average citizen of his day. As one rather fatuous biographer-turned-public-speaker put it, those five years of continuous travel made a true cosmopolite of a farm boy from Franklin County who learned the trade and social conditions of every country he visited and remembered what he saw. "He graduated with honors from the University of the World . . . (and) he felt at home in, and had friends in Kimberley, Johannesburg, Alexandria, Khartoum, Bombay, Singapore, Canton, Tokyo, Melbourne, Auckland, Manila, Porto Rico, Calcutta and Algiers." Even after Wright parted company with the Dukes, he continued to travel as a salesman of the famous Bonsack cigarette machine, and during his lifetime he circled the globe eight times, made ninety-four Atlantic crossings, and sailed fifteen times across the Pacific.

In 1901, when he was fifty years old, Wright decided to spend more time at home, and it was then that he secured a fifty-year franchise to provide the city with electric light and power, and to run its streetcars with that same miraculous power, instead of with mules. The going was not always smooth, and altercations with the town commissioners about the condition of the car tracks continued to plague him, just as it had plagued the former owners of the street railway. But Wright had long since adopted a cavalier attitude toward friction and spilt milk. "Pick up your milk pail and go for the next cow," was part of his philosophy, which also included absolutely no belief in luck.

Ignoring the possibility of luck, either good or bad, Wright believed that "purpose should be behind every endeavor," and that the way to succeed was to "select a business for which one has a natural talent and taste and master it until you love it above all other pastimes or amusements." Apparently acting on that premise, he built a factory to manufacture tobacco machinery, electric motors, electric fans and a number of other mechanical contraptions, including one that made ice. All of these innovations were under the umbrella of the Durham Traction Company, which by 1910 was a thriving business. It had eighteen streetcars running on seven miles of tracks and electric lights on streets, in homes, and in businesses. But most important of all in a tobacco town, it had power in the factories to run the machines, and because Richard Harvey Wright was manufacturing many of them, he was well on his way to becoming Durham's fifth resident millionaire.

Maybe it was then that he began to think about leaving Dillard Street and building himself a mansion, as the other four had done. He already had the land—275 acres of prime farmland out on the Roxboro Road, only a few miles away from downtown Durham—so maybe it was time to move on to greener pastures.

IN 1916, WRIGHT BUILT his mansion, a beautiful house with the beautiful name of Bonnie Brae. Located about four miles from downtown Durham, it bears many distinctions, not the least of which is its significance as the only one of Durham's "tobacco boom" mansions still standing, all the others having fallen victim either to the Great Depression or to urban renewal, which swept through the city from the late 1950s until well into the 1970s. Fortunately, Bonnie Brae escaped that devastation for two reasons: it was anything but "urban" and, even more fortunately, it was still occupied by family members, who cherished its history and could afford to keep it in the fine style that made it one of the prettiest sights you could see on a sightseeing drive through northern Durham County.

Riding out Roxboro Road was something many families did on fine Sunday afternoons back in the "olden days," before traffic got to be such a problem and wholesale development fouled up the landscape and television pre-empted much of what used to serve as weekend entertainment. And it was a drive worth taking, especially in May, when the flowering trees were flowering and the meadows of Bonnie Brae were unbelievably green and the fence surrounding that whole vast property looked freshly-painted and unbelievably white.

Beyond the fence, at the end of a long gravel driveway, the house stood in a protecting grove of tall oak trees, clearly visible from the highway and gleaming white as a frosted cake above the dark green boxwoods that hugged its base. A friendly, sprawling two-story house, pinpointed architecturally as "Colonial Revival," with a wide one-story porch supported by Doric columns and giving off, as one admirer has stated, an atmosphere of "comfort, tranquil domesticity, and . . . leisured country living that today is mostly memory."

Whether or not domestic tranquillity prevailed there at all times is a matter of conjecture, since Richard Wright built Bonnie Brae not just for himself, but also for his spinster sister, Mary, his deceased brother's wife, Bettie, and Bettie and Thomas Wright's six children: Tom, Dick, Lila, Nannie Bet, Cora and Mary Ruth. Apparently, Wright was a man who placed responsibility for kith and kin above desire for tranquil domesticity and saw the opportunity to care for two women and six normal, growing children as a Christian duty not to be shirked. Tragically, he had lost his own wife, Mamie Exum, a year after their marriage in 1884, and because his only daughter died four years later, it is entirely possible that he welcomed the chance to provide for his large and, at times, undoubtedly noisy adopted family.

Certainly there was ample room for them at Bonnie Brae, with eight bedrooms opening off a large center hall, a bathroom for each bedroom, and a sleeping porch "of sufficient size to accommodate large house parties." Downstairs, a long living room, secondary hall and sitting room on the right side of the main hallway all opened, through French doors, onto the porch and a porte cochere that protected arrivals and departures from inclement weather. To the left of the hall were a library, dining room, kitchen, "miscellaneous service areas (and) farther to the north, through the library, a screened porch used as a summer dining room." Some years later, a swimming pool "designed almost as a wing of the house, as well as an element in the landscaping" was built just beyond the summer dining room.

Wright lived at Bonnie Brae for thirteen years before he died, but he never retired and was on a business trip when, according to *The News and Observer*, "He was stricken on August 19 [1928], was removed to a Roanoke hospital, and later moved to Durham" where he died at Watts Hospital seven months later, on March 5, 1929. The Raleigh newspaper devoted almost a full page to his accomplishments as "a Durham capitalist and the last surviving member of the group which amassed fortunes in the tobacco business there." The paper also described him as "a man who kept his business to himself" and that "little is known of his holdings in this country and abroad"; but then it went on to say that "estimates place his wealth from $10 million to $20 million."

Nine months later, the stock market crashed and America was plunged into the Great Depression, but Wright's heirs apparently were not affected by it to any great extent, at least for a while.

IN 1932, THOMAS DAVENPORT WRIGHT, JR. and his wife, Claudia Lewis Wright, acquired Bonnie Brae, and there they reared their own six children: Meriwether, Thomas, Richard, Elizabeth, Claudia and Diana. To say that these children grew up in a privileged environment is an understatement, but it is no exaggeration to add that countless others also enjoyed the Wright home. For over twenty-five years, well over 2,000 of Durham's young women experienced its hospitable charm, thanks to Claudia Wright, who presided over it until her death in 1981. As founder of the Durham Debutante Ball, each year

Bonnie Brae House

she opened the doors of Bonnie Brae to approximately fifty-five local debutantes and their escorts, beginning in 1955; and the parties she gave for them, always highly proper (no alcohol was ever served), were such beautifully executed examples of southern hospitality at its best that they became legendary.

In 1990, seventy-four years after Richard Wright built it, Bonnie Brae stood empty, denuded of its protecting trees, open to the elements, and in danger of dying. Like Somerset Villa, Fairview, Beverly Hall and Four Acres—the homes of Julian S. Carr, Washington Duke, George Watts and Benjamin N. Duke—it seemed destined for oblivion. Unless somebody thought it was worth the high cost of restoration and preservation, Bonnie Brae, too, would fall victim to the wrecking ball.

AUTHOR'S NOTE: *Fortunately, somebody did. A local developer, Gary Hock, has owned Bonnie Brae House for over a decade and uses it for office space.*

# TWENTY ONE

# Hacks vital to Durham in "Gay Nineties"

*I*f getting from one place to another had not been of prime importance to human beings, man would not have invented the wheel. Or the boat. Or the train, the bicycle, the hot air balloon, the automobile, the plane, the rocket.

It seems that getting around has always been a top priority for *Homo sapiens*, and getting around in Durham before the twentieth century was much harder than it is today.

Now, almost every family has at least one car, and buses and taxicabs are available to anybody who can pay the fare; but until the electric trolley came on the scene in 1902, most local citizens who couldn't walk, or didn't want to, had to hire a hack.

Rich folks, of course (and Durham had more of those than any town of comparable size in the state, thanks to tobacco), owned their horses and carriages and had their own stables behind their fine houses, and the coachmen they employed often wore splendid uniforms, tall beaver hats and haughty expressions.

Durham's hack drivers, on the other hand, neither looked nor acted like family retainers, and their rattletrap surreys and phaetons usually were castoffs,

bought either from private citizens or livery stables for anywhere from $15 to $25. The horses that pulled these conveyances had cost about $15 or $20 at the most, and most had swollen knees and could only "amble along in a painful manner," heads bobbing, eyes dull, ears limp.

In spite of the initial cost, all but six of the twenty hack men who worked in Durham in 1898 owned their own rigs; otherwise, they would have had to turn over fifty percent of their proceeds to an employer. With fares only ten cents in the city during the day and twenty-five cents at night (beyond the city limits they were fifteen cents and fifty cents), a family man wouldn't have much to take home if he had to part with half of every dime and quarter he collected, and sixteen of the drivers were married. Only one was a native of Durham; the rest, with the exception of a lone Virginian, were from various parts of Orange County.

For the above statistics, and the information that follows, we salute one Henry M. North, as without his research a piece of Durham's social history would have gone unrecorded.

North, long dead, was a Trinity college student when he interviewed eighteen of these forerunners of today's taxicab drivers and then published his findings in *The Archive*, the student magazine that still exists today. Evidently a painstaking young man, he described his subjects as generally well-behaved, genial and polite even with unruly passengers, or with "young, white sports" who rode where they wanted to go and then refused to pay.

Given the opportunity to voice their feelings to North, however, it became apparent that they were not a happy lot. With the exception of "one cheerful Methodist preacher," all were disgruntled, thought $10 a year for a license was too high, and fares were too low. After all, they said, it cost from $1.50 to $2.50 each week "to keep a horse in running order," and although an unwritten law decreed that drivers could not cut rates, some drivers cut them anyway.

All agreed that they were barely making a living and that it was impossible to save any money. And if they filled their surreys with four passengers, instead of two, the front seat had to be reversed and then the driver, forced to crouch on his knees in the small space behind it, suffered a bone-bruising ride over the rocky, potholed surfaces that passed for streets and roads in and around Durham.

One of the men, apparently voicing his distaste for Durham, told North he had been "born at the University," and that Chapel Hill was "the garden spot of the whole land and the front yard of the state," and that he was tired of being a hack man. It interfered with his religion.

Nobody could be a hack man and be a Christian at the same time, he said, because of the abuse, and the temptation to work on Sundays. It was all too much, and he would rather be "a common day laborer."

Whether this irate chauffeur of ordinary citizens carried out his threat or not will never be known, but North relates that most drivers did quit after two or three years, which indicates that the burnout rate for Durham's hack men was pretty high.

It was time for taxis, apparently, and the first one appeared here in 1909.

# TWENTY TWO

# Early taxi journeys exciting in Durham

Real people telling us the way it was is the best way to go, I think, when I'm searching for the way we were.

Take Marvin Doyle Harris, for instance, and his store of information about the taxi business. Although Harris admits he does not know just when the concept of a chauffer-driven, passenger-carrying conveyance for hire came into existence, he does know that "in the days of the Roman Empire you could hail a chariot, get aboard and tell the driver your destination" and, in due time, arrive there. For a fee, of course.

According to Marvin Harris, who speaks with authority about such things, some enterprising Romans (their names, unfortunately, have been lost to posterity) saw a definite need and decided to fill it, thereby making travel easier for people who owned no wheels and, at the same time, increasing the contents of their own personal moneybags.

No doubt with some trial and error, these ingenious entrepreneurs rigged their chariots with a lever, gears, a tray and "a cylindrical-type basket, or drum, containing a number of small stones." By flipping the lever and simultaneously engaging the gears as soon as the vehicle was in motion, the drum would rotate "in a ratio with the wheels and . . . let the stones drop into the tray as the chariot traveled," and thus it became a taxi, complete with meter and driver. As soon as the designated destination was reached, "the driver counted the stones in the tray, collected X number of lira per stone from the passenger, disengaged his 'meter,' put the stones back in the drum, and began to look for another fare."

So says Marvin Harris, former owner of Durham's Yellow Cab Company, which he sold to a friend, Louis Carver, in 1968. Harris is the son of Mack Doris Harris, better known as M. D., and a nephew of John Harris, two brothers who "wouldn't admit they had moved to Durham from Shake Rag," and told folks, instead, that they came from "just up the road a ways" from that elusive and unidentifiable community. The brothers first worked as machinists at the Erwin Cotton Mill, but as soon as automobiles began to appear on the local scene in the early 1900s, they decided to learn how to drive, sell, service and rent the marvelous new contraptions that were destined to change forever the way the entire world lived.

By 1911, M. D. and John Harris had opened a garage on Main Street just east of Five Points, where the Snow Building now stands. They got their gasoline the old-fashioned way, from "a horse-drawn wagon driven by a Mr. Carlton," but the Cadillacs and Overlands they had for sale were modern to the hilt. Cars being too expensive for the average citizen, however (around $2,000 and up), they also had automobiles for hire and, of necessity, drivers to operate them. One of their first chauffeurs was nineteen-year-old Charles C. Haynes, a native of Rutherford County who had married M. D. Harris's sister. Others who drove for the Harrises were Stewart Cole, Frank O'Brient, George Sewell and "a Mr. Clayton," and their expeditions often carried them to neighboring towns. To Raleigh and back cost $10 per passenger and took two hours each way, provided nothing went wrong; and each round trip fare to Chapel Hill was $1.25 and required an hour's drive both to and from the village.

Given the nature of the so-called horseless carriage, all such journeys were "iffy," especially in wet weather, because the machines were frail, balky and unpredictable. They "shook and trembled and clattered" the moment they were started and often "spat oil, fire, smoke and smell," so Durham passengers headed for the state capital or the state university or anywhere else, for that matter, were apt to be delayed. Blowouts, overheated radiators and time-consuming waits, while the driver peered into his vehicle's "innards" to see why it had suddenly stopped, were all part of the excitement that cars engendered.

But that didn't stop people from hiring them

Marvin D. Harris

from the Harris brothers, who remained involved in automobile-related businesses as long as they lived. They acquired dealerships, filling stations and storage garages; they sold tires, parts and accessories; and, inevitably, they became owners of a taxi business that evolved from the "for hire" concept. Fortunately, Marvin Harris has had the good sense to record some of their history, which I fully intend to preserve in this space, God willing.

Incidentally, Shake Rag has been claimed by Granville, Person and Lee counties, in spite of the fact that the name seems to be tied to bootlegging before, during and after Prohibition.

# TWENTY THREE

# Streetcars recalled as gas prices climb

Contemplating skyrocketing gas prices and ever-increasing air pollution evokes nostalgia for certain "good old days" when Durham folks rode streetcars if they had to go farther than their legs would carry them. And no matter where they went, it was a bargain. They could go from Ramseur Street way down in East Durham clear across town through Five Points to Trinity College, which was practically in the country, for a nickel.

For a dime, a courting couple could enjoy a summer evening ride from Thomas's Drug Store, on Main Street, to the Reservoir at the end of Broad Street before the conductor changed the cable and they could begin to enjoy the ride back. It was a leisurely journey that absorbed most of that particular date, but did leave enough time for refreshments. At Thomas's, where revolving fans turned lazily overhead, customers sat in wire-backed chairs at small round tables and ate big bowls of ice cream that Mr. Thomas "hand-cranked" behind a partition at the back of the store. It was, by mutual agreement of all who came and went through the swinging doors, the best ice cream in the world, and it cost a nickel a bowl. So two bowls, coupled with two street-car fares, came to less than a quarter, money well-spent for a young man's romantic encounter with his true love.

A family of six could pack a picnic and ride to Lakewood Park, which was also out in the country, for thirty cents; and there they could swim in Durham's first cement pool after they had rented black woolen bathing suits and white rubber caps and once-white towels from the man who managed the bath house and made everybody take a shower before they got into the water. In addition to the pool, there was a roller coaster, a merry-go-round, a skating rink, a dance pavilion and a casino where traveling stock companies put on plays and musical shows, so it is not surprising that the park manager, Tom Foster, advertised it as "The Coney Island of the South."

Lakewood Park had come into being because of the streetcars and drew many out-of-town pleasure seekers to Durham. These visitors from neighboring cities arrived at Union Station by train, then walked up Church Street to Main and caught the cars headed for Lakewood. They paid their fares through open windows to a conductor who walked around a platform on the outside of the trolley collecting coins, slipping them into a metal box fastened to his belt, and displaying remarkable nonchalance while barreling along at a rate of at least fifteen miles per hour.

On rare occasions, a car rounding a curve too fast would jump the rails and hit the street curbing, but by some miracle not a single one ever completely turned over, and nobody ever was hurt. Riders were scared silly, without a doubt, but not enough to give up riding those wonderful conveyances that operated from five-thirty in the morning until eleven o'clock at night and took them within walking distance of any place they wanted to go for just five cents. It was not all that great for the motormen, however, who worked in nine-hour shifts for nine cents an hour and frequently got cold and wet while collecting fares. They also had to put up with boys who jumped on cars and rode free until they were discovered; belligerent dogs who barked and chased and snapped at their ankles; and drunks who had to be kept in line until they could be deposited at the police station.

Electric streetcars made their debut in Durham on May 23, 1902 and were met with great excitement by the public. Promised transportation to an important baseball game at George Lyon Park, which was also way out in the country at what is now Maplewood Cemetery, people lined both sides of Main Street and cheered when three cars, filled to capacity, took off on what may have been one of the shortest maiden voyages in the history of horseless vehicles. No sooner were they really rolling than the power failed, the cheers changed to jeers, and the trolleys had to be hauled back to the car barn on Morris Street by a team of mules.

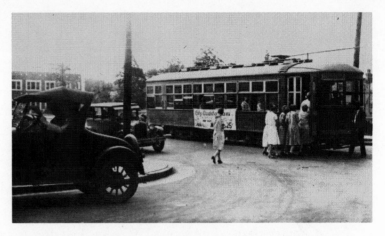

Women are seen waiting to board the Durham Trolley Service. ca. 1920.

Undaunted by this ignominious beginning, the Durham Traction Company had its cars ready to operate in time for commencement at Trinity College on June 2, and with a skeptical crowd watching from the sidelines and the trolleys jampacked, the trip was successful. Soon the company began to profit from its new venture, but R. A. Tippett, a motorman from 1904 until 1928, said he worked a solid year before he got a raise of one cent an hour. He called it a "big day" when that happened, but said an even bigger one came in 1907 when the state legislature passed a law decreeing that all streetcars had to be enclosed. Before that, "the rain and snow would blow all over you," Tippett said, and sometimes "a conductor almost froze to death."

Streetcars were replaced by buses in 1928, but because it was cheaper to pave over the tracks rather than take them up, they're still buried under six inches of asphalt.

Too bad some genius can't discover that resurrecting them would profit both the city and the citizens.

# TWENTY FOUR

# For-hire cars lead to profitable taxicab firm for Durham

*M*arvin Harris, former head of Yellow Cab, Inc., later owned by Louis Carver, may have inherited his affinity for automobiles from his father, M. D. Harris, who began to operate a garage on Main Street shortly after the first cars appeared here around the turn of the century. M. D. Harris must have known instinctively that the "horseless carriage," rickety, graceless and unreliable as it was in those days, would soon be mankind's main mode of transportation, for automobiles became his way of life. With his brother, John, he sold them, serviced them, fueled them and taught people how to drive them; and when he began to hire them out to the public, he laid the groundwork for a profitable taxicab business.

M. D. Harris's son Marvin, born in 1913 "in the 800 block of Mangum Street, delivered by Dr. W. W. Olive," and occasionally cared for by young Wylanta Rochelle (before she outgrew babysitting and became Mrs. Brodie Leonidas Duke), has recorded some of his father's early experiences, and we applaud him for that. Not only do those experiences profile a successful entrepreneur, they also resurrect a long-departed group of Durham residents who came of age when "the automobile was new, exciting, and a thrill to drive, its possibilities unlimited," and the cars they hired from M. D. Harris enlarged their horizons significantly.

Douglas Hill, who married attorney J. Lathrop Morehead; Mary Sasser, who married attorney H. G. Hedrick; and Helen Gribble, who became the wife of Dr. Foy Roberson, were popular local belles before they ventured into matrimony, and "We used to go to Chapel Hill to the Zeta Psi dances, and [our] mothers never used to worry about us if we went with Mr. Harris in his car," Mrs. Morehead told Marvin Harris many years after the fact.

But M. D. Harris was not infallible, especially on the narrow, twisting road that snaked its way from Chapel Hill to Durham. "As we were coming home one night," Mrs. Morehead continued, "we rounded a curve and Mr. Harris hit a mule and wagon. You know, there were no lights on the wagon—and the lights on the car weren't too good—and although none of us was hurt, the car sure was messed up."

Apparently relegating mule, wagon and wagon-driver to limbo, Douglas Morehead went on: "Once

I had some girls from Charlotte visiting me and we called Mr. Harris to come by and take us to ride. Will Minor (future secretary-treasurer of the Durham Buggy Company) and Tom Worth (future banker at Durham Loan and Trust Company) had come calling, and they went with us, out Cole Mill Road to the Eno River bridge. Most girls in those days wore 'rats,' which was false hair—but not wigs like they have now—and one of the girls lost hers, so we had to come back real slow, looking on both sides of the road for that hair piece.

"There were very few cars then. Buck Lyon had one, and Angier Duke (both grandsons of Washington Duke), but most of the time we had to call Mr. Harris to come and carry us around. When Lathrop and I were married on February 24, 1917, Mr. Harris took us to Apex to catch the train to go on our honeymoon. Lathrop was attorney for the railroad, so we could travel on his pass.

"I talked with Annie Laurie Newsom (wife of long-time Durham mayor M. E. Newsom) and she said Mr. Harris took her and Gene to Raleigh to catch the train when they got married. And he also took Mr. and Mrs. R. M. Kinton when they got married." (R. M. Kinton owned one of Durham's leading jewelry stores.)

Later in 1917, some months after he had seen the just-married Moreheads safely embarked on their wedding trip, M. D. Harris and his brother, John, left Durham temporarily to launch a new business venture. No doubt aware of America's impending entry into World War I and a consequent need for in-

M. D. Harris

creased public transportation, "we went to Camp Lee, Virginia just outside Newport News," says Marvin Harris, "and operated the for-hire cars between Camp Lee and Newport News, and wherever. It was a busy time."

No doubt it was a profitable time, as well, and may have convinced M. D. Harris that he should eventually go into a taxi business. How he did it is another little known piece of Durham history that should be in the books. But I got it first, thanks to Marvin Harris.

# TWENTY FIVE

# Sidewalk chat finances taxicab firm

The Yellow Cab Company first appeared in Durham in 1926 under the aegis of W. T. High, who operated it from the Washington Duke Hotel and managed to keep it going until 1932 in spite of the 1929 stock market crash that caused so many businesses to fail.

In 1933 the name was noticeably absent from Durham's city directory, but Mack Doris (M. D.) Harris, who would reinstate it twenty-nine years later, was already planning to start a taxicab business as soon as he could raise enough capital, and in the meantime he was selling tires. Seemingly undeterred by the Great Depression, M. D. Harris was looking ahead to the day when he would be competing with existing local cab companies (Blue Bird, East End, Hawk, Duke and U-Drive-It-Yourself) and in 1934 he decided the time had come.

It was not a good year to borrow money. In spite of President Herbert Hoover's insistence that America's economy was sound, corporations and banks that had not already failed were shaky, to say the least, and in many cases were "undermined by skull-duggery and fraud." But most people really wanted to believe times were getting better, and apparently M. D. Harris was one of them. So he set out to set himself up in a new business, and in the words of his son, Marvin Harris, this is how it happened (parenthetical statements are mine):

"M. D. needed some start-up capital to go in the cab business, so he went to the Citizen's National Bank (M. E. Newsom, president; R. E. Dillard, vice president), the Homes Savings Bank (John Sprunt Hill, president; W. E. Sledge, vice president), the Fidelity Bank (J. F. Wily, president; Jones Fuller, vice president) and the Durham Loan and Trust Company (George Watts Hill, president; B. R. Roberts, vice president) to borrow $700, and they all turned him down.

"He was coming up Parrish Street, headed for his office in the Hotel Gas and Storage building (Harris's brother, Walter, owned Hotel Gas and Storage), and he happened to meet Mr. R. L. McDougald, a vice president of Mechanics and Farmers Bank (Charles C. Spaulding, president). They paused to speak, and

Some of the
Founders of
Mechanics &
Farmers Bank.
ca. 1900.

in a conversation out on the sidewalk M. D. told Mr. McDougald he had been trying to borrow money to go into the cab business, but couldn't get a loan.

"McDougald: 'How much do you need?'

M. D.: '$700.'

"McDougald: 'What can you do with $700?

M.D.: 'For that down payment I can get five new Chevrolets from Carpenter's (Carpenter Motor Company).'

"McDougald: 'Come by my office in the bank tomorrow and let's see what my people can do.'

"Next day M. D. went by the bank, Mr. McDougald had the note and the check made out, M. D. signed the papers, took the check to Carpenter's, and was very soon in the taxi business. That same day, he moved his banking business to Mechanics and Farmers, and the Broadway Taxi-Yellow Cab accounts are still there."

Broadway was the name Harris chose for his taxi venture, which was listed in the 1935 city directory at 111 Rigsbee Ave., "all new cars, radio equipped." In 1942, Harris moved it to the new bus station on the corner of Main and Dillard, and it was then that son Marvin left his uncle Charlie Harris's Bull City Oil Company, where he had been employed since 1935, and "went to work for Daddy, managing the

Louis Carver, partner of Marvin Harris, Jr. Taxi Service.

taxi office and doing the bookkeeping. The war years were hectic," he remembers, but those years also were catalysts for economic recovery, and in 1948 he was able to resign his job and set his sights on becoming a college graduate.

Married since 1936 and a father since 1941, with two years of credits from Mars Hill Junior College, Harris entered the University of North Carolina at the same time his daughter, Patsy, started first grade at the George Watts School in Durham.

"I graduated from Carolina in 1951 with a B.S. in accounting and went to work at Elkins Motor Company as office manager," he says. Then in 1956, when the company his father had owned until he died in 1951 came up for sale, history repeated itself. Marvin Harris "went to Mr. John H. Wheeler at Mechanics and Farmers Bank, borrowed money, and went into the taxi business."

During the next decade, Broadway acquired several smaller operations, and in 1962, after buying the Yellow Cab Company from R. B. Ashley, Harris incorporated that name into his own business rather than dropping it.

Louis Carver, who left a sales manager's job at Long Meadow Dairy to work for Harris in 1968, bought the company when Harris retired in 1970. He called it Yellow Cab, Incorporated, and as such it served the public with thirty-seven cars and three wheelchair vans for the next twenty years.

It goes without saying, but I'll say it anyway: Durham's foremost taxicab company continued to bank at Mechanics and Farmers.

# TWENTY SIX

# Two companies offered phone service

*I*n 1991, a writer for the *New York Times* stated that the United states was rapidly running out of telephone numbers, and blamed "the proliferation of fax machines, cellular phones, pocket pagers, computer modems and business telephones" for the fact that every telephone switch in the country would have to be replaced

The rest of the story was so technical it proved beyond my comprehension (I don't even understand the doorbell, much less the telephone), but it did underscore my long-held conviction that (a) there are too many people in the world, and (b) too many of them are addicted to the telephone.

As a result of its ever-growing dependence upon Alexander Graham Bell's invention, North America today is in dire need of more area codes, but new ones cannot be created until "all of the nation's telephone switches are reprogrammed, a complex and time-consuming task." It also will be expensive and frustrating, and the change will be difficult for the telephone companies and create serious problems for business, said the *Times*. Furthermore, when it is

completed, callers may have to dial eleven digits, rather than seven.

All of these doom-and-gloom prophecies make me wonder if bringing the telephone to Durham in 1888 was not tantamount to setting Pandora's Box down among us. At the time, of course, citizens applauded the local Commonwealth Club (forerunner of today's Chamber of Commerce) for inducing Southern Bell Telephone and Telegraph Company to locate here, but within a short time subscribers were up in arms over Bell's exorbitant rates. For nearly six years they grumbled and complained about having to pay $48 a year for a business phone and $36 for one in the home, and finally, in 1894, Julian S. Carr, Louis A. Carr (no relation) and George W. Watts decided to remedy the situation by organizing a local company and undercutting Bell's rates.

Their Interstate Telephone and Telegraph Company, located on the third floor of Carr's First National Bank building, charged only $30 and $20 per year, respectively, for business and home phones, so it is not surprising that the new company snared a number of Bell's old customers as well as some potential new ones. This may have prompted Bell to issue a statement in its 1895 directory prohibiting non-subscribers from ever using its phones "except to call a physician or give a fire alarm." Bell also warned legitimate callers not to use the instrument during a thunderstorm and never, under any circumstances, to say "Hello, Central," or otherwise try to engage the operator in conversation.

In 1897, having acquired almost twice as many customers as Bell (200 to 103), IT&T moved its headquarters to a building on the southwest corner of Main and Church Street, where it continued to thrive, apparently, as it was able to buy out the Bell operation in 1903.

By 1910, company president Julian S. Carr, with his usual flair for hyperbole, was advertising it as "one of the most complete and perfect telephone exchanges in the State of North Carolina," but Carr also was toying with the idea of selling it. Having reached the venerable age of sixty-five, he aimed to retire from all commercial interests and devote his remaining years to travel, and in 1913 he sold the phone company to Richard H. Wright, who had previously collaborated with him in a number of business ventures, usually to their mutual profit.

Wright made his brother, Thomas D. Wright, general manager of the company and retained W. W. Shaw, the former manager, as secretary-treasurer,

and by the end of that year IT&T had 1,363 subscribers. Under Wright's twenty-year regime the company prospered and progressed (dial phones were in by 1927), and when he sold it to the Theodore Gary Company in 1933, it was still a good investment in spite of the Great Depression, as the following statistics will show:

Renamed Durham Telephone Company by Gary, in 1940 subscribers numbered 10,000; in 1950 they had increased to 25,000; in 1955, with 32,452 subscribers, Durham Telephone merged with General Telephone; and in 1957 it became General Telephone Company of the Southeast, with headquarters in Durham.

As of August 2000, GTE (now Verizon) has 191,000 lines here, and there's no doubt about it, that's progress. But I still remember, with a kind of homesickness, the first time I climbed on a chair, took the receiver off the hook, and breathed into the black mouthpiece of our telephone, which hung high on the east wall of the back hall and was forbidden to children, except by special permission, which was rarely granted.

For what seemed like forever I waited, and then, magically, Central spoke to me. "Number, please?" she said, as if I were a Real Person, and in that moment I gained considerable stature in my own eyes.

"Three seven," I told her, and it really didn't matter when nobody answered at my best friend's house.

*I had used the phone.*

*. . . a fantastic place to start a business.*
TRAVELING SALESMAN

# Durham—once a city of exciting stores . . .

In the spring of 1911, when Reuben Lynwood Baldwin drove his wife and two little girls from Lynchburg, Virginia to Durham to live, it took him seven days to travel 110 miles, he had 125 blow-outs on the way, and his car had to be pulled out of the mud fifty-seven times. But he never thought of turning back. His mission was to establish a branch of his family's mercantile business in North Carolina, and neither the idiosyncrasies of the new "horseless carriages" nor anything else was going to discourage him.

The year before, on his first trip to Durham, which had been highly recommended to him by a traveling salesman as "a fantastic place to start a business," he had arrived by train late at night, only to find the fantastic place pitch black dark, not a light burning anywhere. Something had happened (something was always happening, he discovered) to "the 127 beautiful arc lights that burned all night the year round," according to a Merchants Association brochure proclaiming the advantages of "The Town Renowned the World Around." He had to grope his way to the Hopkins House, several blocks north of Union Station and Durham's best hotel (it was really nothing but a great big boarding house), but that first visit persuaded him that the salesman might be right, after all.

Although Durham was by no means beautiful and parts of it were downright ugly, its growth since the end of the Civil War had been phenomenal, and showed no signs of waning. Churches of every denomination dotted the landscape; there were thirty-two doctors and twenty-seven law firms profiting from mankind's physical, emotional and financial woes; and five schools and colleges, in addition to fifteen public schools, were educating young people. Of more importance to Baldwin, a population of over 25,000 was able to support thirteen general merchandise stores, two men's clothiers, one hatter, and ten dry goods and notions stores. Foremost among the latter were the Ellis Stone, B. F. Kronheimer and Q. E. Rawls companies, and they, thought Baldwin, could stand some competition.

That decision had sent him to the Fidelity Bank, eventually, to negotiate a loan so he could buy a small milliner's shop that was for sale on Main Street, and shortly thereafter he began to transform it into the fourth Baldwin's in the family chain and the first in North Carolina. When he opened its doors to the public on March 11, 1911 he established a tradition that was to continue for seventy-nine years.

R. L. Baldwin, apparently, was destined from birth to be a merchant. His grandfather, Albert Baldwin of Buckingham County, Virginia, established a store in 1838; his father eventually became the owner; and he and his brothers continued to operate and expand the business, opening stores in Farmville, Lynchburg and Roanoke. So R. L., as he was called, came to Durham accustomed to success, knowledgeable about buying and selling, and confident that the "integrity, fair-dealing and honesty" that had characterized the family's dealings with the public would attract as much trade in the Tar Heel state as the Virginia establishments were drawing.

Progress, however, was not always steady and smooth. Stumbling blocks were waiting, and on a windy Saturday in 1914 a disastrous fire destroyed Baldwin's and the entire block of stores surrounding it. What the owner thought as he viewed the rubble that night is not known, but on Monday he was back in business after buying "another little shop that was available in the 100 block on the southeast side of Main street," and Baldwin's continued to operate at that location for over three quarters of a century.

Major changes took place during those years in order to meet changing conditions, and according to the owner, who had quickly become one of downtown Durham's familiar figures and a highly respected member of the community, each step was "onward and upward."

The year before the stock market crashed in 1929, when business was booming all over the country, Baldwin bought the building next to him and enlarged the premises, and in spite of the Great Depression that soured the next decade and brought on a rash of bankruptcies, his company survived. By then a fixture on Main Street, its presence was reassuring, somehow, as banks and businesses failed, mortgages were foreclosed, stores were vacated, and their owners vanished from the Durham scene to look for a better future somewhere else. If Baldwin's, "Where Shopping Is A Pleasure," continued to serve customers in spite of their decreasing numbers, then, surely, things couldn't be as bad as they seemed. Could they?

# TWENTY EIGHT

*Nobody, of course, had reckoned
on Black Tuesday.*

# Baldwin's remains solid in Depression

*I*n 1927, after sixteen profitable years in "ladies' ready-to-wear," R. L. Baldwin brought one of his Virginia-born nephews, Monroe Baldwin, into the business and began to enlarge his Main Street store, first buying the building adjacent to his on the east side, and then hiring the architectural firm of Atwood and Nash to transform the two properties into a bigger and better whole.

Since arriving in Durham and setting up shop in 1911, competition had burgeoned, and in addition to such old rivals as Ellis-Stone, Kronheimer and Rawls-Knight (formerly Q. E. Rawls), other companies were angling for Durham's female trade. Belk's, Efird's, Gilmer's, Tilley's, Montgomery Ward and Sears Roebuck had moved to town, and catering to less expensive tastes there also were a Charles Store, a United Dollar Store, and a Raylass's. But Baldwin, possessed of a strong positive attitude and accustomed to success, had never been deterred by competition, and as the new store took shape and his nephew assumed part of an ever-growing business load, he began to envision a rosy future. Ten years hence, his fourteen-year-old son, Reuben Lynwood, Jr. (called Lynwood by his elders and "Duck" by his high school peers) would graduate from Duke University. Then he would enter the Harvard Business School, God willing. And after a year in that prestigious institution, he would take his natural place by his father's side, just as R. L. had done back in Farmville, Virginia before he came to Durham. And thus the family tradition would continue, as it had since 1850.

Nobody, of course, had reckoned on Black Tuesday, October 29, 1929. That day, when $5 million in stocks went down the drain, the whole world changed.

Baldwin, in addition to being a leading merchant, had helped organize the Home Building and Loan Association and become its chief officer in 1920. He also was president of the Citizen's National Bank, so he had double concerns during the catastrophic era that was to go down in history as the Great Depression. "But he never brought any of his business worries home," his son, Lynwood, remembers. "To my knowledge, my father never had a bad mood, and he had one tremendous asset, the ability to compromise. So no situation ever was impossible to him, because he could always figure out some way to keep going by compromising. He could adjust. And he had a great sense of humor."

Thus armed, the owner of Baldwin's weathered the economic depression, and only in the year 1932 did his store not make a profit, however modest. To many in Durham, it was comforting, somehow, to see that it was "business as usual" at Baldwin's, and that its proprietor remained the same friendly, cheerful gentleman he had always been.

There can be little doubt that Baldwin also inspired confidence at the two financial concerns he headed, the Home Building and Loan Association and the Citizen's National Bank. When FDR's unforgettable Bank Holiday occurred in 1933, Baldwin went to Richmond on that Friday, when every bank in Durham closed its doors, and Lynwood Baldwin recalls that "whatever Dad said to those folks at the Federal Reserve about the bank and the building and loan must have done some good, because both of them opened up again on Monday."

R. L. Baldwin

Fortunately, the tobacco industry and the creation of Duke University, with a $40 million gift from James B. Duke, kept Durham from suffering as keenly from the Depression as did other parts of the state. By 1934, the economic picture was a little brighter, and by 1937, just ten years after the first major enlarging of his store, R. L. Baldwin was ready to do it again. As planned, his son was at Harvard, following graduation from Duke, and by 1938 he'd be ready to begin the career that, unbeknown to him, had begun the day he was born, on December 6, 1913.

Baldwin's was a grand store in Durham.

And he would not start in a small, refurbished millinery shop, as his father had done. Lynwood Baldwin would start in elegant new quarters containing 30,000 square feet of beautifully decorated space housing eighteen departments catering not just to women, but to men and children, too. Beginning with babies, and going right up the ladder to grandparents, the new Baldwin's would be a store for the whole family. Designed by well-known architects T. C. Atwood and H. Raymond Weeks, and built at a cost of $130,000, it would be "a monument to the spirit of integrity, fair dealing and honesty" that had prevailed since its inception, and it was bound to boost "Durham's standing as the shopping center of North Carolina."

Happy days were here again!

Or, at least, just around the corner.

*The last word in*
*department stores.*

# Baldwin's used advertising for profit

Because the owner of Baldwin's knew the value of keeping the public's attention, both he and his son, R. L. Baldwin Jr., advertised regularly in *The Durham Morning Herald* and *The Durham Sun* from the store's opening in 1911 until its demise in 1990, and some of those early ads are still extant. Preserved on the brittle pages of old newspapers and apt to shed yellow flakes at even the slightest touch, they are fragile doors to a past long gone, a time when every store in town was closed on Sunday and the eternal verities were love, work and duty.

Scanning one of the earliest of these, which appeared on September 18, 1918 in *The Durham Sun*, I realized that while America was fighting Germany in the war to end all wars women's skirts rose from just above the floor to above the ankle, barely clearing the tops of the laced-up high-heeled dress boots that were so popular. That same year the pelts of two or three small mink, each biting the other's tail in order to stay draped around milady's shoulders, cost "$15 each" at Baldwin's and were the height of fashion.

Coats were "from $25 to $50," coat suits "from $25 to $65," dresses "from $20 to $39.75," and millinery, described as "very reasonable," ranged from "the very smooth small Hat to the large and more dressy." Blouses, then called "shirt waists," were "from $5 to $8.50," and the most popular colors in the fall of 1918 were burgundy, plum, gray, taupe and Belgian blue.

(Exactly fifty-four days after that ad appeared in the evening paper, the Armistice was signed and my father announced, at the supper table, that there would never be another war. America had won and

Baldwin's set the pace for the latest fashions and home trends.

the world was now safe for democracy, he told us, and I believed him. Papa had spoken, and that was that.)

Seven years later, on April 1, 1925, prices had fallen. Baldwin's advertised Easter coats "as new as tomorrow (and) the ultimate in style, quality and value" for "from $24.75 to $49.75"; and "Frocks for every daytime occasions . . . made on lines so adorable to youth and so flattering to the older women," ranging "from $15.85 to $24.85." Evening gowns "for the Easter socials" were made of satin, tulle or taffeta "in every lovely new color of the season." They fell almost to the ankle in back, rose almost to the knee in front, and exposed the back almost to the waist.

(My big sister had one of these, and the night she wore it for the first time to a high school fraternity dance at Forest Hills Club House, I went upstairs and fell on the bed and wept with envy and wished I were old enough to go out with boys, wished I had a gorgeous new dress made of taffeta, wished I knew how to dance, wished I didn't have freckles, et cetera et cetera.)

By April 1, 1938, when *The Durham Morning Herald* published an entire section about the formal opening of a brand new Baldwin's and called it "the last word in departments stores," the Great Depression had begun to ease its grip on the economy. But prices were still low, with ladies' coat suits that had sold for $25 in 1918 now priced at $5.95. Jackets were fitted, shoulders were padded, skirts ended just below the knees, and Fraberlyn hosiery "so beautifully flattering to the ankles" was being sold exclusively at Baldwin's for "$1 a pair, or three for $2.85."

The store's innovations included the use of blue mirrors and photographic murals in decorating; modern pneumatic tubes replacing the old wire baskets as a system of money control; a luncheonette that would accommodate fifty diners at a time; an air-conditioned kitchen with both gas and electric facilities; a Youth Center, a Babyland, and a Beauty Salon with an outside terrace. Patrons could dry their hair in the sunshine, sip cool drinks sent up from the luncheonette, and enjoy the ministrations of "Mr. Frank," who was trained in Hollywood, California, and worked there, among the movie queens, before coming to Durham.

The men's wear department was touted as the ultimate answer to the sartorial needs of the most exacting customers; and in a "special paradise" for women called "The Fashion Bowl," there were "so many things to see you must take it like champagne—a little at a time or you'll get dizzy," said one *Herald* reporter. Lingerie, dresses, coats, suits, hats, skirts, sweaters, blouses and even nurses' uniforms could be found in the "Bowl," and shoes to go with all this finery could be found on the street floor. That department, with its "entrancing bleached walnut woodwork and white leather upholstery," had one entire wall covered with a photomural that was "a juxtaposition of shots of . . . the Eiffel Tower, Arc de Triomphe, London Bridge, England's House of Parliament, the opera house in Rome, and New York's own Radio City and St. Patrick's cathedral." It was a far cry from ordinary shoe stores lined with shelves and paper boxes. But it—and all the rest of it—was to be expected at the new Baldwin's, truly the last word in Durham department stores on the eve of World War II, according to the ads in the local newspapers.

(How could Papa have been so wrong about World War I?)

# TWENTY NINE

*Even now there are those who will never
forget The Fashion or its owners.*

# The Fashion was an exclusive shop for women

The Fashion, Durham's first exclusive shop for women, originated in the minds of Charles and Rose Sawilosky while they were operating a small dry goods store in Waynesboro, Georgia. That was a long time ago, right after World War I, but their idea didn't become reality until after they moved here with their two little girls, Gertrude and Henrietta, in the summer of 1921.

They came because they wanted to live in a bigger town, with more opportunities for the good life and better schools for their daughters, and Durham seemed to fill the bill. Greensboro had been an option, too, but in the end they chose the "Bull City," where factory whistles bellowed three times a day and the smell of tobacco had been in the air so long nobody but newcomers noticed it.

After two or three days, they didn't pay much attention to it, either.

By 1920, Durham's population had exceeded 30,000, its public schools ranked with the best in the state, and it even had a college, named Trinity, that some of the town's millionaires—there were five of them—couldn't seem to do enough for, apparently. And as if that weren't enough in the way of educational advantages, the University of North Carolina was only twelve miles away. So the Sawiloskys rented a house on Queen Street, just a few blocks east of the business district, and then they rented a modest store at what turned out to be an ideal location—the corner of Main and Church streets.

One-Twenty-Nine East Main was a lucky number for "Miss Rose" and "Mr. Charlie," as those two ex-

Charles and Rose Sawilosky, above and left.

perts in women's wear came to be known, and The Fashion gave some of Durham's older and larger stores a considerable run for their money. On opening day, Miss Rose shone like a star among the seven professional models Mr. Charlie had imported especially for the occasion. Dark, slender and pretty, she and her cohorts put on a fashion show for the fashion-conscious women of Durham who came to see what the new store was all about, and seeing the subdued elegance of its décor and the quality of its dresses, suits and coats, many of those women became lifelong customers then and there, and loyal friends of the owners.

Mr. Charlie, a mannerly man with thinning dark hair and a ready smile, enjoyed the constant companionship of an unlit cigar, held either in his mouth or in one of his hands, and he had a special way with children. While their mothers tried on his expensive clothes, he offered them sticks of chewing gum and drinks of Huckleberry Springs water from a cooler on the landing of the stairway that led to the store's business office and alteration room; and he listened to their answers to his questions with what appeared to be rapt attention.

Every woman who entered his store was "Little Lady," no matter what her age, size or shape happened to be; and if he couldn't produce the Davidow suit this one wanted, or the Adele Simpson evening gown that one craved, he called Miss Rose and the problem was soon solved. Women of means who wanted to look their best at all times no longer had to go to Richmond, or Washington, or even New York to buy clothes. Now they could tell Miss Rose what they wanted, or she could tell them what they *really* wanted in order to stay "in style," and on her next buying trip to New York she would find exactly the right dress, coat or suit.

Sometimes she would even bring back an extra piece of fabric, should a special customer want to complete her costume with a matching hat; and then she would get Miss Myrtle Albright, the best hatmaker in town, to fill that bill.

"My mother could do anything, and do it well," says her youngest daughter, Henrietta Brandt. "She was a marvelous cook, a beautiful dancer, a good bridge player, and she really knew how to wear clothes. When she walked in a room, she just seemed to light it up, and she would go out of her way to help people. Mother was a wonderful person."

A fitting tribute, I think, to Rose Sawilosky, and one that many others echoed to me as they sorted through their memories of a store that had a certain special "something" that will never be found, I dare say, in any shopping mall.

Even now, eighty-two years after it opened, there are those who will never forget The Fashion and its owners. Some long-time customers also remember some of the people who worked there: Lacey Hargrave, the teen-age janitor who delivered clothes on a bicycle until he learned how to drive; Mozelle Allen, the "alterations lady" whose red hair, in the process of turning gray, took on a surprisingly becoming pinkish cast; and Tessie Huckabee and Mabel Sigmon, the first sales ladies. Among others who followed them were Josephine Fleming, Margaret Bagwell, Ruth Pollard and Frances Rose, to name only a few.

A handful of erstwhile patrons of The Fashion, questioned about their memories of it, admitted that some of the most significant milestones in their lives were inextricably tied to that exclusive little shop:

- The first "grown-up church dress," to be worn with the first longed-for silk stockings.
- The first fur-trimmed coat, with its made-to-order matching hat
- The first strapless evening gown, pale pink satin swirled out at the bottom, like a fish tail.

And, with each one, the opportunity to say, if anybody asked: "I got it at The Fashion."

In some fortunate circles, that phrase was tantamount to the ultimate seal of approval when it came to clothes for going away to prep school, for going away to college, for going to the Terpsichorean Club's debutante ball in Raleigh. Clothes also for going to dances at Duke and Carolina and State, and sometimes to Princeton, or to the Naval Academy at Annapolis.

And eventually, in the so-called orderly procession from birth to death, clothes for getting married.

From the 1920s until the rebellious 1960s, when

long-haired flower children decreed that it was cool to wear something from a thrift shop and go barefooted to your own wedding, that all-important event usually required a long-trained white satin gown and an elaborate veil of tulle or lace. More often than not, it also required a trousseau, designed to tide the bride (and the groom) over the next few years, at least. That meant a number of dresses in addition to the "going away dress," which was always described in detail, along with the wedding gown, by the society editors of *The Durham Morning Herald* and *The Durham Sun*.

The trousseau also meant a coat, possibly two (one for winter, one for spring), and the requisite number of skirts, sweaters, hats, gloves and scarves. Although The Fashion did not carry shoes or lingerie, if one wanted Miss Rose to supply these essentials with the rest of the trousseau, it was as good as done. What she didn't have in stock, she would go to New York and buy, not only for the bride, but also for her mother, her sister(s), her bridesmaids and her diminutive flower girl.

And when all was in readiness at last and the great day finally arrived, Miss Rose would go, if asked, to the bride's home to help her dress, and then on to the church to see that gown, train, veil, bouquet and bride were in a state of perfection and ready to proceed down the aisle, accompanied by a doting father who would be considerably less solvent, come next month, but all for a good cause.

As the years passed, more and more women from Durham, Chapel Hill, Oxford, Henderson, Roxboro and Raleigh became walking advertisements of The Fashion's perennial chic. Some scrimped and saved to acquire the store's expensive clothes, others took the largesse of a parent or a husband for granted and wore them like a second skin, and all of them felt the impact of Miss Rose's personality. Her uncanny knack of knowing exactly what style or cut or color would bring out a customer's best look engendered trust, and her warmth and friendliness encouraged the kind of confidences that made her privy to most of the joys and sorrows of her "special ladies."

Small wonder that The Fashion prospered during the 1920s, withstood the depression of the 1930s and continued to thrive until urban renewal and the subsequent demise of downtown Durham brought about its closing in 1979.

# THIRTY ONE

*She simply acted on a hunch that women
were inveterate shoppers.*

# Energetic woman puts spark into ads

ack in the 1930s, there was no such thing as a shopping guide for Durham consumers, and nothing in the newspapers that faintly resembled today's emphasis on the creative sales pitch. On the contrary, ads aimed at Durham shoppers back in the 1930s were short, to the point, and almost completely devoid of imagination.

In the spring of 1937, for instance, Ellis Stone, a leading department store, offered *Latest Fashions For An Early Easter* and listed, without further persuasion, "Easter Dresses $16.95, Easter Coats $29.95, Easter Suits $19.95." Baldwin's, another popular establishment, was equally terse: *High Fashions For Low Temperatures* was the banner above "Warm Coats $9.95 to $27.50." But Baldwin's did lean a little more toward eloquence with "200 New Dresses to Double Your Charm With Prices To Balance Your Budget."

All in all, however, the ads people read with their morning coffee, or after their evening meal, were statements of fact, such as "Men's Fine Shirts $1.65" and "Half Wool Blankets $2.98," until a certain Durham lady decided, in 1932, that the time had come for a new approach to advertising.

Douglas Hill Morehead, well born, well-to-do and well endowed with native intelligence and a quick wit, was married to a prominent attorney, J. Lathrop Morehead, a grandson of North Carolina governor John Motley Morehead and only son of Durham's first banker, Eugene Morehead. She also was the mother of one daughter and the mistress of an imposing estate on "Morehead Hill," but motherhood and manor-tending were not enough to consume all of her considerable energy. As for doing good works, she had long since done her share of good works in both church and civic affairs, so she began to look with growing interest at Durham's business arena.

Douglas Hill Morehead (right) and John Moorhead at Hope Valley Country Club in the 1980s.

The fact that she was well into middle age and had no special training in those professions generally open to women at the time (teacher, nurse, secretary, seamstress) was no deterrent. She simply acted on a hunch that women were inveterate shoppers, whether times were good or bad, and launched herself into advertising.

Having made up her mind to eschew a life of ease and "do something actual," Douglas Morehead proceeded, in the very teeth of the Great Depression, to become publisher, editor, reporter and advertising manager of a four-page, nine-by-seven-inch newspaper she elected to call *DurHaM's Buy-Ways*, capitalizing her own initials, D.H.M., in the masthead. She

defined the sheet as "A Guide for Distinctive Shoppers," and it was a far cry from what the public had become accustomed to reading.

Mrs. Morehead's headlines caught the eye, and her copy helped to boost the city's sagging economy and, at the same time, the little paper enhanced her own growing reputation as a "classy" huckster. *DurHaM's Buy-Ways* was regarded as highly sophisticated advertising, larded with just enough snob appeal and name-dropping to attract not only women, but "all sorts and conditions of men"—bankers, drycleaners, house painters, retail grocers, garage and mill owners were among her clients.

Full of chit-chat, doggerel, puns and snappy headlines, the paper was an immediate hit, and six years after its first appearance in 1931, it was still going strong. On March 18, 1937, there were six pages, instead of four, and they contained ads for nine clothing stores, three banks, two bookstores, two hat shops, two florists, two beauty shops, two grocery stores, a garage, a drugstore, a laundry, a dry cleaner, a decorator, the Erwin Cotton Mill, the Durham Public Service company and the Washington Duke Hotel.

A small success story, perhaps, but it gave Durham a new view of advertising, and among the local merchants who profited from it, I give you the following excerpts:

WEEPING WILLERS [the headline]: "Many men shy off from making a will and become sad and mournful if wills are mentioned. A perverse sentimentality. They should weep at the prospect of unwilled property, unplanned division of estate, and heirs unprovided for. These are the real causes of mournings, because estates left undisposed of by will become the prey of amateur executors or the victims of state law, which, planned to suit every case, suits none.

So weep no more, my laddie. Face the facts, take your estate to the Trust Office of THE FIDELITY BANK, discuss your dispositional objectives with these men, have your plans incorporated into a will, and name this Bank as the executor . . . Use sense, not sentimentality, in your estate disposition."

EATER'S DIGEST: "Free souls who abhor regular meals and like to let digestion wait on appetite will appreciate the flexibility of the housekeeping at the TAVERN of the Washington Duke Hotel. Here such non-conformists can eat when they please, what they please, and as much as they please to pay for. Try a sample of this freedom at the TAVERN and discover how pleasant a meal is when there's no mother to chide you about clocks and vitamins."

QUIT BEEFING: "Switch to turkey . . . HARRELL'S MARKET can supply you with this memorable fowl in any size or either sex. Harrell's turkeys, grown on his own farm, are scientifically bred and housed and are of a delicacy undreamed of in your fowlosophy. Call L-7251 and order your Thanksgiving turkey now. You'll give thanks on November 24th if you've been this foresighted."

CROWNED HEADS: "Easy is the head that wears a crown from BALDWIN'S HAT SHOP. A chic little crown of felt tiara-ed in fur—a diademic model of jewel-trimmed suede—a coronet of velvet crested with plumes—even an amusing half-crown of fuss and feathers for evening. Any of these numbers will give you the serenity that comes from style. BALD-

WIN's is also featuring the small 'coat-collar' hats that fit into your neck lines."

FOR GOODNESS SAKE: "If you want really good party refreshments, 'ham-what-am' biscuits, cara-mel pies like Hillsboro used to make, white-meat chicken salad and other eat-ceteras, call MRS. J. C. MICHIE F-2731. She knows her stuff. You should know it, too!"

A "NEW FASHION" COCKTAIL: "To make Easter Parade the stimulating draught appropriate now take 1 jigger-coat of BALDWIN'S style, add several dashes of BALDWIN'S Vernal Accessories, mix with a coupla hot shots of Valcraft shoes and you'll create a 'New Fashion' that will do wonders for your jaded feelings . . . Altogether, BALDWIN'S new styles are positively intoxicating."

Re-reading took me back, with the speed of light, to the sedate, marble-floored Fidelity Bank, where I opened my first account; to the exciting Washington Duke Tavern, where I drank my first beer; to Harrell's Meat Market, where my mother bought turkeys; to Baldwin's downtown Main Street store, which outfitted me for more years than I care to count, and I saw them again, even though all are gone, vanished, the victims of progress and urban renewal.

And Mrs. Michie, who really was a gourmet cook before the word became familiar in America, is gone, too. So is Douglas Morehead, herself a free soul who abhorred the mundane, who raised conservative eyebrows by going to work when she really didn't have to, and who made shopping—and reading about it—more fun.

I miss them all.

# THIRTY TWO

*The only trouble with this damn business
is that it's dying of improvement.*

BENJAMIN R. ROBERTS

# Davison, Hill take lead in health care insurance

*N*obody really knows how much talk has to transpire before an idea finally takes form and becomes reality.

Dr. William Preston Few, the first president of Duke University and one of the least talkative men in Durham unless he was promoting a cause, talked for ten years, off and on, with James B. Duke about establishing a medical school here before Duke finally decided to do it. And Dr. Wilburt C. Davison, who left the Johns Hopkins Hospital in Baltimore to become the first dean of the Duke Medical School, began talking in 1928 about a hospital insurance plan that did not materialize as the Hospital Care Association until 1933.

When Davison arrived here in 1927 to assume his position at a university that had not yet been built and to some degree was still in the planning stages, North Carolina had only one doctor for every 1,244 people and only one hospital bed for every 382 people. Over sixty percent of the population viewed medical care as a luxury, and there was a widespread tendency among certain segments to regard hospitals as "death houses," to be avoided at all costs, if possible. North Carolina, no doubt about it, was one of the most backward states in America as far as health care went. Only South Carolina was worse.

Davison, still in his mid-thirties, was an optimistic soul with a buoyant personality and considerable determination, and changing that bleak picture became one of his top priorities. Highly trained under some of the biggest names in the medical profession, he brought with him a number of new concepts re-

DUKE HOSPITAL STAFF - APRIL I, 1931

I. JONES, 2. PERLZWEIG, 3. CEKADA, 4. RUFFIN, 5. CRAVEN, 6. JOHNSTON, 7. CALDER, 8. TAYLOR, 9. BELLOWS, 10. MACKLER, 11. AVNER, 12. BAKER, 13. OATES, 14. HANSEN, 15. SMITH, 16. REEVES, 17. SMITH, 18. ALYEA, 19. SHANDS, 20. EADIE, 21. DAVISON, 22. MAGILL, 23. PERSONS, 24. AMOSS, 25. FORBUS, 26. BAKER, 27. HOLLINSHEAD, 28. GRIESEMER, 29. SMITH, 30. SWETT, 31. CRAVEN

Thirty-one men stand outside the Davison entrance to what is now Duke Hospital South, the original Duke Hospital Building. Dr. Davison, for whom this first building was eventually named, is #21. ca. 1931.

garding the teaching and practice of medicine in hospitals. And he also brought along a proposed solution to the knotty problem of how the average wage earner could afford to pay the hospital, should he or members of his family need to go there for medical or surgical treatment.

Davison's answer was a prepayment plan based on the insurance principle. He had observed it while he was a student, and later an intern, at Oxford, England, and he was eager to see it established not only in Durham, but throughout the state. Paying in advance for unexpected illness or accident had been

tried before as far back as 1800, when the government built and maintained a Marine hospital in Norfolk, Virginia by deducting twenty cents per week from every sailor's pay. Closer to home, six manufacturing plants in Roanoke Rapids were offering employees and families medical, surgical and nursing care in both the home and the hospital for twenty-five cents per week, but patients could use only the local hospital, which ran counter to Davison's belief that benefits should be transferable, and that hospitals throughout the state should participate.

Needing local support, Davison took his proposal

Dr. William Preston Few

George Watts Hill

to George Watts Hill, grandson of George W. Watts, founder of Durham's first hospital. Hill, a banker who sat on the board of Watts Hospital and handled its business affairs, listened carefully to what might be a solution to the painful fact that the city's pioneer medical center had been operating in the red for some years and often was less than half full.

Responding positively, Hill agreed to help implement the plan, and because his standing in the community was assured and his words carried weight, he gathered enough support to stage an organizational meeting at Watts Hospital on March 8, 1929, with the new dean of the still non-existent Duke Medical School as the chief speaker.

Present at that meeting were Dr. Foy Roberson, representing Lincoln Hospital; Dr. S. D. McPherson, representing McPherson Hospital; Dr. John W. Smith, representing the Durham Ministerial Asso-

ciation; and W. E. Stanley, representing the Durham Board of Public Health. Absent were representatives from the Chamber of Commerce and Durham Hosiery Mills, but they, along with the Duke Endowment, the Durham Hospital Medical Association and the Durham-Orange County Medical Society, had already endorsed the plan, which received unanimous approval from those attending.

Davison and Hill's joint effort was a giant step in the right direction, and what they named the Durham Hospital Association would have been the first such company in America, had not the stock market crash the following October quashed it. Its demise was temporary, however, and its resurrection, in 1933, as the Hospital Care Association was to prove the truth of an old adage turned cliché: Big oaks from little acorns grow.

AS A GENERAL RULE, most people don't appreciate hospital insurance until an unexpected illness or accident disrupts their lives and assaults their bank accounts.

For example: You head for the coast on a beautiful Saturday in May, get hit by a drunk driver before you've reached Raleigh, and wake up in a strange hospital surrounded by strange people wearing masks and white uniforms. Chances are, you don't immediately think about how you're going to pay for what's happened to you, but sooner or later you remember a certain document salted away in a lock box back home, and you not only appreciate it, you thank God for it.

The above scenario, which took place in 1938 before doctors and nurses wore green, involved two young people married less than two years and a Wake County farmer with a big taste for "white lightning" and no liability insurance. The farmer escaped without a scratch, and the young wife was able to limp away from the collision with nothing more than superficial cuts, a few bruises and a sprained ankle. But the husband was admitted to Rex Hospital, in Raleigh, with multiple fractures, internal injuries and a fifty-fifty chance of survival, and thus began the first episode in a long-running personal soap opera that might well be called "Life Can Be Beautiful, But Not Without Hospital Care."

It was Certificate of Membership GA1166, issued by the Hospital Care Association of Durham, N.C. on the first day of December 1933 that eased the physical and psychological pain of the male protagonist in that drama. For a registration fee of two dollars and a commitment of twenty cents a week, his hospital care policy provided him with "a $5 private room, board, general nursing care, nursing supervision, routine laboratory blood count and urinalysis, dietetic service, the use of operating or delivery room, surgical dressings and ordinary drugs, anesthetics, X-ray service and medications provided by the hospital."

Because it did not provide for the services of "physicians, surgeons, special nurses or their board, any specially ordered laboratory work, special drugs or antitoxins, or orthopedic appliances or casts," the out-of-pocket expenses for No. GA1166, who had required almost all of the above items in order to beat the odds against him, were enough to obliterate a carefully hoarded savings account. But there were few regrets. Money, after all, was only money, and in 1938 nobody had much anyway, Hospital Care included.

BORN DURING THE WORST depression this country has ever known, the company was chartered on August 5, 1933 by W. E. Avery, Dwight Snyder and J. D. Reeder, all of Raleigh, who had lofty objectives but no cash. However, they must have had a hunch that George Watts Hill, grandson of the founder of Durham's Watts Hospital, might be interested in their scheme, because they approached Hill and "were cordially received in the home of his father in Durham." The younger Hill's interest in hospital insurance dated from 1929, when he and Dr. W. C. Davison, dean of the new Duke University Medical School, started what would have been the first such company in America if the stock market crash had not aborted their venture, and his belief in the concept had not diminished.

After hearing them out and perusing their documents, Watts Hill gave the three entrepreneurs from Raleigh his endorsement, in the form of a rent-free office in the Durham Loan and Trust Company building and his signature on a note for $250. As soon as both Watts and Duke hospitals granted them a $1,000 credit extension for eighteen months, they were ostensibly in business, and by the middle of November, 1933 the Hospital Care Association was a reality.

Henry Groves Connor, a Wilson attorney, W. H. Glasson, a Duke professor, and Elisha M. Herndon and Dwight Snyder, former insurance salesmen, were president, vice president, sales manager and secretary, respectively; and twenty-year-old Elizabeth Marshall Davis, with a degree from St. Mary's Junior College in Raleigh, and a post-graduate degree in business from Durham High School, was assistant secretary and, essentially, a Jill of all trades who virtually ran the office while Snyder and Herndon beat the bushes for members.

A stunning blonde who trotted to proms up and down the eastern seaboard, "Lib" Davis, now Mrs. J. H. Mallard of Durham, had just returned from a weekend of dances at the University of Virginia and was still sleeping off fatigue when a mid-morning call from Herndon changed the course of her life.

At a time when jobs, especially for women, were almost non-existent, she had been offered one with a title: Assistant Secretary of the Hospital Care Association.

It opened on borrowed money in one room in Durham's Trust Building, and the young woman who minded the store, so to speak, while her bosses were out trying to sell an entirely new concept of

Elizabeth Davis, Mrs. J. H. Mallard

insurance to the public, came highly qualified to her first job. She proved to be a definite asset to the fledgling company in more ways than one.

"I did everything in that office," the now stately and still stunning grandmother remembers. "Typed all correspondence, kept the books, answered the phone, acted as cashier, made the bank deposits, swept and dusted, and after a while, when we began to do better and needed more help, I trained all the girls we hired." (Among those girls, who came and went over a period of years, were Doris Green, Evelyn Ennett, Josephine Mangum, Mary Lucy Pyne, Bertha Ragan, Helen Shaw, Josephine Shelton, Carrie Lockhart, Dorothy Gaddy, Gertrude Isenhour and Lucille Blalock.)

Dr. Davison's guests at Josh Tarnage's barbecue included on right side: Ann Altvater, Dr. Davison, Barrie Altvater, Peggy Altvater, Vernon Altvater, Dr. Daryl Hart, Mary Hart. Roy Crenshaw is pictured at left front.

Davis herself was hired for $10 a week, "but we were operating on almost nothing, so I told Mr. Snyder and Mr. Herndon to just hold back my salary until I really needed it, and when I finally did need it —I was invited to Princeton for a set of dances in March—I asked for it and got $120 and went off for the weekend and had a perfectly grand time."

But grand times, or even reasonably good times, were not on the immediate horizon for company officials. To begin with, almost all of Durham's wage earners, with the exception of its tobacco and textile barons, had been hit hard enough by the Great Depression to believe that keeping food on the table and a roof overhead was far more important than

paying in advance for an accident or an illness that might or might not happen; so selling the plan was difficult.

The first buyer, a printer by trade, was Charles L. Medlin, of Raleigh, and the fact that the company had hired him to print its literature may have influenced him to own the first policy that came off his press, Certificate No. GA1001.

"We thought it would impress the public if we started with 1000," sales manager E. M. Herndon confessed three decades later after he had become president; but going under the assumption that all was fair in economic depression, as Shakespeare said it was in love and war, did not have the desired effect.

Vernon Altvater in his office at Duke Hospital. ca. 1941.

By the end of 1933, only 309 members of the public had been sufficiently impressed to buy a policy, and Hospital Care lost $9.52 on each one.

A year later, although enrollment had increased dramatically to 4,734 and the loss per member had dropped to $4.50, the company recorded a deficit of $10,837.25. In 1935, that figure increased to $13,601.95, in spite of the fact that the membership had more than doubled. Dwight Snyder, who had been promoted to executive vice president, became highly concerned about the financial condition, "as well he might have," Herndon admitted later. The sound of an ambulance siren often made Snyder hope that the occupant of the speeding vehicle

wasn't a member of Hospital Care, because there wasn't enough money in the bank to pay the claim, and before the year was out he resigned.

If Duke and Watts hospitals had not had a significant stake in the success of Hospital Care, it probably would have gone under like so many other businesses that failed during the Great Depression. The two hospitals, however, needed insurance monies to help cover their operating costs, and Duke, especially, needed "clinical material" (patients) for the education of its medical students.

So it happened that early in 1935, Duke and Watts decided to invest $6,000 each in the foundering insurance company's future, but with strings attached, of course. Dangling from that princely sum of $12,000 were the following stipulations: Hospital Care was to pay off all debts, buy out the original stockholders, and adopt new by-laws, under which the association "could assume special obligations in favor of the two hospitals in return for cash or credit advanced." Furthermore, after a general "house cleaning," (all but six of the fifteen employees were released) Duke and Watts hospitals would name five of the company's seven directors, "including all of the Executive Committee."

It was this new committee that requested, and got, the services of Frederick Vernon Altvater, superintendent of Duke Hospital, to reorganize the company and put it on a solid business base. A Duke graduate who had majored in economics under Dr. W. H. Glasson, Altvater was so disappointed when he failed to land a coveted job in a northern bank that Glasson suggested he "go ask Dean Davison if there isn't something you can do at Duke Hospital," and the young man from Central City, Colorado took what may have been one of the best pieces of advice he would ever be offered.

The highly perceptive dean of Duke's medical school must have sensed considerable potential in the quiet, good-looking young man whose thoughtful conversation was threaded with dry, understated wit. Davison forthwith gave Altvater a responsible job in the purchasing department, and in 1932 sent him to four major medical centers, in Illinois, Iowa, Colorado and Minnesota, to study their methods of book-keeping, collection and financial administration.

In 1933, Davison appointed him superintendent of the hospital, and in that capacity he was "loaned" to Hospital Care during the summer of 1935.

Under Alvater's guidance, new accounting and recording systems were adopted, and on his recommendation Donald E. Deichmann, a salesman with Monumental Life Insurance Company of Baltimore, was hired as secretary-treasurer and office manager. Deichmann, another Duke graduate and, incidentally, one of Altvater's fraternity mates, was big, blond, handsome, outgoing and extremely likable. A former co-worker remembers him as "over six feet tall, played football and was real friendly. Don had a nice way about him, folks liked him. Another thing about him was, he made a very good impression on the public, was a good family man." Deichmann also was able to implement Altvater's ideas, and to move forward toward the company's original goal of enrolling not just white collar workers and professionals, but the working classes, as well.

Nevertheless, it was slow going. In spite of the fact that by the end of 1936 the company had offices in Durham, Raleigh, Asheville, Fayetteville, Greensboro, Charlotte and Concord, it lost just under $11,000 that year and continued to lose for the next two years. It also continued to grow, with the membership doubling through 1937. Benjamin R. Roberts, who had succeeded Henry Groves Connor as president of Hospital Care in 1935, opined not once, but many times, that "The only trouble with this damn business is that it is dying of improvement."

But it did not—would not—die. Instead, it became one of Durham's famous "firsts," which Dean Davison insisted was "the first statewide hospital insurance plan in the world, the first to provide prepayment coverage for any group to any hospital, the first to enroll groups on a waiver basis and the first to give family dependents the same coverage as the employed certificate holder."

And, eventually, it evolved into Blue Cross/Blue Shield of North Carolina which, on December 31, 1999, reported that membership had reached 1.9 million, revenue from premiums and fees stood at $1.9 million, and the company had a net profit, after taxes, of $18.6 million that year. Branch offices across the state include Charlotte, Hickory, Greensboro, Raleigh, Greenville and Wilmington, with headquarters in Chapel Hill.

# THIRTY THREE

# Going into debt was no way to start a family

Twelve years ago, in the spring of 1991, I wrote this: Having observed for many years and with ever-increasing dismay an inexorable rise in the cost of health care, I recently succumbed to a sudden impulse and asked a young friend if she would mind telling me just how much it was going to cost to have the baby she was obviously going to have in a few weeks, if not sooner. Because my own initiation into motherhood had occurred during the Great Depression, I knew there would be a sizeable difference between what my spouse had paid for that mutually earth-shaking experience, back in 1939, and what hers would be liable for in 1991, but I was shocked at the "ballpark figures" the young mother-to-be was able to give me off the top of her head, so to speak, at a party.

Needing documentation, I learned from the horse's mouth (Durham County General Hospital) that excluding the obstetrician's fee of "around $1,730" for prenatal care and delivery, $540 is the cost of a normal delivery and a Caesarian section is $767. The patient's first hour in a labor room costs whoever is to pay for it $52, and each additional two hours in a recovery room add up to $90. Succeeding hours, should there be any, are $22 each. For a private room, the tab is $296 per day, and a crib in the nursery for the baby is almost as much—$277, to be exact, provided special care is not needed. Special care raises the cost to $333.

Thus a normal *accouchement*, with no extras (drugs and anesthesia are extras), followed by two days in the hospital (that's all insurance companies will cover) comes to approximately $3,358. And that, I was told by my expectant friend, is very reasonable. Compared to what a normal delivery costs in places like Dallas, Houston and Atlanta, she said, it is extremely reasonable.

Today, in the spring of 2003, the cost of giving birth has escalated, to put it mildly. Now, the obstetrician's fee for normal prenatal care and delivery is $2,100; and normal delivery at Durham County General costs $825, plus a post-delivery charge of $132, plus $523 per day for postpartum care of the mother in her room, plus a newborn charge of $489 per day for the baby, whether it stays with its mother or goes to the nursery.

But if parents-to-be know, in advance, that delivery will be by Caesarian section, they also know that prenatal care and delivery by most obstetricians will cost $3,100, and the hospital charge will be $1,650, plus a recovery room charge of $350.

Mulling over these facts took me back in time to an era when Durham was not yet known as "The City of Medicine" but as "Tobaccoland USA"; and as memories began to surface, I gradually came to the conclusion that giving birth in Tobaccoland was far less costly and infinitely more pleasurable (all things considered, of course) than it may be today in the City of Medicine. For instance: In my case, nine months of prenatal care, followed by nineteen hours of labor (I was a slow starter) and subsequent delivery at Duke Hospital, Durham's newest and finest in 1939, cost around $200; and two weeks in a private room cost $98 and constituted, for me, the most restful time of my life, before or since. Most of that blissful and never-to-be-repeated interim I spent in bed, either sleeping, eating, reading, and receiving flowers and baby presents, or enjoying my absolutely-perfect-brand-new daughter and her brand-new father's frank admiration of me as a producer of perfection. The rest of the time, I came to know and love my very own registered nurse, who arrived each morning at seven and ministered to me until three in the afternoon.

Nurse Cole's starched white uniform rustled when she walked and her starched white cap sat perkily atop her dark hair, cut short according to regulations. Regulations also governed her lack of fingernail polish and lipstick, and the whiteness of her stockings and her shoes; and on those cold, dark December mornings she wore, according to regulations, a navy blue woolen cape lined with red over all that pristine whiteness, and Florence Nightingale herself could not have been a more welcome sight. She gave me leisurely bed-baths, comforting back-rubs, fresh bed linen every day, and the verbal assurance that I had, indeed, produced an exceptional and beautiful child. Between times, she regaled me with stories about her chosen profession, some of them hair raising and others hilarious, and for all that tender loving care and superb entertainment, she billed me, according to regulations, $4.25 a day.

We couldn't afford her, of course, but the baby's father, in a fit of anxiety brought on by nineteen hours of labor (mine *and* his), insisted that we splurge. So for him the "ballpark" price of parenthood was under $400, considerably less than what it costs today, but still a lot of money if your yearly income is about $2,200 (ballpark). If we hadn't had a policy with Hospital Care Association, for which we paid $21 a year, we might have had to float a loan, and going into debt, as everybody knew back then, was no way to start a family.

# Movers & Shakers

*Anyone can succeed
if he's willing to
apply himself.*

J. B. DUKE

# THIRTY FOUR

# A dour façade hid Wash Duke's sense of humor

Washington Duke, the oldest of Durham's pioneer tobacco manufacturers, lacked the benefit of a formal education and the polish that goes with it, but native intelligence coupled with a strong streak of shrewdness made him a wealthy man after the Civil War and, in due time, a leader in this community. Eventually, Duke became a philanthropist, and today his statue broods over one of the campuses of a great institution of higher learning that bears his name.

Go out to Duke University and take a look at that statue. Better still, go to the university library and look at pictures the sculptor must have studied in order to create it. Those pictures do not indicate, by any stretch of the imagination, that Washington Duke was prone to levity. On the contrary, they make it hard to believe the fellow ever enjoyed a good belly laugh. But there is evidence that, although he was a laconic man with little use for banter, a sense of humor did lurk beneath the dour facade the elder Duke consistently presented to photographers. If it was slightly "skewed" at times, so be it. Better a little humor, even at somebody else's expense, than none at all.

Having said as much, I herewith give you a Duke story as it was told to Claude V. Jones, city attorney from 1937 to 1972, by the late Jones Fuller, himself a highly competent lawyer noted for his Chesterfieldian demeanor, precise delivery and quick wit.

Recreating for Claude Jones the following encounter between Washington Duke and John F. Wily, which took place many years ago on the corner of Main and Corcoran streets in downtown Durham, Fuller said:

"As you may know, Claude, the Dukes in the early part of their businesses banked at the old Morehead Banking Company on Main Street, but as their businesses and holdings grew, they decided to establish their own bank, the Fidelity Bank, at the northeast corner of Main and Corcoran Streets. A vacant lot now occupies that site.

"In establishing the Fidelity Bank, the Dukes had to have someone run it for them, so for this purpose they went up North and hired a gentleman named John F. Wily, who came down here and undertook the task of operating the bank and did so in a very efficient and successful manner.

"One afternoon about four-thirty, after the bank had closed, Washington Duke was walking along

Washington Duke

Main Street and encountered Wily, who was standing on the corner of Main and Corcoran waiting for someone in his family to come pick him up and take him home.

"Duke walked up to Wily and said, 'Wily, you look like you're in deep thought. What are you thinking about?'

"Wily replied, 'Mr. Duke, I was thinking that when I came to Durham this street that is now Corcoran Street was an unpaved, narrow, dirt street that went only one block north from Main. Now it has been extended to Chapel Hill Street, and it has been paved and curbed, and gutters have been placed on it, and sidewalks have been constructed, including a nice paved sidewalk right here by the bank. This street

also goes southwardly to and across the railroad tracks to Pettigrew and beyond.

'When I came here, Main Street also was a dirt street, so muddy in rainy weather that horses hitched to buggies and wagons were not able to pull them through it, and in dry weather, clouds of dust were raised by vehicles traveling along it. Now, as you can see, Main Street is paved, with curbs and gutters and sidewalks, and it represents one of the finest streets in the state.

'When I first came down here, Main and Corcoran were dark at night, having only one gaslight in a block. This condition was certainly inconvenient for our citizens, and, in many instances, was unsafe. Now we have electric streetlights, and in addition to contributing substantially to the convenience of the public in the use of these streets at night, the level of safety has greatly improved.

'Without detailing all of the improvements and advances which have been made since I came to Durham, the entire town has gone forward in many aspects, some of which are evidenced in our public school system, in the arts and culture of the community, and in our public library, which is located just a few blocks from here on this street and is one of the finest in the state.

'All in all, since I came here, our town of Durham has blossomed into a fine place in which to live and work.'

"About this time, Wily's ride came for him, and as he started to move down the street, old Washington Duke shifted the wad of tobacco in his mouth, spat a stream of brown juice onto the sidewalk, and uttered this parting remark:

"'Wily, I shore am glad you come!'"

# THIRTY FIVE

# Benjamin Duke quietly aided education

*J*ames Buchanan Duke has always gotten the lion's share of credit for present-day Duke University because he was the Duke who gave a whopping $40 million to Trinity College in 1925 and said, in essence, "Change your name to mine."

But "Buck" Duke wasn't the only member of his family to benefit the little Methodist college that began as Union Institution back in 1838. Washington Duke, the man Buck liked to call "my old daddy," was the first—he gave $85,000 to bring Trinity from Randolph County to Durham in 1892—and Benjamin Duke, Buck's older brother, was the second—he gave the college $24,000 in 1897 and, to tell the truth, never really stopped giving to it.

Ben, the diffident one, the frail one, the dark-eyed Duke with the Van Dyke beard who stood with such quiet dignity in the long shadow cast by Buck, his red-headed brother—he was the first one of his clan to single out higher education as perhaps the worthiest cause a rich man could espouse, and his thinking undoubtedly influenced both his father and his brother. After his initial gift of $24,000 he gave Trinity $90,000 in 1899; financed the building of a granite wall around the entire campus in 1905; gave $250,000 in 1910; and in 1920 donated $100,000 toward the construction of Southgate Building, a dormitory for women.

Thus the college received, over a period of twenty-three years, $1.5 million from Benjamin Newton Duke, who left an Orange County farm in 1873 and came to Durham to manufacture tobacco. He was poor, like almost everybody else in the South after the Civil War, but four years later he was well off enough to marry and settle down to the business of raising a family and being a good citizen, which he was for the rest of his life.

To say that he prospered is to put it mildly; to say that he was a good and faithful steward of the bounty that came his way is an understatement. But all of that is a matter of record, and generally well known. What's not so well known today is the way Ben Duke spent some of his vast wealth on February 22, 1902, when he and his wife, the former Sarah Pearson Angier, celebrated their twenty-fifth wedding anniversary at "The Terrace," their home on West Chapel Hill Street.

Benjamin Duke

It was the leading social function of the season, Durham by that time having acquired a society worthy of a "season." It was also one of the most elaborate ever given in the city, according to a *Durham Morning Herald* reporter who offered subscribers an inside look at how twenty-five years of connubial bliss could be celebrated, providing one had the wherewithal, as Ben Duke did, to hire the Hollow Brook Orchestra of Raleigh to play Viennese waltzes while a Washington, D.C. caterer and his "corps of assistants" served an elaborate supper to the assembled guests.

Those guests, definitely Durham's upper crust and doubtless wearing their finest, were greeted first by Mrs. Lyda Duke Angier, Mrs. Rufus L. Patterson, of New York, and Mr. and Mrs. Gordon McCabe, Jr., of Petersburg. Then they were greeted by the bride and groom, who stood in the wide front hall beneath two large silver initials, A and D, and two large silver dates, 1877-1902, which had been suspended from the ceiling. Duke, a slight, dark, bearded man who had inherited his father's flaring ears, was nevertheless elegant and impressive in full evening regalia, and so was his wife.

As befitted the occasion, Sally Duke outshone everyone else in a Paris gown of white chiffon over white silk with silver embroidery and "incrustations of black lace." Living proof of her husband's success, she wore a bertha draped with turquoise and diamonds, a girdle of silver, a diamond necklace with opal appendants and, on her upswept hair, a diamond tiara.

Assisting the host and hostess in entertaining were Mrs. J. E. Stagg, Mrs. E. M. Graham, Miss Florence Roney, Miss Inez Angier, Miss Mary Clucas, of New York, and four gentlemen: W. A. Erwin, J. H. Southgate, C. W. Toms and J. E. Stagg. These relatives and/or business associates of the Dukes steered guests to the sitting room where coffee and lemonade were being served (no alcohol ever came into "The Terrace"); to the dining room, where the table groaned with the Washington caterer's exotic viands; and to the upstairs hall, where "several hundred presents representing a small size fortune" were on display.

Free to examine these gifts at will throughout the evening, people trooped up and down the stairs at a steady pace, and "many were the exclamations of

"The Terrace," home of Benjamin Duke, was located between Chapel Hill and Willard Streets. ca. 1895

admiration" overheard by the *Herald* reporter, who was particularly impressed by the thousand dollar bill, framed in silver, that Mr. Duke had given Mrs. Duke; and also by a silver vase, "the most beautiful and costly one in Durham, and perhaps in the State," that had been sent by James B. Duke, the little brother who now was president of the giant American Tobacco Company and a permanent resident in New York City.

Ben Duke, too, was destined to leave Durham and make his home in Manhattan, where he would live in a mansion on Fifth Avenue from 1923 until his death in 1929. But that exodus was still far into the future on the night he and Sally entertained "hundreds of friends" at a party no one was likely to forget, least of all the ladies. The ladies, especially, probably would always remember that gala evening, when each one of them received a silver wedding bell engraved with the Duke's monogram and dated 1877-1902.

I wonder how many of those gleaming little "favors" still exist in Durham today, and if any of those that did survive the ensuing years are kept polished and proudly displayed as the heirlooms they are. I do hope so.

# THIRTY SIX

*Be duly thankful for those who*
*clip and save our social history . . .*

# Durham had rich and famous long before TV show

At least a century before television gave America *Lifestyles of the Rich and Famous*, Durham newspapers were giving their subscribers tantalizing glimpses into the lifestyles of Washington Duke, B. N. Duke, J. B. Duke, George Watts and Julian S. Carr, five millionaire manufacturers of tobacco who had achieved a degree of fame in their own hometown simply by being rich.

In 1896, with a population of not much more than five thousand, having one millionaire per one thousand people gave Durham something to boast about, especially in view of the fact that in 1870 only three hundred souls called the place home, and not one of them was either rich or famous.

But thanks to man's craving for tobacco, the three Dukes, their partner, George Watts, and their highly competitive rival, Jule Carr, became ex-

tremely wealthy in a relatively short span of time, and curiosity being part of the human condition, the rest of the town became extremely interested in how they lived. Of special interest were the social activities of these men and their families, and although the press was happy to oblige whenever possible, "high living" in those Victorian days usually consisted of ladies' literary club meetings, church socials, picnics in season, and occasional lectures or debates at the Lyceum, the city's first cultural organization open to both men and women.

Such events gave reporters scant opportunity to focus on "human interest," but now and then there was a wedding in one of the "first" families, and judging from *The Durham Morning Herald*'s account of one such nuptial, it is plain to see that the paper's readers wanted more than bare facts. Infinite detail, apparently, was what they craved, and that's exactly what they got when Washington Duke's granddaughter, Mary Lyon, married James E. Stagg in "one of Durham's most dazzling triumphs." Not surprisingly, the wedding at Trinity Methodist Church drew a large crowd of "interested spectators" who watched invited guests arrive and craned their necks to see inside the church each time the doors swung open.

Decorated by Mrs. Mattie Southgate Jones, a friend of the Dukes, Trinity had been "resplendent" with pink and blue lights and was, according to next morning's *Herald*, "the loveliest scene these people have ever been permitted to look upon." Electricity having been a commodity in Durham for only ten years, it was still something of a novelty and, definitely, a status symbol.

Large initials of the bride and groom, fashioned of pink and blue lights, hung from an arch over the sanctuary. Pink and blue lights twinkled above the organ loft, festooned the altar rail, and glowed in matching candelabra placed at each end of that rail. Only the choir rail, draped in maidenhair and asparagus fern interspersed with pink carnations, lilies-of-the-valley, and pink and blue satin "love knots," escaped electrification.

Participants in the wedding were, for the most part, kinsmen, friends, business associates of the Dukes, and members of the "society" Durham had created for itself in the space of twenty-five years. Miss Lily Parrish, daughter of pioneer warehouseman and ex-mayor E. J. Parrish, played the organ while her father, accompanied by C. A. Jordan, F. L. Fuller, W. H. Branson, G. W. Watts, T. B. Fuller, W. A. Erwin and J. H. Southgate, ushered guests into the pews.

Mary "Mamie" Lyon Stagg

When the ceremony began, groomsmen Macon Alston, Paul Sneed, Arthur Lyon, Ben Lyon, Albert Kramer and J. F. Wily came down the aisle with bridesmaids Vera Lyon, Etta Heartt, Maude Morgan, Daisy Green, Pearl Duke and Bessie Langhorn, all gowned in blue chiffon and taffeta.

Florence Roney, maid of honor and cousin of the bride, wore pink chiffon and taffeta and preceded the groom, who "entered leaning on the arm of his best man, John C. Winder." At the appropriate moment, he "gallantly went forth and met the bride, who walked down the aisle alone wearing a tulle veil over a pearl-and-lace trimmed wedding gown and "an elegant diamond brooch, gift of the groom."

The Reverend John C. Kilgo, president of Trinity College, friend of Washington Duke, and soon to be a bishop, assisted the Reverand John N. Cole in the ceremony, and following the benediction four small "flower children" stepped into the breach and captured the congregation's attention. Mary Duke Lyon, Edwin Buchanan Lyon, Beatrice Whitaker and Lyell Jones led the just-married Staggs out of the church and "literally made for them a pathway of roses, emblematical of their tinted roseway through life," so the public was informed the next morning. That particular issue of *The Morning Herald* was, no doubt, passed from hand to hand, with much comment and conjecture, in many Durham households throughout the city.

Fortunately, at least one subscriber cut out the story of the Stagg wedding and the reception Washington Duke gave afterward at "Fairview," his home on West Main Street, not far from his factory.

It was a gala affair "which for brilliancy of conception and completeness of appointments has never been excelled in the country;" and Duke, ordinarily a rather dour gentleman who didn't give a fig for "society," stood with the bride and groom under a canopy of smilax, roses and pink ribbons and managed to be "most entertaining" to the hundreds who attended, among whom were "many distinguished visitors from a distance."

Be duly thankful for those who clip and save our social history, the kind that rarely gets into books.

AUTHOR'S NOTE: *Mrs. J. E. Stagg, known to her friends as "Mamie," was, like her grandfather, an exemplary and generous citizen and an ardent supporter of Methodism. For many years she financed the carillon programs at Duke Memorial Church, and in memory of her mother she gave Trinity Church its present hand-carved chancel rail, which is considered a work of art. She was also one of the largest donors to the erstwhile Washington Duke Hotel, which was imploded on December 14, 1975.*

# THIRTY SEVEN

*Anybody can succeed*
*if he's willing to apply himself.*

J. B. DUKE

# Introducing Duke students to their benefactor

*I*t's entirely possible, even probable that no more than a handful of seniors who graduate from Duke University each year know much if anything about their alma mater's founder, James Buchanan Duke. I assume they know who he was and what he did, in a general sort of way—don't brochures take care of all that?—and they must know a little of what he looked like in his prime because of the statue that dominates the quadrangle fronting the chapel on West Campus. But a majority of seniors, I dare say, go away from here oblivious to many of the fascinating facts, and some of the equally fascinating legends, about J. B. "Buck" Duke.

To prevent that from happening when commencement rolls around next year, I herewith offer a few bits and pieces of incidental information about Duke University's biggest benefactor to this year's graduates (and anybody else who's interested): Buck Duke was six feet two inches tall, redheaded and good looking. He had a broad forehead, calm, deep-set eyes, a rather small mouth, and the high coloring of the typical Scot. He dressed conservatively, but didn't seem to care much about clothes and often looked rumpled, the seat of his pants shiny with age.

Although he was what you might call a taciturn man, he was never at a loss for words when he wanted to speak. He would state his reasons for making any judgment about anything, and he was prepared to argue when it was necessary, but when he was wrong he was willing to admit it. He had a highly accurate memory, seemed never to forget anything, and although he was prudent in his actions, for the most part, he was certainly not timid. He hated flattery and was quick to spot it, and he

Nannaline Duke, second wife of J. B. Duke and mother of Doris Duke, only child.

Doris Duke

J. B. "Buck" Duke (sitting) and B. N. Duke

didn't like what he called "putting on frills." In conferences, if the discussion went on too long, he'd say, "Cut out the town meeting," which meant: Get down to brass tacks, do something, and do it quick.

In his elegant New York office at the American Tobacco Company, hanging directly across from his desk where it was easy to see, Buck Duke kept a picture of his father, Washington Duke, standing by the small log building that was their first Durham factory. He attributed much of his success to "my old daddy," and for years he gave big sums of money to his daddy's favorite charities, mostly schools and churches and especially Trinity College.

Finally, in the early twenties, he decided "It's time I was beginning to think about a monument," and that's when he gave $40 million to Trinity and suggested that the trustees change its name to Duke University. "I want to leave something in North Carolina that 500 years from now people can look upon and say, 'Duke did that,'" he told a reporter in an interview, and then he added, "Every man owes something to the state he was born in."

But what Buck Duke liked most was to give the opportunity of work to those who wanted to help themselves. He liked that best because he loved work for its own sake. He loved it so much he never took vacations. He said the pleasure he got out of work was all the recreation he needed, and he often planned and schemed and mapped out the strategy for many of his big deals while he was lying in bed at night. Lack of sleep never bothered him. He was working, lying there in the dark. Perfectly happy, just working.

He also was happy when he was riding around in his limousine, for which he paid the vast sum of $11,000. "People ought to buy good cars, good men, good anything," he once said to a man he knew was going to quote him. "Take this car. It's been driven 100,000 miles, and it only costs me seven cents a mile. It's a good car. Anything you buy that's good pays profits."

And that included the men he hired. "Cheap men don't pay," he said. "If you have a company, build it up with costly men, and let them make profits. Give them part of yours and you'll get it back." A good philosophy, and one that worked for Duke. But he also believed that he had succeeded "not only because I had more brains, but because I worked harder, stuck it to it longer than most. Application and determination are what count . . . Anybody can succeed if he's willing to apply himself. Superior brains are not necessary."

If Buck Duke had been alive to say those words to this year's graduates, would they have made a lasting impact? And just out of curiosity, would they have been politically correct? And what about "not only because I had more brains"? Could that have been a Freudian slip, perhaps? Or just a typo?

We'll never know.

# THIRTY EIGHT

# Library research is no small challenge

*B*ecause recollection needs the reinforcement of research to give it authenticity, considerable physical effort goes into writing about the way we were in times past.

For instance, just getting yourself from where you live to either Perkins Library at Duke, or Wilson Library at UNC, can be an enervating experience, especially if you've been out of college for more than fifty years.

But if something you're writing about has to be documented, and none of your own reference books will do that, you switch off your typewriter or your computer and prepare yourself for the outside world: Put on something that looks halfway decent, then pick up your briefcase, get in your car, drive to the library that's most likely to have what you need, and start looking for a parking place.

Because practically everybody connected to an institution of higher learning drives a car there too, it usually takes from ten to thirty minutes to find a spot on campus that doesn't require a special decal and is within a mile of your destination.

Eventually you stand on tired feet before a card catalogue until you locate what you think you want. Then you collapse, as gracefully as possible, into a very hard straight chair and contemplate a very large collection of papers that is, in reality, the haystack in which your absolutely essential needle of information is hiding.

At that moment, what you really want to do more than anything else in the world is lie down and take a nap. What you do, instead, is begin to read. You read until you forget fatigue, forget your surroundings, forget everything except these marvelous papers so carefully preserved in their neat, sturdy boxes.

And if it really is a lucky day, you finally root out not only the needle in a haystack you're looking for but something else, too—something exciting, something as seductive to the mind as buried treasure can be to a digger's eye. You experience that small, special miracle called serendipity.

Serendipity. Five lilting syllables that trip from the tongue like musical notes. The dictionary says it means "the faculty of making desirable but unsought-for discoveries by accident," and for you it also means another trek to this same library tomorrow, thanks to the unsought-for clipping from *The New York Times* you just happened to see as you were returning papers to boxes.

Dated November 27, 1919, it begins "While high-price physicians and nurses hover near in soft-footed attendance, a $100,000,000 baby, probably the richest mite of humanity in all the world, lies cooing today in the Fifth Avenue home of Mr. and Mrs. James Buchanan Duke."

Less rich babies, you discover as you read on, were those fathered by W. K. Vanderbilt ($60 million), Edward V. McLean ($50 million), John Nicholas Brown ($10 million), and John Jacob Astor (a paltry $3 million).

Obviously, little Doris Duke was newsworthy in the eyes of *The Times* because she was due to inherit the bulk of Buck Duke's $150 million estate; but throughout her lifetime she continued to interest the media for many reasons, most of them due more to her eccentricities than her wealth.

*The Times* story about her birth in 1919 was only the beginning of a saga reporters would find irresistible for years to come. In 1935, especially, the arresting, sloe-eyed, strong-chinned face of Doris Duke became a familiar sight everywhere, for all the world loves a lover, and that was the year Doris fell in love and married socially prominent James Cromwell. She also managed to outwit nosy reporters and do it in secret, so she and Cromwell became even more of an "item."

Doris and "Jimmy" Cromwell were married at the same Fifth Avenue mansion where she first cooed her way into her famous father's heart, and only a handful of relatives and friends witnessed the cere-

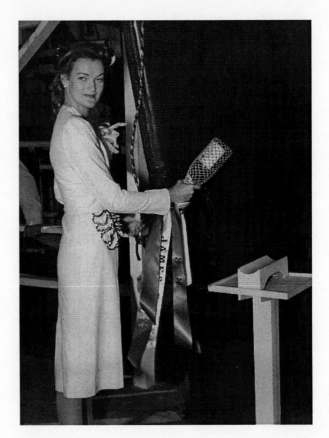

Doris Duke

mony performed by Supreme Court Justice Burt J. Humphrey of Brooklyn, New York.

There were no bridesmaids, no groomsmen, no ushers, no white satin gown, no gossamer veil, no orange blossoms, no Mendelssohn, no Lohengrin. There were just two people standing before a man who was not even a minister. Although the bride's grandfather, Washington Duke, might well have looked askance at that fact, he probably wouldn't have cared a bit about the lack of nuptial folderol.

But Washington Duke had long since departed this world, so he never knew that after an unconventional wedding his granddaughter and her husband eluded the press and left for a honeymoon around the world. They traveled by steamship, airplane, boat, automobile, elephant and rickshaw, and they were gone almost a year.

So serendipity, which produced that first clipping about Buck Duke's only child, undoubtedly will lure this writer into even greener Duke pastures, if time and stamina permit. Meantime, the following data, found while looking for something else, indicates that Doris Duke's uncle, Benjamin Newton Duke, was one of Durham's most popular citizens.

When he died on January 8, 1929, at age 76, approximately 513 people came to his home on Chapel Hill Street and left their calling cards; 392 sent telegrams to his widow; more than 300 wrote letters of condolence; and 440 stories about his life and death, culled from magazines and newspapers, were pasted into a handsome scrapbook now preserved in the Manuscript Room at Perkins Library.

It's worth a trip out there to see it—if you can find a parking place.

# THIRTY NINE

*Like a long and difficult labor, the cumbersome process of passing, reconsidering, tabling and reinterpreting motions finally gave birth to Durham County on February 28, 1881, but not without the skilled assistance of Williamson Whitehead Fuller, physician in charge.*

# Young lawyer aids at the birth of Durham

Back in 1881, when twenty-three-year-old Williamson Whitehead Fuller moved with his wife and infant son from Raleigh to Durham, some of the older citizenry may have viewed him as not quite dry behind the ears, but in spite of his youth he had already gained a reputation for brilliance as a lawyer. Earlier that year, he had co-authored a bill for the creation of Durham County, and despite furious opposition from highly experienced politicians, he had been mainly responsible for its passage in the North Carolina General Assembly. So he came to Durham trailing clouds of glory, as it were, and leading tobacco manufacturers and city officials, who stood to gain most from his accomplishment, gave him a lavish welcome.

The movement to create Durham County was spawned in a series of smoke-filled rooms by smokers who believed passionately in smoking and would like to have seen every man in Christendom take up the habit. These men were W. T. Blackwell and Julian S. Carr, manufacturers of Bull Durham Smoking Tobacco; Blackwell's brother, J. R. Blackwell; Carr's brother-in-law, E. J. Parrish; and businessmen S. T. Morgan and J. C. Angier. Having profited greatly from the success of the tobacco industry, they were having to deal with increasing amounts of legal business resulting from that success, but most of it had to be transacted in the county seat of Hillsborough, and Hillsborough was fifteen miles from Durham. Every time they went, they lost valuable time that otherwise would have been spent on making more money, and the situation, they agreed, could not go on.

So they took their problem first to W. K. Parrish

Williamson
Whitehead Fuller

and Caleb Green, two state legislators who lived in Durham; and then they hired the prestigious law firm of Merrimon and Fuller, in Raleigh, to draw up a bill to establish a new county called Durham, and to assist in getting that bill passed in the General Assembly of 1881. Augustus A. Merrimon and Thomas C. Fuller, one a former U.S. senator and the other a future federal judge, were among the best legal minds in the state; and Fuller's son, Will, newly admitted to the bar and his father's firm, had distinguished himself at both the University of Virginia and the Dick and Dillard Law School in Greensboro, so the six catalysts for what was to be a new chapter in Durham's history felt they were in good hands.

As it turned out, they were. But carving Durham County from valuable parts of neighboring Orange and Wake was an extremely painful operation that generated howls of protest from powerful lobbyists in Hillsborough, Raleigh and other parts of the state. They saw no reason why Durham, a bumptious little town of money-grubbers, should be allowed to confiscate three of the richest townships in Orange, and also two from Wake, but after much heated debate the bill managed to pass its third reading in the House on February 10, 1881.

Elation among the Durham contingent was drowned when the bill, after passing its first reading in the Senate, was strongly opposed by Senator William T. Dortch of Goldsboro (who happened to have a number of relatives in Hillsborough). Contending that the creation of any more counties would prove too costly for the state to administer, Dortch moved that a decision on the bill be postponed indefinitely, but as soon as his motion passed, Senator J. M. Staples of Greensboro (who happened to be Will Fullers' father-in-law) immediately made another motion to reconsider the vote to defer action.

For the next week, Staples' motion was postponed repeatedly while supporters attempted to garner support for the bill. In spite of their efforts, it fell six votes short of passage on its second reading, and a determined Dortch attempted to put a "clincher" on its defeat by moving for reconsideration of the bill and then tabling the motion without a vote. A few hours later, the senator from Goldsboro apparently suffered a lapse of memory and endorsed a new county, to be called Vance, near Oxford, and his blatant inconsistency aroused a wave of support for Durham County.

Acting on Will Fuller's advice, proponents argued that simple justice required the legislature to correct its own mistakes when new evidence (Dortch's inconsistency) came to its attention, and that it was entirely legal for the Senate to "reconsider the vote by which it had voted to reconsider and lay that motion on the table."

Traditionally, no bill could be reconsidered more than once, but the president of the Senate agreed with Fuller's "sound proposition" that no power existed that limited a legislative body where its own actions were concerned.

Like a long and difficult labor, the cumbersome process of passing, reconsidering, tabling and rein-terpreting motions finally gave birth to Durham County on February 28, 1881, but not without the skilled assistance of Williamson Whitehead Fuller, physician in charge.

I WAS MARRIED AND had two grown children before I read everything that has been written in history books and biographical collections about Williamson Whitehead Fuller, who was called Will, or sometimes Willie, by his kinsmen, and W. W. by his business associates. At the age of twenty-two, after distinguishing himself by playing a large role in the creation of Durham County, in 1881, he left his father's law firm in Raleigh and moved to Durham with his young wife, Annie, and their infant son, Staples.

Buying a house on the corner of Main and Dillard streets, Fuller remodeled and expanded it so extensively, in order to accommodate his growing family, that at least one historian described it as a mansion.

Young Will Fuller practiced at first with an older attorney, W. S. Rhoulac, and after an interim alone following Rhoulac's death, he formed a partnership with his brother, Frank Lanneau Fuller, which continued until 1895. During this time he gained an enviable reputation as one of the most able lawyers, with one of the most lucrative practices, in the entire state. Other attorneys noticed, as did judges, spectators and the press, that Will Fuller could be any way that would best serve his cause in a trial— terse and homely, urbane and gracious, scholarly and philosophical, or practical and persuasive, and this unusual talent did not escape the shrewd eye of James Buchanan Duke.

In 1890, W. Duke Sons and Company retained Fuller as its legal counsel in Durham, and in that capacity he helped to organize the American Tobacco Company, of which J. B. Duke became the head. Duke also became increasingly dependent upon Will Fuller for advice, and in 1895 persuaded him to move to New York as the American Tobacco Company's chief legal counsel. For the rest of his life, which began in Fayetteville just before the outbreak of the Civil War, W. W. Fuller lived, worked and eventually retired in New York, but he never forgot his kinfolks and frequently came to Durham, where many of them lived.

It was on one of those visits that I met him for the first time, and I remember it vividly. I was playing in the backyard when my mother called me inside, told me Cousin Will Fuller was coming to see us, and that I was to help her entertain him until my father came home from the office.

When I was scrubbed, dressed and combed to her satisfaction, and she was equally pleased with her own reflection in the mirror, I was led downstairs, directed to a chair in the living room, and told to sit still and not wrinkle my dress. After what seemed like forever, the doorbell rang, the front door opened, and I heard my mother's cry of welcome, a deep voice rumbling her name, and the smack of a cousinly kiss.

Then my Cousin Will appeared, huge and smiling, a vast benevolent Presence that seemed to fill the room. He wore a swallow-tail coat and striped gray trousers, there was a diamond stickpin in his tie and a red rosebud in his lapel, and his eyes, under heavy dark brows, were large and very bright and almost smiling, like his mouth under an iron gray mustache that matched his hair.

I slid from my chair and smoothed my dress, and when he bent to kiss the top of my head I smelled him—clean skin and starch and Bay Rum, my father's smell, almost. Not quite Papa's, but almost.

"Ah, Wilhelmena," he said, and the luminous eyes regarded me steadily, and with great kindness, as I answered his questions.

It seemed to matter a great deal to him how old I was (six), what grade I was in (first), if I had learned to read (Yes, Sir), and, finally, if I liked horses (No, Sir). He laughed then, and told me I would change my mind if I came to Haymount, his home in New York, and met one of his horses whose name was Black Bear, because Black Bear could talk.

Not with his mouth, of course, but with his foot. By stamping his right foot, Cousin Will explained, Black Bear could say how many hours were in a day, how many days were in a week, what two times two was, if Warren G. Harding was president of the United States (three stamps for yes), if money grew on trees (two stamps for no), and a lot of other things I would find out when I came up to see him, and Cousin Annie, at Haymount.

"Now, you will come, won't you Wilhelmena?" he asked, and I said, "Yes, Sir," although I knew, somehow, that I never would.

Such encounters never get into the history books, nor the biographical sketches, nor the eulogies, but they burrow into the mind of a child and stay there forever. So now when I read about W. W. Fuller's "personal magnetism" and his "positive genius" for friendship, I know, first hand, whereof the writer speaks.

# FORTY

# Julian Carr helped to found a famous coastal resort

*I*n 1857, former North Carolina Governor John Motley Morehead founded the town of Morehead City and became largely responsible for building both its port and its railroad terminal. About two decades later, Julian Shakespeare Carr, of Durham, joined forces with two eastern North Carolina friends, Frank W. Barnes, of Wilson, and Ashley Horne, of Clinton, and established the Morehead City Hotel Company, in which they sold stock with enough success to build what was to become one of the most famous resorts on the eastern seaboard.

At the time, Carr was well on his way to being the richest man in the state, a pinnacle he would reach in 1887. Because he took to luxury like the proverbial duck to water, it is easy to imagine his enthusiasm for a plush hotel on the coast, where he might occasionally escape the hottest part of the summer with his family and, at the same time, increase his income and enhance his reputation as the outstanding entrepreneur of his day.

The Atlantic Hotel, like Carr, was the "last word" when it came to embellishments and trappings. It had a 100-foot-square ballroom with a gleaming hardwood floor and a balcony for spectators; a large, beautifully appointed dining room (plus a separate one for children and their nurses); writing, reading, card and smoking rooms; a bar, a billiard room, a bowling alley and a barbershop; a steam laundry and a store; an electric-light plant with 2,000 light capacity; telegraph and long-distance telephone offices; and the finest seafood to be had. The Atlantic featured stone crabs, scallops, shrimp, terrapin, many kinds of fish and, on at least one occasion, venison (a guest killed a deer not far from the hotel).

Completed in the early 1880s (one source says 1881, another 1883) at a cost of $15,000, the rambling, three-story structure overlooking Bogue Sound was topped by two large cupolas and adorned with two sections of double porches across the front. There were 300 guest rooms, many with baths and all with gaslight and running water, amenities that were by no means usual then and ones that proved to be a definite drawing-card for the establishment.

The sort of comfort and elegance provided by the Atlantic immediately attracted "the elite of North Carolina," who spread the word so successfully that

The Atlantic Hotel in Morehead City around 1885.

before long people from New York, Baltimore, Chicago, Cincinnati, Atlanta and Augusta, Georgia; Nashville, Tennessee; and Columbia, South Carolina, were traveling to Morehead City, which was fast becoming "a Mecca for all who sought the refreshing southwest summer winds on the Carteret Coast," at a cost of $23 a week for a room with a bath and $18 for one without.

In 1887, the original owners sold the hotel to Dr. George W. Blacknall, of Raleigh, proprietor of that home-away-from-home for legislators, the Yarbrough House. Two years later, Blacknall sold it to the Atlantic and North Carolina Railroad, which wanted to increase traffic on its road to Morehead City. Later, when the state leased the Atlantic and North Carolina to the Norfolk and Southern for a period of ninety-nine years, the hotel went with the contract and "the new management gave it new life" for the next two decades.

Until World War I, the hotel catered to well-heeled

vacationers who enjoyed deep-sea fishing, swimming, boating, tennis, golf, cards, bowling, dancing and the convenience of a covered railroad stop with a boardwalk leading straight to the Atlantic's front door.

Surf bathing on Bogue Banks, now Atlantic Beach, was one of the hotel's big attractions. In the afternoon, when the sun had lost most of its blistering heat, sailboats transported bathers across the sound to the north side of the banks where, after plodding through sand to the ocean side, they welcomed the sight of open pavilions and dressing rooms provided by the hotel. It also maintained a livery stable there that made drives down the beach possible during the season that extended from June through Labor Day.

For less adventurous guests, bath houses at the rear of the hotel made bathing in the sound easy and pleasurable, and because the medical profession approved it as beneficial to health and well-being, entire families, from babies to grandparents, bobbed around every day in the relative calm of Bogue Sound.

Numerous families throughout the state visited the Atlantic Hotel every summer, some for two weeks, others for a month or more, and a few for the entire season. These "regulars" usually had their favorite sleeping quarters, their favorite tables in the dining room, their favorite white-coated waiters, and their favorite fishing-boat "Cap'ns."

Cap'n Arthur Midgett, Cap'n Tean Piner and Cap'n Gib Willis were held in high regard because of their expertise in handling boats and locating fish. When Durham attorney Frank L. Fuller (who moved to New York to become legal counsel for Liggett & Myers Tobacco Company) bought a forty-foot yacht that he named the *Frank and Susan* for his grandchildren, he retained Arthur Midgett as its skipper for many years.

In addition to Fuller, other Durham devotees of the Atlantic Hotel were T. J. O'Brien, T. F. Southgate, George Watts Carr, Mrs. J. E. Stagg and Mrs. V. S. Bryant Sr. In later years, Mrs. Stagg and Mrs. Bryant, along with the S. D. McPhersons, the St. Pierre DuBoses, the Watts Carrs and the E. M. Camerons, either built or bought summer homes fronting the sound in Morehead City. The Watts Nortons, also of Durham, opted for a house on the beach, which was developed after a bridge across the sound made it accessible and, inevitably, extremely popular.

On Easter Sunday, April 15, 1933, the wonderful old Atlantic Hotel caught fire. Nobody knows how the blaze started, and, fortunately, nobody was in it at the time. Watts Carr, Jr., formerly of this city, happened to be on the beach that morning, and he remembers: "We were playing ball with Anne Norton (Mrs. Watts Norton), and we saw this black cloud rising over Morehead, and then we began to smell the smoke and even feel the heat. When somebody said the hotel was on fire, we went over there to see what was happening and we watched it burn to the ground. I still have a picture that somebody took of the ruins."

Not a pretty sight to countless lovers of what has become a legend, the fabulous hotel that, for over half a century, drew its clientele from North Carolina's "first" families, and attracted so many Tar Heel governors, senators and congressmen that it was called "the Summer Capital of the State."

# FORTY ONE

# Carr's love for his wife defied death

here are many aficionados of graveyards, believe it or not, and those who are new to the area and interested in Durham's history should consider exploring the Julian Shakespeare Carr plot in the old section of Maplewood Cemetery. Like everything else the tobacco and textile magnate had a hand in creating, Carr's burying ground bears the mark of his flamboyant personality, and it also speaks eloquently of his love for Nannie Graham Parrish, the woman who shared his life for forty-two years.

During the year following her death on August 18, 1915, her grieving husband wrote their eldest daughter, Lida Carr Flower, of Kansas City, that he was planning a tribute to "dear sweet Mother" that was going to "make the world sit up and take notice." He had decided on a marble tablet depicting Leonardo da Vinci's *Last Supper*, to be placed in Trinity Methodist Church, where they had worshipped together throughout their married life, and he also wanted to put several large sculptures at the gravesite in Maplewood. And to get the very best artisans, he was willing to import them from Italy and give them free housing during their stay in Durham.

The replica of Leonardo's masterpiece was going to be "one of the most beautiful pieces in the world when it is finished," and as for the statuary and the landscaping in the cemetery, there would be "nothing as beautiful in any cemetery which I have ever visited, but your dear sweet mother deserves (it) all, and more," Carr told Lida. There can be little doubt that he later impressed that fact on the stonecutters, whom he did import from Italy and supplied with all the Carara marble they needed to do the job.

The plot these artisans embellished dwarfs most of those surrounding it, where other prominent Durham citizens sleep. A semicircle curbed in granite and shaded by cedar and magnolia trees, it is 160 feet across at its widest point. The entrance is marked by stone gateposts topped with bronze lions' heads that snarl at each other above a wide stone step inscribed CARR above the words: *Ashes to Ashes and Dust to Dust.*

Beyond the entrance are three ivy-blanketed graves with elaborately carved headstones bearing the names of Carr, his wife and his youngest son, Austin. To the right, tucked away and almost hidden beneath a boxwood bush, a small rectangular stone, marked JSC-CSA, attests to the fact that Julian Carr

Monument, sculpture
honors "Mother."

was a Confederate soldier. Not surprisingly, perhaps, it is noticeably tilted, as if someone has tried to kick it over.

Directly beyond the graves three small nymphs in clinging robes, standing back-to-back and holding hands, form the pedestal for a fountain; and behind the fountain is what Carr called the "Seat of the Resurrection." This twelve-foot granite bench, carved with a large sun above the words: *I Am The Resurrection and the Life*, is where he sometimes went "to talk with dear Miss Nannie" and contemplate the white marble statues facing each other from opposite sides of the garden. One is a seated woman with her arms around two young children. *Many Daughters Have Done Virtuously But Thou Excellest Them All*, carved on a seal of red marble above the woman's head, obviously reflects Carr's open admiration for the mother of his six children. The second group, comprised of two angels guarding a large cross with a prone female embracing its base, is inscribed, *Simply To Thy Cross I Cling*, and may have represented to Carr the sum total of his wife's faith. But judging from other letters to his daughter Lida about the cemetery project, Carr apparently spent more time and thought on a single kneeling angel supporting an open bronze book on its back than he did on the other figures. Two poems are engraved on the book, one called *Mine* (author unknown) and the other, by Eugene Cowles, entitled *Forgotten*.

Carr was not entirely pleased with Cowles' composition. With total disregard for the laws of copyright, he wrote to Lida and asked her to change it. "I am enclosing the poem *Forgotten* and want your help with reference to it," he said. "I don't like the last line of the first stanza, which reads, 'Yet I have forgotten, you say.' It seems to be in bad taste to talk about a dead person, 'You say,' and I want you to correct that verse for me and make it in good taste and good rhythm.

"Now I have objection to the sixth line in the third stanza, which reads, 'To be held in your arms again.' That sounds to me in bad taste, too, and I believe it could be very materially changed for the better. Then again, in the fourth stanza it says, 'Of two strong arms and two warm lips and eyes of steadfast gray.' I don't like the expression, two strong arms and two warm lips. Besides, Mother's eyes were blue. Correct these lines for me, preserving the rhythm and general beauty of the poem."

What Lida wrote for her father must have pleased him, but one wonders if her mother's memorial garden in Old Maplewood is ever haunted by the ghost of Eugene Cowles, hovering over the angel with the book on its back and groaning, maybe even swearing, over the sight of his "corrected" poem.

Today the cedars and magnolias Carr planted almost eighty-seven years ago cast long shadows over the graves, and their roots protrude from the earth like the swollen veins of the very old. Brown cedar needles lie in the white marble palms of the statues' forever-young hands, in the crooks of their forever-smooth elbows, and in the folds of their white marble tunics. There are moss stains on the "Seat of the Resurrection," and a McDonald's hamburger wrapper, crumpled beneath it, suggests that someone has been enjoying this special place, where pigeons coo, and the traffic sounds beyond the cemetery are muted, and Julian Carr's small, lopsided Confederate marker takes on a certain wry dignity among all these stone angels and sentiment.

# FORTY TWO

# Tiffany window honors Tar Heel troops

*I*t's highly possible that almost everybody who recognizes the name, Tiffany, associates it with the famous store on New York's Fifth Avenue, where only the very finest jewelry and artifacts are for sale and only the very rich can afford them.

Tiffany, however, also connotes stained glass windows, which can be looked at and appreciated by anybody, rich or poor, and one of the most beautiful windows in one of the finest Tiffany collections in America honors the state of North Carolina. It is there thanks to the efforts of Julian Shakespeare Carr, a Durham man who never missed an opportunity to boost either his home town or what he was prone to call "the dear old Commonwealth of North Carolina."

Carr, a veteran of the Civil War and an honorary general in the United Confederate Veterans of America, learned in the summer of 1906 that plans were being made to fill the Old Blandford Church, in Petersburg, Virginia, with memorial Tiffany windows representing each of the southern states. With typical dispatch, he wrote immediately to his friend and fellow Confederate, Henry Clay Roper, of Petersburg,

asking for information regarding the matter and stating his intention of seeing to it that the North Carolina Division of the U.C.V. placed a "handsome window to the memory of the 'Tar Heels' in this church."

Roper, a member of one of Petersburg's most prominent and affluent families, was, like Carr, a dedicated and generous member of the U.C.V. Also like Carr, he frequently paid for impoverished Confederate veterans to attend annual reunions, which were held in various southern cities. On one occasion, when Roper was approached by someone in the railroad station and asked, "Who is paying the train fare for all these men?" he replied with some asperity, "My heirs."

Apparently, Roper gave Carr instructions as to whom to contact and how to proceed, for within eight months the Ladies Memorial Association of Petersburg received a letter "from General Carr. . . saying that the amount for the N.C. Window had been raised and the order could be sent on to Tiffany of N.Y." The association's goal was a complete restoration of Old Blandford Church "as a shrine to

Window honors sacrifice:
Tiffany window memorializes
Civil War soldiers. This is
one of the 15 windows in
Old Blanford Church.

those who gave their lives in the defense of Petersburg" while it was under a ten-month siege by Union forces. So great was the faith of these ladies that even before they had any cash on hand, they commissioned Louis Comfort Tiffany to make "fifteen opalescent windows to commemorate the thirteen states of the Confederacy." One of the two extra windows contains the only Confederate flag ever produced by Tiffany Studios, and it was dedicated to the Ladies Memorial Association. The other, known as "The Cross of Jewels" window, was donated to Old Blandford church by Louis Tiffany himself, "in recognition of the work accomplished by the Ladies."

Louis Comfort Tiffany (1848-1933), whose father had founded the prestigious Fifth Avenue store, was above everything else a painter, and a very good one, long before he began hand-crafting stained glass windows, the first of which he created in 1876. He had his own furnaces at Corona, New York, and there he made a special glass he called "Favrile," a name he coined and used as a trademark. Describing Favrile glass in 1896, he claimed that it had never before been equaled "in range, depth and brilliancy of color," and that because "all our windows are built in accordance with the mosaic theory, without the intervention of paint, stains or enamels, they are practically indestructible and will not corrode, peel or fade."

Tiffany fused color into his Favrile glass by adding crushed metals—fourteen-carat gold, or copper, or cobalt, for example—while the glass was still in a molten state, and his particular way of doing this made his windows like no others in the world.

Old Blanford Church, Virginia

Those at Old Blandford depict thirteen saints, and Saint Bartholomew, holding a knife "to symbolize his being flayed alive," represents North Carolina. It is not known who chose that particular martyr to commemorate the Tar Heel state, but it is entirely possible that Jule Carr, "the little general" who was the catalyst for the window, had something to do with the inscription. It reads: "In memory of North Carolina's Soldiers, of whom 40,275 proved their devotion to duty by their death. God bless North Carolina."

Put Old Blandford Church on your list of weekend getaways (it's about 125 miles from Durham). When you view the intricate beauty of North Carolina's window, reflect on its cost: $350 to make it, and $35 to place it.

A real bargain.

This 100-year old window graces the University United Methodist Church located on Franklin Street in Chapel Hill.

# FORTY THREE

# Julian Carr commissioned work of art

Astounded best describes the way I was almost all day long on May 6, 1990 after going to a Sunday morning service at the University United Methodist Church on Franklin Street, in Chapel Hill, to witness the rededication of a magnificent stained glass window that had been given to the church over 100 years ago by Julian Shakespeare Carr. For nearly thirty years it had lain in a jumble of who knows how many pieces on the floor of the church basement, and had I been forced to walk from Durham to Chapel Hill to see it in its resurrected state, instead of riding there in comfort, the trip still would have been worth the effort.

My first sight of what has been described as "a dramatic pictorial representation of the meeting of Ruth and Boaz in the fields" left me breathless for a moment, and subsequent visits continue to evoke a similar response. Far too large for the present church—it's approximately twelve by twenty feet— this depiction of one of the Bible's classic love stories was patiently reassembled (it took over a year), ingeniously back lighted, and finally mounted in the stairwell adjacent to the sanctuary, and the effect of all those jewel-toned reds and blues and greens blazing away in a wash of golden sunlight is, as I said before, breathtaking.

The fact that the window is there at all seems nothing short of a miracle to me, because from the late 1920s until 1962 it was stored in a corner of the basement in the old sanctuary, which was used by the citizens of Chapel Hill as a recreation center for several years. One member of the committee that launched a campaign to restore the window told me that "kids played all kinds of games down there, even basketball—can you believe it? And when the stained glass expert finally got all the pieces over to his place in Raleigh, he found he would have to replace only three small sections."

Michael Bonn, co-owner with his brother, Robert, of B and B Glassworks in Raleigh, is the expert who restored Boaz, a wealthy Bethlehem landowner, and Ruth, the beautiful Moabite who became his wife, to their original glory. Another expert, the late George C. Pyne, a Durham architect who knew just about all there is to know about stained glass windows, said this particular one was "very valuable . . . because of its quality and the period in which it was designed." Pyne was referring to the 1880s, when the South was riding a wave of post-Civil War prosperity and Durham was booming, thanks to tobacco.

One of its wealthiest citizens, manufacturer Julian S. Carr, was a native of Chapel Hill who had been born on Franklin Street and raised in the Methodist faith. It was at his father's urging that he moved to Durham in 1870 and bought, with $4,000 of his father's hard-earned money, a partnership in the W. T. Blackwell Tobacco Company. That alliance started him on a remarkable career, and as a businessman, entrepreneur, and pioneer in the field of advertising, he made a great deal of money. At the height of that career, when he was involved in the establishment of railroads, utilities, banks, newspapers, hotels and textile mills, he decided to publicly honor his parents, John Wesley and Eliza Bullock Carr.

John Carr had been a successful merchant, a handsome man with bright blue eyes, a hearty laugh, and "a fine, natural red in his cheeks." Miss Eliza Bullock, of Granville County, had been a stylish, energetic young woman whose square, determined jaw rescued her face from mere prettiness and stamped it with a look of quality. They had met in 1837, and on Christmas Day in 1838 they were married and began their life together in a house on the corner of Franklin and Columbia Streets. Nine children, six of whom lived to maturity, were born to them, and in the little village that housed the University of North Carolina they were known as good parents who "raised their children well, a hard thing to do in Chapel Hill."

Their son, Julian, a flamboyant man who delighted in spending and giving away his money, would have been out of character had he not commissioned the biggest stained glass window in Chapel Hill to their memory, and only by the grace of God, I believe, does it still exist. Carr realized "the importance of the arts to the religious experience," and I urge you to go and see what his mother and father inspired him to give to the church that nurtured him as a boy.

It'll be worth the trip.

# FORTY FOUR

*When I was around sixteen, my mother wrote to
General Carr and asked him if he didn't want
to send me to college, and he said yes, he did.*

LUCY CARR OLIVER

# Beneficiary doesn't forget General Carr's generosity

Julian Shakespeare Carr, the millionaire tobacco manufacturer who made Bull Durham tobacco world-famous back in the 1880s, seldom refused any young person who came to him asking for help with an education, and the late Mrs. A. B. Holland, of the King's Daughters Home on Buchanan Boulevard, bore witness to that fact. Sprightly, stylish and outgoing, Mrs. Holland's zest for life shone in her smile, bounced in her walk, and bubbled in her speech, and it was difficult to believe she had already had her ninety-first birthday well before our interview in the summer of 1990.

"I was named for General Carr," she said, "and he sent me to college. There were seven of us children, six girls and one boy, and when I was around sixteen my mother wrote to General Carr and asked him if he didn't want to send me to college, and he said

yes, he did. He told her he would send me to Oxford College, over in Oxford (N.C.), because he liked Professor Hobgood, the man who ran it, and so that's where I went."

Lucy Carr Oliver was one of numerous babies who received the Carr name because either one or both of their parents admired the "little General" whose personal charm equaled his Midas touch. Her father, George W. Oliver, postmaster and owner of a general store in Top Knot, near Yanceyville, had an aunt in Durham whom he and his family often visited; and no doubt they were impressed by Carr's importance and also by his friendliness and accessibility. Unlike many wealthy men, he never distanced himself from the public, and his unfailing courtesy, like the carnation he always wore in his lapel, was a hallmark, of sorts.

Lucy Carr Oliver in 1917, in Oxford College piano recital dress.

Carr's love for children was well known, and being an ardent believer in higher education, he grieved for boys and girls who longed to go to college, but could not afford it. A notorious "soft touch," he kept few records of his private charities and rarely spoke of them, either, so there is no way of knowing how many youngsters were the beneficiaries of his generosity. Lucy Oliver was one of them, however, and she liked to talk about her years at Oxford College, a venerable institution that began in 1811, the year the town of Oxford was "laid out" and, simultaneously, both a male academy and a female seminary were established there.

Forty years later, in 1850, the Oxford Baptist Female College came into being. And in 1871, while North Carolina was still reeling in the aftermath of the Civil War and Reconstruction, the original seminary and the Baptist College merged into a single institution. Four years after that, Frank B. Hobgood, of Raleigh, moved his private school from the capitol city, combined it with the existing female college, and named it the Oxford Baptist Seminary. The school flourished until it was destroyed by fire in 1904, but Frank Hobgood, undaunted, rebuilt it as Oxford College, enlarged it from one to four buildings, and moved it across town from its original site on College Street to a campus bounded by Raleigh and Front streets.

So it was to that campus that Lucy Carr Oliver went in 1916 to major in education, Oxford being primarily a teachers college, and also to study piano and voice. While she was there, Julian Carr sent her an unusual necklace of azure-blue beads that she always wore on special occasions. Carved from lapislazuli, it was probably one of the many gifts he bought for family members and friends while traveling in the Orient during the spring of 1917.

After leaving Oxford College, Carr's protégée taught school until she married Marion Polk Sanford, of Stem, on December 22, 1922. Prominent among the wedding guests was her benefactor, who had responded to her invitation with this letter:

*My dear Lucy:*
*Charmed to acknowledge receipt of your good letter of the twenty second, and yet, I am not surprised, please understand. I had been told by the little "Bluebirds that sing their beautiful song" that I might expect something of this sort and I am glad that my suspicions are confirmed. You can rely on my being on hand to help do the clapping and to congratulate you and wish you all the good and happiness, and my love. I am happy to tell you that the young man, as far as I can learn, is of very good repute and I believe you are going to be happy and do well.*

*Again with my congratulations and best love,*

*Sincerely yours,*
*General Carr*

Carr's gift to the bride was a string of pearls that she treasured, along with the blue necklace and her wedding certificate. Not surprisingly, one of the witnesses who signed that important document was Carr, who told the new Mrs. Sanford that if she'd let him take it home he'd have it framed, so she could hang it on the wall and look at it every day.

"When I went by his office to get it," she told me, "the first thing he said was, 'Are you still happy?' and every time he saw me after that, he asked me the same thing."

Like the man she was named for, Lucy Carr Oliver Sanford Holland was born with a happy nature and retained it throughout a long and varied life, during which she lived first in Stem and later in Bahama with Marion Sanford and their two children, Edward and Louise.

After her husband died, she resumed teaching and also worked at both Belk's and Efird's department stores in Durham, and in 1954 she married A. B. Holland and moved to Fuquay-Varina. There, in 1978, she received the Sertoma Club's Mankind Award "for service to the community, state and nation," and for sixty years she was active in the Order of Eastern Star, the Democratic party, and the Methodist church in Bahama. Going to Oxford College undoubtedly enriched Mrs. Holland's long and happy life, which ended on February 3, 1991, shortly after her ninety-second birthday.

As Shakespeare said: "The good men do lives after them . . ."

*... he swore like a sailor ... and slept with his favorite dog.*

# Salty law dean shocked pious Duke, attacked status quo

Around the turn of the century, James B. Duke and his brother, Benjamin, agreed to underwrite the establishment of a law school at Trinity College, and thereby hangs a tale of one of Durham's most colorful characters, Samuel Fox Mordecai (1854-1927). Mordecai electrified the pious atmosphere of the little Methodist school for twenty-three years and, as dean, laid the foundation of a law school that eventually would rank with the finest in America.

A stocky, handsome man with regular features, a ready smile, an expressive face, and eyes that could literally dance with humor, Trinity's first dean of law was dapper and dignified in appearance, but he swore like a sailor, attacked the status quo whenever it offended his intelligence or sensibilities, and often slept with his favorite dog.

Needless to say, as the years passed he became, more and more, a legend in his own time.

Educated in Raleigh's private schools, Oxford's Classical and Mathematical School (forerunner of the Horner Military Academy) and the University of Virginia, Mordecai was a brilliant scholar. His extraordinary grasp of the law put him, at the age of twenty-two, into practice with Richard H. Battle, of Raleigh, and later on the faculty of Wake Forest College, where he lectured three times a week until Trinity College president John C. Kilgo invited him to become head of the new law department.

By that time he was fifty years old, had been happily married long enough to father nine children (five boys and four girls), and was, therefore, in need of a large house. He also wanted sufficient grounds for a flower garden (he raised exquisite roses), a vegetable garden (he had a lot of mouths to feed), and a large assortment of animals, mostly dogs and chickens.

Fortunately, a twelve-room house was available on the college campus facing Buchanan Boulevard, and the fact that fireplaces and stoves were its only source of heat undoubtedly contributed to Mordecai's propensity for profanity. It was he who stoked them at night and fired them up in the mornings, and his swearing was the only alarm clock his family needed to rouse them out of bed. One of his daughters said that whenever her Papa yelled, "God damn son of a bitch!" the children knew it was a very cold day indeed, and dressed accordingly. But they were never threatened by their father's irreverence, she insisted. On the contrary, they had a "wonderful, comfortable childhood" on the Trinity campus.

Swearing on that campus, and also in the classrooms of an institution rooted and grounded in Methodism was tempting fate even for a scholar of the dean's stature, and inevitably a movement to fire him was instigated by a disapproving and possibly envious faculty member. But the effort failed, probably for two reasons: Mordecai's ability to slash through seemingly endless legalese to the core of a problem and come up with an exquisitely simple solution made him a great natural teacher; and, according to one of his fellow lawyers, "His students idolized him, his associate teachers venerated him, and all who possessed the privilege of his friendship loved him."

So Mordecai remained, often bullying and badgering his young men into learning something of the law, and as they walked the tightrope between

Samuel Fox Mordecai

his approval and disapproval, they also learned humility. To a student who was not well prepared he was apt to shout, "What the hell are you doing in college? You got no business studying law. The only thing you'll ever be good for is planting corn and picking cotton!"

But knowing all the answers did not necessarily guarantee his approbation either, as one student discovered when, after replying correctly to several questions others had missed, Mordecai fixed him with a look and said, "Just because you're in here with a bunch of jackasses is no reason for you to think you're some kind of stud horse."

Nominally an Episcopalian, but no churchgoer (he was also a Democrat and a member of the Zeta Psi fraternity), Mordecai described himself as a Methodist Episcopalian Baptist Jew, and to quote a Raleigh friend and admirer, "How he did love the sound of his Hebraic name, and the tingle of his portion of the Patriarchal blood!"

The fact that his parents, Samuel and Ellen Mordecai, were first cousins may have contributed to his eccentricity, and his early years on an antebellum plantation, surrounded by doting relatives and slaves who addressed him, from birth, as "Marse Sam," no doubt contributed to a self-assurance that allowed him to speak his mind whenever and wherever he pleased, with no regard for consequences. But in spite of all that, his obvious love for children, animals and flowers revealed the essential gentleness of his nature and prompted one of his colleagues to say "he would not needlessly set foot upon a worm."

One love of Mordecai's life was Pompey Ducklegs, a registered dachshund given to him by Durham resident Ernest Seeman. Mordecai said Pompey, whom he sometimes addressed as "you darling precious dog," ate the entire Book of Genesis right out of the Bible, and could tell a fool from an intelligent man just by the sound of his footsteps. Pompey also chewed tobacco, he said, but "only if it was R. J. Reynolds' Level Best." For years the two were inseparable, the dachshund following the dean wherever he went and sleeping at his feet while he taught. Once, when Pompey began to moan and cry, and finally coughed up something he had eaten, Mordecai, visibly alarmed, shouted to the class, "Get out of here, you numbskulls! You're so dumb you're making my dog sick!"

As a lovable curmudgeon, Samuel Fox Mordecai had no peers on the local scene, and as a teacher of law he had few equals. Of the seven books he wrote, *Mordecai's Law Lectures* was the most widely used and best known of all the North Carolina legal texts of that day, and no student he recommended for the bar exam ever failed to pass it.

Quite a monument to a man who sidestepped stuffiness and marched through life to the beat of his own drum.

*He laughs and the world laughs with him,*
*he weeps and the world dies laughing.*

ANONYMOUS

# Bill Stauber, a non-stop comedian for life

There are a few television comedians who make me laugh, and sometimes I snicker at something I read in a book or newspaper—I have more luck with A. C. Snow, of *Fifty Plus* and *The News and Observer* —but discovering humor around town these days is pretty fruitless, for the most part.

Multiple concerns—crime, drugs, low SAT scores, political correctness, tornados, floods, dishonesty in high places, et cetera, et cetera—seem to have numbed everybody's sense of the ridiculous, and that's why I like to remember the late William E. Stauber Jr., of Durham, who never failed to offer me, and anybody else he happened to run into, the priceless gift of laughter that God, undoubtedly, had given him. And I never failed to take it. Sometimes I took it with a stitch in my side and tears in my eyes, and for that I am truly thankful.

Bill Stauber was born in 1917 in Rural Hall, a small town in Forsyth County where, he said, everybody turned out the lights at 8:30 p.m. and the main industry was the production of toilet seats.

Stauber further claimed that the most severe crises Rural Hall ever suffered through was when the Methodist preachers changed, and that the town's biggest problem was trying to keep a town drunk.

In 1934, when he was seventeen, he entered the University of North Carolina, enrolled in Commerce School, and started becoming, by degrees, "a campus celebrity who put Rural Hall on the map," chiefly by "writing funny" for *The Buccaneer*, the college humor magazine, and *The Daily Tar Heel*, the student newspaper.

In addition to his journalistic endeavors, Stauber organized a musical comedy group called "Sound

Quiet genius at work.

But the boys (they were called "college men" in the 1930s) at Carolina saw Stauber in a slightly different although equally benevolent light, for the most part.

One cohort in the fourth estate who later became publisher of *The Chapel Hill Weekly*, regarded him as a "medium-sized, sad-looking fellow who had a comeback for any and all remarks," adding that his quiet appearance and soft voice could fool a lot of people, but "really, Stauber was tops. He could write a volume with one hand and roll a cigarette with the other."

During his junior year, Bill Stauber was made editor of *The Buccaneer* and his first issue, in the spring of 1939, "heralded the reign of the belly laugh," according to *The Daily Tar Heel*, where his columns appeared regularly and were "the white hope of the editorial page."

Not surprisingly, his love affair with writing affected his grades, a situation he shrugged off later by admitting, "I made so many Ds at Carolina that folks thought I was a four-letter man at Duke." Printer's ink was definitely in his veins by then, and in the fall of 1939 it may have gone to his head.

That November, Stauber brought out a "Sex Issue" of *The Buccaneer* that got the publication banned before it even reached the newsstands, chiefly because of its cover (raw jokes were a given in "*The Buc*" long before Stauber took over), which depicted "a lady of questionable morals seated comfortably on a sofa." The caricature shocked enough faculty, alumni and members of the student government to censure the editor and relegate 4,000 copies of the magazine to an incinerator.

In spite of the brouhaha that kept the campus

and Fury" and then wrote an original script which he helped to produce, (and in which he starred) that won an ASCAP award, thus adding another feather to one of the many hats he wore as a student.

One co-ed described him as "essentially a very serious-minded person, despite the fact that he is a natural-born comedian," and said that his baby face "brought out the mother in all the girls"; while another admitted that she "expected him to be sort of wise-cracking and satirical and stuff, but he seems to be a gentle sort of person."

Bill Stauber holds mock-up of cover for banned issue of campus humor publication *The Buccaneer.*

On stage in drag.

and much of the state buzzing for weeks, the boy from Rural Hall took the incident in stride, to all appearances. Tongue doubtless in cheek, he later told a reporter that "the magazine wasn't all that bad . . . I sold several thousand copies to the Methodist Church for Sunday School literature."

Actually, Stauber did save one copy of his infamous "*Buc*" from the holocaust that destroyed the remaining 3,999, and he was right. Compared to most of today's popular magazines—*Playboy, Hustler, Cosmopolitan*—it wasn't all that bad.

I WISH I COULD LOOK forward to more time on this fascinating planet than I'm likely to get. For one thing, I wish I had time to write a book about Bill Stauber, who wished he had time to write a book about Samuel Hamilton Rivers, the father of two sets of twins, one set named Jessie Bethel and Bessie Ethel, and another one named Samuel Hamilton Rivers Jr. and Samuel Hamilton Rivers II (Sam and Ham). Stauber called his prospective opus *Rivers Stay Away* (he wrote one chapter), but I'd call mine, if I had time to write it, *Stauber Don't Go.*

Unfortunately, Stauber did go in the summer of 1983, after a long battle with lung cancer that, despite the pain, never took away his phenomenal ability to make people laugh. "Bill is funny without trying," a fellow student at the University of North

Stauber as a "shavetail."

Carolina once said. "He laughs and the world laughs with him, he weeps and the world dies laughing." And that's why I wish I had a little more time, because somebody definitely should get William Erwin Stauber Jr., of Rural Hill, N.C. down on paper, in depth.

In case somebody ever decides to try, here are a few bare facts about his life after he graduated in 1940 from UNC: He worked in radio and advertising in Raleigh, Salisbury and North Wilksboro, joined the Naval Reserve in 1942 as an ensign, served as a deck officer in both the Atlantic and Pacific theaters, and was retired at the end of World War II with the rank of lieutenant commander.

In 1947 he came to Durham and joined the advertising firm of Knox Massey and Associates, where he put his creativity to good use dreaming up ads for Long Meadow Farms, Erwin Oil Company, Clark and Sorrell, the Durham Tobacco Market, Newcomb's Reproductions, Southland Associates, Model Laundry and Dry Cleaning, Style Craft Interiors, Yager Drug Company and Massey's largest account, the B.C. Remedy Company.

B.C. Headache Powders, invented and produced by Germaine Bernard and Commodore Thomas Council, two Durham businessmen, was Stauber's "baby" for about twenty years (he oversaw all creative and production functions), but he probably cured more headaches with his jokes and one-liners than the powders in their blue-and-white packets did. Or so we like to think, for laugher is, after all, the best medicine.

Stauber's particular brand found its way into everything he did, and some of the things he did, outside of advertising, were with the Chamber of Commerce, the City of Medicine Advisory Board, the North Carolina Jaycees, the Salvation Army, the Durham Tobacco Market, the Red Cross, the March of Dimes, the United Fund and the Merchants Association. And when he became a county commissioner in 1970, he was instrumental in establishing the Triangle J Council of Government.

Stauber also was instrumental in getting Epworth United Methodist Church established. A charter member of the congregation, he taught Sunday School in both the adult and junior departments, and once said of that experience: "I taught four different classes. One was nine- and ten-year-olds—my favorites. Another was the eleven- and twelve-year-olds (and) I did pretty good. Another was thirteen- and fourteen-year-olds (I wasn't so successful). And the fourth was adults. I was a complete flop."

Few would agree with the latter assessment, however, and there were those who thought he had a mission in life "and it had nothing to do with reforming the world . . . his mission was to add a little joy (and) this was a lifetime project for Mr. Stauber."

One way of adding joy, if indeed that was his mission, was through writing. "I am one of the few people I know who decided at an early age what I wanted to be and ended up doing just that," he said. "From the time I won the five dollar first prize in the county-wide Savings and Loan contest for fourth graders, I wanted to be a writer. Of course, I really didn't write the winning essay. My mother did. But I liked the money.

"Later I learned that writing really didn't pay all that much, but I still wanted to pursue it [even though] people who want to be writers really don't like to write. The hardest part of writing is tying yourself down to a pen and paper or a typewriter and actually turning out anything [so] I guess that's why I finally ended up in radio and then later advertising. Very seldom do you compose anything of more than one minute in length. Most radio and television commercials are thirty seconds and even folders or booklets aren't more than three to five minutes. Anything beyond that is too much."

But Stauber didn't stick to that premise. For at least a decade he wrote a column called *It's Not Funny* for the *Chapel Hill Newspaper*, and it was usually the funniest piece on the op-ed page. It often deplored or ridiculed many things, including computers, stores that stay open all day and all night, HEW (should be PHEW), government handouts, Saturday weddings (interfere with golf), co-ed dormitories, massage parlors, Congress, Christmas shopping, too much bigness, co-ed fraternities (frasorities), supermarket cash registers (he preferred himself, the clerk, a pencil and a paper bag), charge accounts, and Howard Cosell.

Stauber was positive about many things, however: summer camps for dogs, so he could enjoy no barking; the Masters Golf Tournament; one six-year term in office for every elected government official; his wife, Sarah; his mother-in-law, Mrs. Benjamin D. Gaddy; making downtown Durham off-limits so people would want to go there; TLC in hospitals; something big to look forward to; and his dog, "Li'l Bit," who was struck deaf and dumb after a car hit him, but learned to bark again, and also to read lips. Then, miraculously (we think) Li'l Bit learned to sing like John Denver.

And so on and on went the cherub-faced Bard of Rural Hall up to the day he died in August 1983. As far as I'm concerned, it's the only thing he ever did that made me cry, instead of laugh.

For weeks after Bill Stauber's death, I found myself thinking often about what the Greek poet, Euripides, had to say regarding good men. Way back in 400 B.C. Euripides opined that "When good men die their goodness does not perish, but lives though they are gone;" and the reason his words kept coming to mind was because of all the people who either wrote, or telephoned, or buttonholed me in stores and supermarkets to comment on my reminiscences about Bill. And not just to comment, but also to add their personal memories to an ever-growing legend about a remarkable man who was advertising executive, promoter, columnist, versifier and non-stop comedian, a man who ambled through life making folks laugh. A good man.

Especially during World War II, Stauber's contagious sense of the ridiculous boosted the morale of his shipmates aboard the *USS Biloxi*, a light cruiser named for a Mississippi city and commissioned in Portsmouth, Virginia in 1953. According to Stauber, who later put the Biloxi's story into seven stanzas of verse, *"She was authorized by Congress and built in Newport News / A strictly wartime baby with four super-powered screws / With the accent placed on shooting; a minimum on looks / She's the Navy's one and only fightingest cruiser in the books."*

The *USS Biloxi* operated for eighteen months in the Pacific and took part in ten major engagements, beginning at Kwajalein and ending at the coast of Japan. To the tune of "From the Halls of Montezuma," Bill and his buddies sang, *"From the Marshalls to Manila, from Palau to Tokyo / From Truk down by New Guinea, Okinawa and Iwo / In the Marianas, Philippines, Hong Kong and Camranh too / Few ships can match that record. You heard me, brother—few!"* And those who survived believe it to this day.

Stauber was a free-wheeling bachelor not long out of Carolina when Japan attacked Pearl Harbor. He got his lieutenant's bars at what he called the "90-day wonder school" in Chicago in 1942 and was assigned first to the heavy cruiser *Tuscaloosa*, which took him to Russia, the Arctic and Casablanca. Then the navy made him a deck officer on the *USS Biloxi*, and it was there that his true calling took over. Hear what fellow officer Tom Gary, from Money (can you believe it?), Mississippi wrote recently about the "shavetail" from Rural Hall: "I served with Bill on the *Biloxi* for three years, and it was an experience I still cherish. He had charge of one of the gun turrets, but is best remembered for his collateral duty, a job he invented for himself. Most every afternoon he would get on the ship's p.a. system and comment on current events and anything else that came to his mind, and many wondrous things did.

"Some of his comments on life aboard ship would surely have been considered mutinous in other circumstances, but the captain came to be one of his biggest fans as he recognized Bill's considerable contribution to relieving tension during the long days we spent waiting for something to happen, and tension during the time things were happening.

"As navigator, I tried to give Bill some weather information to include in his spiel. What came out of his fertile brain, however, often bore little resemblance to my words. Drawing on his days in Rural Hall, his weather reports were often oriented to the gardener and the farmer. When I visited him after the war and drove through the town, I felt as though I had come home. Rural Hall was Bill's Lake Wobegon.

"And there was that wonderful camaraderie in the officers' mess, of which he was such a vital part. On the rare occasions when we got ashore on some desolate sand spit for a beer party (we once spent fourteen straight months at sea) the occasion wasn't complete until he gave his famous rendition of 'The Great Speckled Bird.'

"He appreciated a risqué joke as well as anyone, but Bill's humor wasn't built around that theme, which comedians often adopt when all else fails. Nor did I ever hear him make a joke that left anyone feeling put down."

What a tribute. But only one among innumerable others that have surfaced since the summer of 1983 when Stauber, on the verge of losing his final battle with cancer and unable to speak, looked up at his wife, Sarah, and winked.

"Sarah was the perfect complement to Bill's blithe spirit," said Tom Gary, and to that I say *Amen*, and *Amen*.

# FORTY SEVEN

*If I had to live my life over again
I do not believe I would have it any different.*

JACK DALTON

# 'Absent-minded professor' changed Durham through his inventions

Today, when so many people seem to believe that the state and federal governments owe them a living from the cradle to the grave, it's refreshing to remember a Durham man who worked from the time he was five years old until he retired at seventy-seven, never borrowed money that he did not pay back to the last penny, and made significant contributions to the tobacco, textile and tea industries. Nor did he ever fail to provide for his wife and children. In addition to food, clothing, shelter and education, he gave them love, laughter, understanding and, before he died, a highly interesting, often amusing, and occasionally heartbreaking record of his own extraordinary life, which began in Pittsylvania County, Virginia, in 1879.

John Thomas "Jack" Dalton's autobiography, inherited by his youngest daughter, the late Mrs. W. V. Singletary, is written in a crisp, straightforward style many seasoned writers never achieve, and it should be available to the reading public, especially historians and preservationists. Maye Singletary was justifiably proud of her father, a mechanical genius who, with only a few months of formal education in a one-room schoolhouse, invented a bag-stringing machine that revolutionized more than one important industry.

But she did not resent the fact that he was never recompensed, adequately, for the ingenious device that helped a number of businessmen, both in and out of Durham, to become millionaires.

"Daddy was a happy man," she said. "He was sort of like an absent-minded professor, I guess, because he was always thinking so hard about his inventions, but he was crazy about his family. He had a great

179

John Thomas Dalton and his beloved wife, Mary Wilborn Dalton.

sense of humor, too, and told wonderful stories. Macon (her twin brother) and I loved to sit on his lap, inside his coat, and listen to his stories, and we did it until he finally said we were getting too big to sit on him."

Dalton himself said in his diary: "There was always one thing I did and that was to try to look on the bright side of life. I had faith in God and my country and myself. If I had to live my life over again I do not believe I would have it any different."

The life that Jack Dalton would not have changed was never easy. From the age of five until he was seven, he worked with his father, who was a farmer, a carpenter, and an operator of both a plane mill and a gristmill. After his father's death in 1886, and his mother's subsequent marriage to a Mr. Craddock, he worked with his stepfather until he was eighteen. During that time he built a wagon, a pushcart, a handcar and a length of wooden rails on which to operate it, a cider mill, a cradle scythe for cutting wheat, and a set of iron wedges for cutting rock—all of this in his "spare" time, when he was not working in the fields, at the gristmill, or in a blacksmith shop.

It was in a blacksmith shop in Virgilina, Virginia, in 1905, that he heard the Golden Belt Manufacturing Company, of Durham, was offering $100,000 to anyone who could make a machine that would put drawstrings into tobacco bags, and from that day Dalton's life changed. A friend agreed to back him in exchange for a fifty percent partnership, and Dalton set his mind—a mind that understood mathematics but "didn't know how he did it"—to the task of making a bag-stringer.

"I worked at night on my own idea, and worked for my customers all day," he wrote years later. "I don't see now how I went through with it, but this was the pattern for life laid out for me, and I had to follow it out." By then he was married to a girl he called "the queen of them all" and had a new baby, and he sensed that "my stringing machine was going to need more babysitting than any baby that was born in Virgilina or any other place," but he was determined to try to make it.

What followed involved long hours of night work, taking on additional partners in order to get more financing, learning drafting, fashioning a crude machine, refining it over and over, securing a patent, getting the machine built, discovering its faults, redesigning it, discovering more faults, refining it again, and so on and on and on until finally, in 1912, Golden Belt bought it. But seven years of partnerships, debts and expenses swallowed up most of the promised money, so it was fortunate that the company hired him (at 40 cents an hour) to supervise the installation and operation of the machines, to build twelve more like it, and to "take the bugs out" of other machines already in the bag factory.

Jack Dalton's bag-stringer, which put out 540 million tobacco bags a year at a saving of $100,000 for the company, was only one of his many subsequent inventions. Among them was a contraption that tied the strings into bows, another that attached labels to the bags without using staples, and still another that attached bags into bundles of twenty-five. And for R. H. Wright Sr., of Durham, he devised an extraordinary machine that weighed out tea, cut tea bags, sewed the seams, packed in the tea, and tagged the bags. Major tea companies in America, Canada and England bought them, the consumption of tea increased as the ritual of brewing it was simplified and Richard Harvey Wright grew richers and richer, thanks to Jack Dalton.

Nevertheless, Dalton's inventions did not make him a wealthy man because he had to enter into too many partnerships in order to finance them. He insisted on paying back, with interest, every cent he borrowed; he relied on certain "gentlemen's agreements" that backfired; and loyalty to a Durham partner compelled him to refuse the offer of a high-paying job with the American Machine and Foundry Company in New York.

But he was blessed in every other respect that mattered to him. "My wife and I are very happy," he wrote soon after he retired from the American Tobacco Company "If it took everything I had to have my wife, I would give it for her, for she has stuck with me through thick and thin, and no man has ever had a finer pal than I have had to go through life with. We are also happy over our fine children."

Speaking philosophically in his autobiography, Jack Dalton said: "I think everybody should always try to add something to this world everyday [sic] of his life after he has reached the age of twenty-one years or even sooner according to his ability. This would be a wonderful world if this were always true."

*Amen* being the only appropriate word with which to end that statement by a man who never let his genius get in the way of his humanity, again I say *Amen*.

*. . . each quail shot and eaten cost $1,000 apiece.*

QUAIL ROOST HUNT CLUB CONCLUSION

# Hunting joined men of vastly different backgrounds

The traditionally masculine sport of shooting quail often brings together men who otherwise might never meet, much less become companions, and that happened to Caleb C. Dula, a prominent businessman from New York City, and Frank Mangum, a son of slaves owned by Willie (pronounced Wye-lee) Person Mangum. A distinguished lawyer, judge, congressman and U.S. senator from North Carolina, Willie Mangum owned a plantation called Walnut Hall, located about four miles from Durham in Red Mountain, now known as Rougemont, and Frank Mangum was born there on May 3, 1865.

Dula, a native of Lenoir, North Carolina, was raised in Missouri, became a tobacco manufacturer in St. Louis, and was an officer in the Drummond Tobacco Company when James B. Duke's giant "tobacco trust" took it over in the late 1890s. Faced with a career decision in his early thirties, Dula decided to join Duke, who was bent and determined to buy up every independent tobacco company in America, and so he went to work for Duke in New York, first as a department manager and later as secretary and then vice president of Continental Tobacco Company, a subsidiary of the American Tobacco Company. Eventually Dula was made a vice president of American, and when the government dissolved that powerful conglomerate in 1911, he became president of the Ligget and Myers Tobacco Company. Obviously, in the world of big business and also in the eyes of "Buck" Duke, C. C. Dula was worthy of a place on that pinnacle of success inhabited only by Very Important People.

Frank Mangum, on the other hand, was born free only because he came into the world exactly one

182

week after the Civil War ended on April 26, 1865 at Lorenzo Bennett's farm, near Durham. His parents, Louis and Ruth, had met and married at Walnut Hall and already had eight children when Frank arrived, and he was the last of their brood. He learned to read from the senator's spinster daughters, Miss Pattie and Miss Mary Mangum, who conducted a select school for young ladies that drew patrons from many sections of the state; and under their guidance he demonstrated an inborn talent for singing that prompted them to dub him "the little musician."

Frank also learned to grow tobacco, the main crop at Walnut Hall, and when his family eventually left the plantation to live on a farm in Rougemont, growing tobacco became his way of life. While sharecropping on the farm of Dr. Arthur Bowling, he met Minnie Faucett, whose father, Thomas Faucett, carried the mail in the Bahama-Rougemont area, and in 1896 Minnie and Frank were married.

As a boy, Frank had learned that rich men from Durham and their friends from up north liked to come to the country to shoot birds, and by the time he was a man he was well acquainted with the Quail Roost Hunt Club. It had been organized by a group of Durham industrialists that included the Duke family, and as Durham grew and the Dukes became more and more prosperous, Quail Roost became more and more popular with certain of their business associates who regarded killing birds and small animals as the ultimate in rest and recreation. These men were quite willing to pay somebody, especially somebody who knew the territory, to go along and carry whatever their hunting dogs retrieved, so it was probably inevitable that C. C. Dula, a V.I.P.

Frank Mangum, November 1915.

from New York who loved to hunt quail, and Frank Mangum, a farmer who knew where the coveys were, would one day meet and establish a mutually satisfactory relationship.

According to his daughter, Ila Mangum Fozard, for Mangum it was one of many such arrangements. "My father carried game for lots of men," she told me in the summer of 1990. "Mr. C. W. Toms was one, and Mr. John Cobb was another—they both worked for the Dukes—and in 1899 he carried for a prince from somewhere in Europe. His name was Prince Cagasta, and he was visiting the Dukes. My father named my oldest sister after that prince, named her Cagasta Mangum, but we always called her Kate."

Caleb Dula and
Frank Mangum
after the hunt
in 1918.

Ila, one of Frank Mangum's three living children, had not forgotten growing up in Rougemont, where "everything was so plentiful, and we had such wonderful food. My father raised everything we ate, had beautiful gardens all his life, even after we moved to Durham in 1931. His health was poor by then, but he still planted those gardens and worked them, and they were beautiful."

In spite of the Great Depression, all of Frank Mangum's children found jobs. "I cooked for Mrs. C. B. Martin when I wasn't but fourteen years old," Ila remembered, "and Kate worked for the J. Elmer Longs at least thirty years. I worked there, too, and after I left, my sister, Pearl, came and stayed for eighteen years with the Longs. And my brother, Odell Mangum, worked forty years for the M. E. Newsoms, and during that time they let him off every day to go to high school. He would get up and cook breakfast for the whole family, and then he would go off to school when the Newsom children went, and after he graduated from Hillside the Newsoms sent him to North Carolina College and paid for his education there.

"I have worked for a lot of fine Durham people. Dr. J. C. Holloway, Mr. and Mrs. Lawrence Kirkland, and also Dr. and Mrs. Angus McBryde. And Mrs. Charles Downey hired me twenty-eight years ago and I'm still with her. She married Dr. W. K. Joklik after Mr. Downey died, and I still go to her every week."

The then seventy-three-year-old daughter of Frank Mangum, who placed herself in the immediate family hierarchy as "the knee baby," said she had eight children, eighteen grandchildren, and four great-grandchildren, and every Sunday anywhere from ten to thirteen would arrive at her home on Weaver Street for dinner. Their "Mama Ila," as all of them called her, was eager to give them what they liked, and their favorite dishes were fried chicken, rice and gravy, macaroni and cheese, okra and tomatoes, and either strawberry cobbler or peach pie.

Asked what her children did, their mother said: "Levern is a tile finisher, Ronald—he's a twin to Donald—is with the fire department, Donald is the minister at Mount Zion Christian Church, Josephine is a printer, and also caterer, Debbie teaches physical education and is married to a professional basketball player in Houston, Yasmin is a landscape architect, Kim is a chef at La Louisiana, a restaurant in New Orleans, and Jon is on his third tour of duty with the U.S. Army in Germany."

Needless to say, Frank Mangum would be proud of his daughter, Ila, and her children, all of whom are living proof that a determination to disregard injustice and seize opportunity is the way to successful living.

Quail Roost Hunt Club was dissolved in 1926, when members "came to the realization that the expenses of running the vast hunting preserve made each quail shot and eaten cost one thousand dollars apiece." Bought by John Sprunt Hill, it later became a model dairy farm and the home of George Watts Hill, Senior. Today the main house serves as a conference center for the University of North Carolina.

# FORTY NINE

*It was a genteel assembly line with an elegant foreman.*

# The Saunders sisters were artistic stylists

Relatively few people living in Durham today remember the Saunders sisters, four aristocratic maiden ladies who established a dressmaking "salon" at their home on Cleveland Street that drew clients from as far away as New York city.

Forced by financial reverses to make a living for themselves and their widowed mother, the Misses Bessie, Aggie, Florrie and Nena Saunders became seamstresses, one of the few "respectable" occupations open to Southern gentlewomen at the turn of the last century. But the only customers the sisters took were those whom they considered "quality," and their standards were lofty. Unless they agreed that a lady was well-bred, genteel and "to the manor born," she would never succeed in maneuvering an appointment with Miss Bessie to be fitted for a dress that the other three would likely have a hand in creating.

Impeccable background and breeding, however, did not always insure admission to the Saunders' clientele. Other stumbling blocks occasionally prevented it, as was the case with two young ladies who qualified in every way except that their grandfather "never fought a lick in the Civil War."

The arbiter of such standards was the mother of the seamstresses, Mrs. Richard Benbury Saunders. Before her marriage in 1856 to a Chapel Hill druggist, Mrs. Saunders was Mary Ellen Stanton Brandon, whose father was governor of Mississippi from 1826 to 1831. Gerard Chittocque Brandon, described as "a typical planter, genial, honest and hospitable," was a wealthy gentleman who owned several plantations, and Mary Ellen, along with nine brothers and sisters, grew up on one of them, near Fort Adams, Mississippi. Raised to be a Southern belle, she was waited on by slaves, sent to a finishing school in Maryland, and met young Richard Saunders, a graduate of the University of North Carolina, while visiting a classmate in Scotland Neck.

After their marriage they settled first in Chapel Hill, later went to Oxford, and finally moved to Durham. But long before, when Sherman's army had marched through North Carolina, Mary Ellen had been a young mother with a husband away in the fighting, and like everybody else, she hid whatever she could from the marauding soldiers. She managed to keep them from finding most of her valuable possessions; but she never got over the fact that they shot holes in her baby's bathtub, which she hadn't bothered to hide.

Because of this senseless act, her hatred of "damn Yankees" never abated, and whenever she spoke of the incident it was with scorn and considerable bitterness. "I never thought they'd even notice a tin tub," she would say, venom in her voice and fire in her eyes, "much less destroy it!"

In spite of being unreconstructed rebels, however, the Saunders ladies were not above catering to certain people from "up Nawth," as they called the region above the Mason-Dixon line; and two Durham residents, Mrs. B. N. Duke and Mrs. F. L. Fuller, were able to supply them with many customers. When Ben Duke and Frank Fuller moved to New York (Duke with American Tobacco Company and Fuller with Liggett and Myers), their wives became walking advertisements for the Durham dressmakers. The gowns they wore elicited not only admiration and envy from well-heeled Northern women, but requests for the Saunders' address, as well. So it wasn't long before letters with New York postmarks began arriving at the big white house on Cleveland Street; and if they were accompanied by recommendations from "Miss Sally" Duke or "Miss Lillian" Fuller, the orders usually were accepted. If not, they went into the wastebasket.

Dressmaking via long distance was no problem for the four spinsters whose magic fingers had earned them a reputation as "wizards with the needle." All they required was a lady's measurements, a picture or description of what she wanted, and the materials. These could be mailed to Durham, and, in due time, mailed back to New York in the form of a dress, exquisitely made, carefully packed, and guaranteed to please.

The process for local customers was more involved. It demanded a certain amount of ritual that included being greeted at the door by Mrs. Saunders and invited into the parlor for a chat, and it also provided the sisters with what today would be called "job satisfaction." This came in the form of news, news about people. What they were doing, where they were going, how they were dressed, what they were saying, who they were seeing, what they were eating and how it was cooked, and the state of their health—anything and everything. None of this was gossip. It was news. Gossip was a horrid word, a practice not to be tolerated; but news was welcomed eagerly because the ladies rarely left their house except on Sundays when they attended services at St. Philip's Episcopal Church.

Miss Aggie got out a bit more because she did the shopping at Durham's leading dry goods stores, Rawls-Knight and Ellis Stone, for cloth and buttons and needles and thread and hooks and eyes and lace and ribbon. She was the model in the family, thin and always stylishly dressed; and she walked fast, almost sailed along with her head up high and her eyes bright and alert. Miss Aggie never missed a trick, had plenty to tell when she came back home bringing, among other things, the latest Vogue or Bon Ton patterns.

These were not a necessity, however, because Miss Bessie, the eldest sister, could copy the latest styles from Paris or New York simply by looking at pictures in magazines and then cutting her own patterns from old newspapers. Miss Bessie, who was very stout and had a man's haircut "to save trouble," also made forms out of flour sacks stuffed with scraps of cloth and skillfully molded into a semblance of each client's torso. This was done according to measurement, and while Miss Bessie measured ladies in the privacy of an upstairs bedroom she engaged them in conversation. As a skillful dentist draws a tooth, she drew all sorts of information from their mouths while she ascertained the size of their waists, busts, shoulders and hips, scribbling the information on a scrap of paper with the nub of a pencil. Later she would convey this news to her mother and sisters, who were waiting down in the dining room that had been converted into a workshop.

This big room, with tall windows that stretched from floor to ceiling, held two sewing machines; but most of the stitching was done by hand, stitching so fine it was almost invisible to the eye and yet strong enough to last for years without breaking. Hooks and eyes and the elaborate beading on wedding and evening gowns were done by Miss Aggie and the youngest sister, Miss Nena, who was sweet-faced, shy and the least talkative of the four. Miss Florrie, the only redhead, concentrated her talents on the skirts that eventually were attached to the bodices made by Miss Bessie. It was a genteel assembly line with an elegant foreman who strongly resembled Whistler's mother. Mrs. Saunders always wore a lace cap on her white hair and a long black dress that swept the scrap-littered floor when she walked.

A small oval-shaped stove in front of the fireplace held a kettle that simmered constantly, providing water for steaming and pressing and humidifying the air. Miss Bessie's rocking chair by the front window was a sentry post from which she watched the activity on Cleveland Street, reporting whatever she saw and announcing the arrival of customers as they opened the gate in the iron picket fence and proceeded up the walk to the porch.

That spacious front porch was shaded by vines, and in the summer ferns grew in baskets hanging from the ceiling and in pots lining the banisters, making it a cool, green escape from the heat that scorched Durham in July and August. Beyond the front door the wide hall was dim and shadowy, and the parlor on the right, where Mrs. Saunders held her preliminary chats, was almost dark. No sunshine ever touched, for long, the flowered Turkey carpet or the elaborately carved furniture upholstered in black horsehair; for it was only on Sundays and holidays that the shutters were opened and the shades behind the lace curtains raised.

Although there were two bathrooms in the Saunders house, there was also a "garden house," as the ladies called it, at the far end of the back yard.

Grapevines grew on both sides of the walkway leading to it, and when the fruit was ripe the sisters answered calls of nature at the garden house instead of using the inside facilities. That way, they explained, they not only got a little much-needed air and exercise but could refresh themselves, going and coming with handfuls of delicious scuppernongs.

When it was time for a meal, the sewing was taken from the dining room table and the food put on it. The five ladies ate decorously, as ladies should; then they cleared the table, wiped it clean, replaced the sewing, and went back to work. It was a way of life far removed from the one Mary Ellen Brandon Saunders had known as a girl, and would have provided for her children if the Civil War had not wiped out the Brandon fortune. But although war deprived them of wealth, it brought out their courage and resourcefulness, qualities they possessed in a high degree, along with family pride and a genius for creating beautiful clothes.

A roster of their Durham customers would include (in addition to Duke and Fuller) such names as Watts, Bryant, Hill, Carr, Foushee, Lyon, Stagg, Toms, Erwin, Graham, Morehead, Southgate, Wright and many others.

One local woman who had her wedding dress made by the Saunders sisters describes it as being "the long-waisted style of 1923, embroidered in seed pearls and trimmed with lace. The train was three yards long, lined with georgette, and had a scroll design of vines and roses, big satin roses made by Miss Florrie, and beaded leaves by Miss Nena."

Another resident, now a grandmother, who lived across the street when she was a child and was a frequent visitor in the Saunders' home, remembers that she was always welcomed when she knocked on the door and always given a peppermint when she left. Sometimes she was allowed to sit on the floor and play with the wicker baskets that held "fascinating scraps of velvet and satin and lace, and also glittery beads and sequins." She recalls that "velvet felt like a cat's nose when you rub it the wrong way, and satin was slippery, and caught the light from the windows. The sequins made me think of fairies; and lace, I knew, made a dress special."

The house on Cleveland Street, along with others in the same block, has been gone for many years now, and the contours of the former quiet residential neighborhood have been altered to accommodate public buildings, among them the new Police and Fire Stations. Mrs. Saunders and her daughters, Bessie, Aggie, Florrie and Nena—elegant ladies all —have left this world for a better one, perhaps; but they are still alive and well in the memories of a few older residents of Durham, who not only valued their artistry, but their friendship as well.

# FIFTY

*Unlike Dresden china, there was nothing fragile*
*about Julian Carr's first child.*

# Lida Carr Flower: A free spirit soaring ahead of her time

In 1874, a daughter born to Julian and Nannie Graham Carr inspired her father to begin thinking seriously about quality education for Durham's little girls, and by 1881 the Methodist Female Seminary was established and seven-year-old Eliza Morehead Carr was one of its first pupils.

Eliza, called Lida, was an exceptionally beautiful child, and although not much is known about her earliest years, she exhibited an inquiring mind and more than average insight when, at age thirteen, she expressed skepticism about organized religion. She confessed to her father that no matter how hard she tried, she failed "to receive satisfaction" from a revival that was converting Durham sinners by the hundreds. Carr, an ardent Methodist and a pillar of Trinity Church, was highly disturbed by his first-born's reaction to the phenomenon of being "born

again," but not nearly so much as he would have been had he lived to see her abandon the faith of her fathers for the psychiatric teachings of Dr. Carl Gustav Jung, whose mentor was Sigmund Freud.

As the daughter of Julian Shakespeare Carr, an adoring parent as well as one of Durham's wealthiest citizens, Lida had a singularly carefree childhood in opulent surroundings, and there can be little doubt that she was overindulged, for Carr was admittedly fatuous about his family. He once wrote to a friend in Chapel Hill that his wife was so handsome and lovable, and his children were so dear and nice, and that all of them made him so happy that, "I can never approach the subject without 'slopping over,' if you will pardon the expression."

So it is not surprising that Lida Carr was a strong-willed child who kept that trait, along with her beauty, throughout a long and active life. She was extremely intelligent, and did well not only in the Methodist Female Seminary that her father had helped to establish, but also at Miss Summers' School in Washington, D.C., a posh finishing school that later became Mount Vernon College.

By the time she graduated from Miss Summers', Lida could read and speak both French and German, and because Durham's provincial atmosphere bored her, she persuaded her parents that well-chaperoned travel in Europe would round out her education and keep her happy. There also may have been an unspoken agreement between them that a suitable husband was more likely to appear in France or England or Spain or Italy than in Durham, North Carolina.

Eventually one did appear, in the person of Henry Corwin Flower, a young lawyer from Kansas City who later became a highly successful banker. He and Lida were married a week before Christmas in 1895, and their elaborate wedding was the talk of Durham for years afterward. In Kansas City, Lida named the handsome home her husband built "Round Hill," after the Orange County plantation where her mother, Nannie Graham Parrish Carr, had grown up; and it was there that their children, a son and two daughters, were born. As soon as the children were old enough to be turned over to a nanny, Lida began to spend much time in Europe, traveling back and forth whenever it pleased her, apparently.

Henry Flower was fourteen years older than his wife, and as president of the Fidelity Trust Company, which he organized in 1899, he was a very busy man, with important ties in the financial world and not much time for travel. But Lida's active mind was not

Eliza Carr Flower

content with her role as a leader of society, the mother of three, and the mistress of a large estate. Lida's mind needed something tougher to chew on, and she found it in the classroom of Carl Gustav Jung. Jung's break with his own teacher, Sigmund Freud, made psychiatric history, and his theory of the libido and the unconscious mind made a profound impression on the wife of Kansas City's leading banker.

In order to study under Jung, Lida took her children to Switzerland, enrolled them in school, and settled down for a year's stay in Zurich. There she met Edith Rockefeller McCormick, the tractor heiress, and because Edith also was a disciple of Jung, the two became fast friends. Later, in 1924, the year after her father died, Lida and Edith became partners in a healing movement that they offered "to hundreds of wealthy women seeking mental healing." Edith McCormick described the movement as "one which would alleviate the mental misery of the world," and Lida Flower's enthusiasm for it turned her into a public speaker and kept her away from home more than ever. Lecturing to audiences of rich women looking for relief from their miseries, she often took along a large diagram she had made of "the various strata of the human mind;" and she spoke convincingly on structural and functional psychology, the collective unconscious, and behaviorism.

In 1932, after eight years of the movement and thirty-seven years of marriage, Lida went to Reno and sued Henry Corwin Flower for divorce. In her testimony she stated that he was "domineering, insisted on his own ideas being carried out, ignored her suggestions, and was discourteous to her friends unless they were of his own choosing." Henry Flower declined comment, and the property settlement was not made public, but the Kansas City Star reported that "a monthly allowance of substantial amount" was to go to Mrs. Flower.

To all appearances the amount was sufficient for Lida to maintain the lifestyle to which she was accustomed, and shortly after the divorce she sailed on the *President Madison* for Honolulu en route to Japan and China, where she planned to study the comparative psychologies of the Orient and the Occident. Although she intended only a brief stopover

in Honolulu, she stayed for the better part of a year, lecturing to selected classes at the University of Hawaii and also to private audiences of army and navy wives. She attributed her interest in the Orient to her father's Chinese protégé, Charlie Soong, who had lived for a time at Somerset Villa, the Carr home in Durham. Soong, founder of the Soong dynasty and father of Madame Chiang Kai-chek and Madame Sun Yat-sen, had sometimes served as a babysitter, of sorts, for Julian Carr's children, and Lida Carr, the oldest child, had vivid memories of the fascinating stories about China that Charlie Soong used to tell to her and her siblings.

In her lectures, Lida said that Aristotle had been the first man to write about psychology, which he called "the science of the soul and its mishaps and adventures"; and that Chinese philosophy located the soul "just behind the eyes in the daytime, and in the liver at night." Carl Jung, she said, believed it was impossible to define the boundaries of the soul and stressed the importance of God and religion. Lida, herself, believed that "there was no excuse for people being in mental darkness in regard to their individual actions," and that each person should know himself, and "clear up his dark side." The only way to better mankind, she thought, was to throw more light on the unconscious mind, which, in her opinion, was one level above the collective unconscious and one level below the conscious mind.

She told her audiences that the psychic energy with which each individual was endowed too often was absorbed in some useless complex, such as a mother fixation, or a father fixation; and that people should learn to diagnose such ridiculous mental obsessions in themselves and do away with them. But in spite of her brusque and sometimes impatient approach to neurosis, she stressed the importance of "sympathy, understanding, and love in the advancement of modern psychology." It was her premise that only a thin line divides sanity and insanity; and that disturbed people should be treated, rather than shut away from the world in asylums.

After Lida reached Tokyo, she took up residence at the Imperial Hotel, where her father had stopped on his trip to the Orient in 1917. There, in the hotel, she practiced her own brand of psychoanalysis by private appointment, and she also gave lectures to several women's clubs in the American colony.

Thanks to her father, Julian Carr, and to her former husband, Henry Flower, Lida had prominent connections and an entrée into the best society wherever she went; and she saw to it that the press was duly informed of her arrivals and departures, as well as her qualifications as an authority on applied psychology. These included her studies with Carl Jung; her collaboration with Edith Rockefeller McCormick; her series of lectures (fifty-six in all) to nurses at the Henry Street Settlement in New York; and her recently completed translation, from the German, of an interpretation of Confucius's *Book of Changes*.

However authentic, it was an impressive background, and Lida, like her father, was always good copy. An outspoken enemy of the status quo, she scorned the universal tendency to keep things as they were and believed that "old-fashioned religion has no more place in the present world than old-fashioned clothes," which, it was perfectly obvious, she never wore. Lida Carr Flower, formerly of Durham and Kansas City, was extremely stylish and very feminine, with soft, clear skin, bright blue eyes, and the prematurely snow-white hair that "ran" in the Carr family. A Tokyo society editor described her as "not at all formidable in spite of her intellectual attainments," and said that "she reminds one of a piece of Dresden china."

Unlike Dresden china, however, there was nothing fragile about Julian Carr's first child. From him she inherited the stamina to travel constantly and the ability to charm audiences and newspaper reporters, and although she was considered an eccentric, she was, in many ways, simply ahead of her time.

As a woman who extricated herself from the traditional role of wife-and-mother (a role she found stifling), and as a crusader against mental illness, Lida Carr of Durham was a pioneer in both psychotherapy and women's liberation, two theories that have become accepted in most of the world today.

# Urban Growth

*You finally root out not only*
*the needle in a haystack you're*
*looking for, but something else too—*
*something exciting, something as*
*seductive to the mind as buried*
*treasure can be to a digger's eye*

# FIFTY ONE

*I hate to see that hotel go . . . I hate to think about
it all going down in a few minutes.*

JOHN A. BUCHANNAN

# Implosion is an indignity to Durham landmark

*Over twenty-five years ago, I wrote the following
story for* The Durham Sun. *It concerned the then-
pending implosion of the Durham Hotel-Motel,
originally named the Washington Duke Hotel and
Durham's first "sky scraper." Because it's history,
here it is again, along with one burning question:
What on earth happened to all those things that
went into the cornerstone back in 1924?*

On December 7, [1975], a date most people will
recognize as Pearl Harbor Day, the Durham Hotel
reportedly is scheduled to be imploded. That's the
word they're using for this catastrophe, and according to Webster's Dictionary, to implode means to
burst inward, which seems more dreadful, somehow,
than bursting outward. An explosion, in spite of all its
noise and violence, nevertheless has a kind of dignity,

an open and above-board crash and racket infinitely
preferable to the muted horror of inner rupture and
slow collapse.

But of course a sixteen-story hotel cannot be allowed to explode in the center of town, for when it
goes this is what will go with it: 300,000 face brick,
680,000 pieces of hollow tile, 55,350 yards of concrete, 900 tons of steel and sheet metal, 350 tons of
reinforcing steel, thirty carloads of limestone, twenty-
one carloads of terra cotta and ten carloads of mill-
work. One carload of glass has already been removed. The demolition of all this must be no threat
to people, nor to the structures surrounding it, so
the proud building that was once the heart of Durham must die as quietly as possible. Many will mourn
its passing. Some will weep. Others will watch, dry-
eyed and angry, while something they helped to

197

build is destroyed. But nobody's going to be very happy on December 7, when the fifty-year-old hotel falls and one of Durham's outstanding landmarks is gone forever.

John A. Buchanan, presently chairman of the board of Home Insurance Agency, says the idea of a new hotel came to him around 1921 because "people were always stopping by our house on Chapel Hill Street, ringing the doorbell and asking if they could rent a room. It got to be a nuisance, and I told my wife that what this town needed was a big hotel, a really fine, first-class place where people would want to stay." His wife, the former Mattie Toms, agreed with him; and at her suggestion that he do something about it, Buchanan went to the Chamber of Commerce.

"Gene (M. E.) Newsom was president, and he grabbed hold of the idea pretty quickly, thought it was fine," Buchanan says. "Then he and I sold it to the rest of the members. We figured it would take at least a million dollars to build the kind of hotel Durham needed, so we knew we'd have to get everybody in town interested if we were going to raise that kind of money. That's when we formed a Citizens' Committee to decide how we were going to do it, but I had no idea it would take so long, almost three years, before we actually started building."

That initial committee later became the Durham Citizens Hotel Corporation, and was comprised of Buchanan, R. L. Baldwin, E. T. Rollins, M. E. Newsom, W. D. Carmichael, J. B. Mason, J. F. Wily, K. P. Lewis, L. P. Paschall, N. Rosenstein and M. S. Llewellyn.

"We hired a fund-raising organization from Philadelphia to plan our strategy on selling stock to finance the hotel, and they were smart folks," Buchanan says. "E. J. Hockenburg was the name of the firm, and they knew their business, they'd had a lot of experience in this sort of thing all over the country. But a million dollars is a lot of money, and we had to raise it in six months, so we had to help them."

Buchanan laughs, shakes his head. "We," he says, "had to pay 'em, help 'em, and lead 'em to the prospects."

Prospects were hard to sell, at first. Most Durham people liked the idea of a million-dollar hotel but were leery of buying stock to finance it. Hockenburg, president of the financing corporation, and four of his staff members came to Durham in October, 1923. They, along with about thirty local men, "worked like dogs right from the beginning," according to Buchanan, but the response was slow. The committee had hired a Lynchburg, Virginia architect, Stanhope Johnson, to draw up the plans for the building; and when he brought his preliminary sketches to Durham for appraisals, Buchanan knew what he had to do.

"I took those plans and got on a train and went to St. Petersburg, Florida to see Mr. Ben Duke, who had a winter home down there," he says. "I registered at a hotel and then I called his house, but I couldn't talk to him because he was sick. Mrs. Duke came to the phone and said he wasn't well enough to see me, so I told her I'd just wait there until he was." Buchanan smiles. "Tell the truth," he says, "I didn't know how long I'd have to hang around that hotel waiting, but the very next day Mrs. Duke called and said she was sending the chauffeur to get me."

By early afternoon the two men were together, Benjamin Newton Duke propped up in bed and John Buchanan sitting in a chair nearby. "I showed him the drawings," says Buchanan, "and explained what we were trying to do, and then I said, 'Mr. Duke we need you. We need you to help us rouse some interest in Durham, get this started.' He looked at me for a minute and then he said, 'Well, John, what do you want me to do?' and I answered him right back, 'I want you to give me a check for $50,000.' And that's what he did, too. Wrote out a check and handed it to me, just like that."

Aided by this boost in both finances and morale, Buchanan came back to Durham and told his wife he was going to New York to see her father, C. W. Toms, about the project. Toms, then a vice president of Liggett and Myers Tobacco Company, and a former superintendent of the Durham schools, lent a sympathetic ear to his son-in-law. He was able to interest a number of New York businessmen in the venture, including Caleb C. Dula, president of Liggett and Myers, who invested $25,000 in the hotel.

"But one of the finest gestures came from Mrs. J. E. Stagg, who was Wash Duke's granddaughter," Buchanan says. "We still didn't have near enough money, so we held a public meeting at the YMCA down on Main Street, and I asked for a general solicitation. I said, 'Who in this room is willing to put up $25,000 or $30,000 to help us get this hotel?' and little Mrs. Stagg stood up and said, 'I am, John.' Then she walked to the front of the room and wrote out a check for $25,000. That started the ball rolling, and we got another $5,000 that same night."

Unlike the Dukes and their heirs, few Durham

The grand Washington Duke Hotel was located in a block bounded by Parrish, Corcoran, Market, & Chapel Hill Streets. ca. 1928.

citizens could afford to write checks for thousands of dollars; but as the drive went on, they continued to invest in the dream of a new hotel with what they could spare from their earnings and, in some cases, with their life's savings. Eventually over 1,200 people, drawn together in a mutual effort that created good will and better understanding in the community, bought just under a million dollars worth of stock. An intensive sales campaign, under the leadership of Buchanan, M. E. Newsom, T. C. Worth and E. Burke Hobgood was held from November 5 through November 13, 1923, with teams meeting each day at noon at the YMCA to report on progress. A pep sheet called "Jas'm" was printed and distributed, and a life size replica of a goat was awarded daily to the team leading all others in sales. At the end of the campaign this prize goat was awarded permanently to J. Mallory Hackney for having led all sales three times.

Another part of the drive was a contest with a prize of $100 offered to the person suggesting the best name for the hotel. Because thirteen people entered "Washington Duke" as their choice, the prize had to be divided, and the winners received only a little over seven dollars each. They were: Mrs. W. M. Lipscomb, Mrs. L. Watts Norton, Mrs. W. F. Franck, Mrs. A. M. Harris, Mrs. C. W. Toms, Mrs. W. D. Parrish, Mrs. W. E. Allen, Alice Pirie, Bernice Daniel, Eunice Chaplain, Lelia Montague, J. D. Ferrell and C. J. Roberts.

Construction began on July 15, 1924 on the site of the old Academy of Music, a city block bounded by Corcoran, Chapel Hill, Market and Parrish streets, and on November 21 the cornerstone was laid. "If they ever go into that, they'll find a bunch of stuff," Buchanan says. "Newspaper clippings, coins, packs of cigarettes and tobacco, lists of names, pictures . . . heck, they even put a picture of me in there."

In addition to the items mentioned by Buchanan, also included in the cornerstone box were a photograph of Washington Duke; pictures of the hotel; a copy of the agreement with the city relative to the sale of the hotel site; a copy of the notice of sale; a copy of the agreement whereby the Academy of Music was purchased; a copy of the agreement with the William A. Foor Company for operation of the hotel; a formal announcement of the laying of the cornerstone, with a program of the exercises and a copy of the address given by Dr. R. L. Flowers; the latest financial statements of banks in the city; copies of *The Durham Morning Herald* and *The Durham Sun*; samples from various manufacturing firms in the city; a copy of "Jas'm," the sales pep sheet; and the following lists of names: stockholders, stock salesmen, board of directors, executive committee, architects, contractors, operators and others connected with the planning and erecting of the building, and the hotel-naming committee.

"It was a rainy, cold day," Buchanan says, "but we had a platform all decorated with bunting and a band and plenty of speeches." In addition to the main address by Dr. Flowers, other speakers included Dr. J. M. Manning, M. E. Newsom and Buchanan.

Eleven months after the laying of the cornerstone, the Washington Duke Hotel held its formal opening October 20, 1925. An editorial in *The Durham Morning Herald* said, in part: "Certainly in this generation, and probably in the history of Durham, there has been no such an achievement on the part of the men and women of this city as will be found in that magnificent sixteen-story building which will blaze with hundreds of lights this evening in honor of those who brought it into existence . . . There is nothing that will do more to stimulate a community and make it go forward than for it to put over some great local enterprise . . . The Washington Duke Hotel is a community monument, the result of community effort and community money. When in future there is hesitation in undertaking some great project, this monument will serve as an incentive to go ahead."

Durham's "community monument" contained over 200 rooms for guests. Although there were only twenty-seven showers, there were 259 bathtubs, 293 toilets, 320 lavatories and 291 drinking fountains, with 17,000 square feet of roofing over all of it. The dining room had a white marble floor and its furnishings included 9,309 pieces of silverware costing $14,000. There were forty-six dozen each of knives, forks and teaspoons; twenty dozen orange spoons; forty dozen salad forks; 223 meat platters; seventy coffee pots; seventy-five sugar bowls; 700 creamers; thirty sauce boats; fifty-eight vegetable dishes; twelve compotes; fifty corn prongs; forty combination oyster and fruit cocktail cups; 100 salt and pepper shakers; thirty glass-lined water pitchers; and forty finger bowls.

On the mezzanine above the dining room and lobby were the Palm Room, the Fountain Room, the Assembly Room, the Ladies' Room and the Ballroom. Three fourteen-carat gold and crystal chandeliers, each equipped with thirty-six lights, hung from the Ballroom ceiling; and the Fountain Room, designed for small groups of eighteen or less, boasted a sizable fountain and pool at one end. The Assembly Room was planned mainly for conventions, and the Palm Room for ladies' parties.

In the basement, thirty cooks and waiters worked in a completely electric kitchen equipped with ovens, broilers, steam table, meat machine, coffee urn, silver burnishing machine, dish washer, bottle washer,

Down comes the cornerstone of the Durham Hotel on December 1, 1975.

dough mixer and roll warmer. Also in the basement were the laundry, with chutes from each floor; a barber shop employing seven barbers and a manicurist; and an ice machine, which could manufacture a ton of ice a day.

The exterior of the building was equally elegant, the first two floors being made of stone, the next eleven of white brick, and the last two of stone and terra cotta. There was no numbered thirteenth floor, but counting the basement there were actually sixteen levels, as advertised. The top floor housed the governor's suite and the bridal suite, both of which attracted much attention during the open house on October 20. It was a time of celebration, and a steady stream of visitors inspected the new hotel from basement to bridal suite, many coming from the neighboring towns of Chapel Hill, Hillsborough, Raleigh,

Oxford and Roxboro. The lobby was decorated with baskets of flowers and potted plants; and the new silver gleamed on spotless white tablecloths in the dining room. The gold and crystal chandeliers glittered in the ballroom, where Tal Henry and his North Carolinians were to play for dancing following a banquet for 500 people. Men, women and children talked and smiled and exclaimed and pointed as they wandered through the hotel, already being described by newspapers as "one of the finest in the South."

At six o'clock, guests for the banquet began to arrive. "A lot of folks wore formal evening clothes, top hats and tails and long ball gowns," says Buchanan, reminiscing. "But everybody had on his Sunday best, and everybody was happy. William Foor, the man we'd hired to operate the hotel, really knew how to put on a good show, and he gave us a fine meal that night for five dollars a plate."

The program, arranged by R. L. Felts, a local physician, included an invocation by W. W. Peele, pastor of Trinity Methodist; and speeches by Dr. W. P. Few, president of Duke University, Dr. W. S. Bernard of the University of North Carolina, and J. Elmer Long, lieutenant governor of the state. The president of the Chamber of Commerce, W. P. Budd, presided; and John Buchanan made the formal presentation of the hotel to the William Foor Hotel Operating Company.

"After I got through talking, the Chamber of Commerce gave me a watch for what I did," Buchanan says. "There were a lot of speeches, and Judge [R. L] Sykes was the toastmaster. After the banquet, the orchestra started playing and people got up and danced; some of them danced until almost morning. It was mighty fancy there in the big ballroom, and a good wind-up for all the work folks had been doing for so long."

Most of that work had been done by Durham people, for Durham. Local firms that had a part in the hotel were the Blackford Company, general contractors; D. C. May Company, Budd-Piper Roofing Company, Dermott Heating Company, Hunt Plumbing Company, Noell Brothers, and Pollard Hardware Company, which furnished 12,500 pounds of nails and the locks and hinges for 1,225 doors. Erwin Mills sheets and pillowcases were bought through Rawls-Knight Company, and two grand pianos were purchased from W. R. Murray Music Company.

"I hate to see that hotel go," Buchanan says. "It took a lot of time and money and hard work from a lot of folks to get it, and I hate to think about it all going down in a few minutes."

A great many people feel the same way, for Durham won't be the same without the old Washington Duke.

# FIFTY TWO

*Love in bloom in '23*

# In the Roaring '20s, teenagers got high on a Durham roller coaster

When fifteen-year-old Frances Foushee completed her sophomore year at Durham High School in June 1923, she began to keep a diary that somehow has survived the ensuing seventy-nine years and today is owned by her daughter, Mary Sweaney Andersen of Chapel Hill. Written in an ordinary school composition book bearing the inscription, "Let There Be Light," the slim volume illuminates three weeks in a decade historians have dubbed the "Roaring Twenties," and it spotlights a group of high school students whose fathers were among Durham's leading business and professional men.

"The gang," as Frances Foushee called her friends, were sons and daughters of John Sprunt Hill, Alphonsus Cobb, Jones Fuller, Howard A. Foushee, R. L. Baldwin, S. H. Hobgood, W. M. Piatt, W. H. Borland, J. F. Wily, W. P. Farthing, D. W. Horton,

W. B. Guthrie, F. L. Walker, W. G. Frasier, R. E. Dillard and J. C. Michie, and by today's standards of behavior they were complete innocents. Because there were no youth centers, no shopping malls, and no beer joints, these teenagers had no place to "hang out" except at their homes, where they were always under supervision.

They got their "highs" on the roller coaster at Lakewood Park, and they got their drinks at Five Points Drug Company, where "dopes" (slang for Coca-Colas) were the strongest beverages available and milkshakes were the most popular. Movies also were popular with the gang, but in 1923 an organization called the Hays Office censored anything that smacked of sex or violence on the screen, and "picture shows" did not need to be rated R or PG. Parental guidance was hardly necessary, however, according to Frances Foushee, who saw *The Rustle of Silk* and described it, in her diary, as "rather slow . . . and what we really wanted to see was Larry Simon, in *The Barnyard*." But she and three of her friends, Margaret Farthing, Rose Frasier and Lib Borland, did like *Garrison's Finish* with Jack Pickford. "It was a thrilling story about horse racing," she commented on June 12, 1923. "The plot was rather old but I never get tired of such pictures." Other pictures playing in Durham that month were *Mighty Lak' A Rose*, at the Paris Theater; *The Face on the Barroom Floor*, at the Academy; and *More To Be Pitied than Scorned*, at the Savoy.

Frances, youngest daughter of Howard Alexander and Annie Wall Foushee, lived with her widowed mother, her sister, Annie Wall, and her brother, Alex, in a fourteen-room house that sat square in the middle of a city block bounded by Vickers Avenue, Proctor Street, Shepard Street and Cobb Street. Also part of the household were Gertrude Green, who was cook, nurse and surrogate mother to the Foushee children; and George White, who was yardman, handyman and chauffeur. Known as "The Terraces" because of the unusual landscaping of the sloping yard that surrounded it, the house had a deep, inviting porch across the front and down one side. In spring and summer, when it was furnished with tall-backed rockers, wicker tables holding pots of flowers and ferns, and a slatted wooden swing that hung from the ceiling, it made an ideal gathering place for the gang. "Tonight the gang came over [to] my house and we had a wonderful time," Frances wrote on June 18. "Everyone says my porch is divine."

According to the current *Durham Architectural Survey*, the Foushee house was "an elegant . . .

showpiece of the neighborhood" with an impressive stained-glass window on the main landing of the staircase. Following Mrs. Foushee's death in 1953, a group of Carmelite nuns lived there from 1960 to 1961. Later, when it became headquarters for the Durham Arts Council, the stair landing was converted into a stage for local theater productions. Today the house is owned by the Durham YMCA, which operates a morning child-care program and also provides activities for both adult members and Y-Teens.

Unlike the so-called flaming youth in more cosmopolitan regions of America during the twenties, Frances and her gang did not drink bathtub gin or indulge in flagpole-sitting and goldfish-eating, but they were not unsophisticated. On the contrary, they were very much aware of trends, and as clothes-conscious as today's young people. The girls had their hair bobbed at John Leach's barbershop (beauty parlors had not yet come on the Durham scene), wore silk stockings and cloche hats, and hoped they would somehow develop "IT," the mysterious female magnetism personified by Clara Bow, a popular Hollywood movie actress.

Rudolph Valentino, another star of the silent screen, inspired the boys to slick back their center-parted hair and hope they resembled "shieks," a term synonymous with "lady-killers" and a look much to be desired. "Cake-eater britches" (slang for bell-bottomed trousers) were favored by lady-killers, and cardigan sweaters with rolled collars were "the style" for both sexes. Although most of the boys in the gang had summer jobs, the girls worked only at certain household chores designed to build character and prepare them for their future roles as wives and mothers. Once their chores were done to their own mothers' satisfaction, they were free to enjoy the rest of the day; and when they were not swimming at Lakewood Park, or playing tennis, or simply lounging around discussing boys, Frances and her friends were usually playing auction bridge. This popular card game spawned bridge clubs that met frequently, bridge parties for out-of-town visitors, and random games that always included refreshments.

During the three weeks before she left for Camp Merrie Wood, in the mountains of North Carolina, Frances Foushee played bridge eleven times and, according to her diary, consumed quantities of angel food cake, mints, sherbet, ginger ale, orange ice, olives, punch and sandwiches. "Dear Mrs. Farthing gave us some delicious ginger ale, sandwitches (sic) —I know I ate ten dozen—and olives," she wrote on June 16; and the following Tuesday, at the Julian S. Carr home, she had "the best punch and angel food cake I ever tasted" and commented that Nancy Carr's bridge party was "lovely" and "Nancy and Mrs. Carr are charming hostesses."

In addition to being a gregarious card player, Frances was bookish, and during lulls in the teenage social whirl she managed to read and pass judgment on four novels. The first, "a silly book called *Greatheart*," was followed by "a pathetic story about an ambitious son of a hard-working tenant and the daughter of a prosperous landowner" called *In the Land of Cotton.* Philip Gibbs's *In the Middle of the Road* documented "an ex-soldier's readjustment of affairs since the War (World War I)," and *Anne Of the Island*, by L. M. Montgomery, was "a beautiful story and although I have read it before I read it over and over."

Frances and F. Lewis Walker III in 1923 on porch steps near library of Francis's mother's home, "The Terraces," 810 West Proctor Street, Durham.

Reading was confined to the daytime, however, because almost every night the gang gathered at somebody's house, to talk and giggle and flirt and play the victrola and dance to such tunes as "Five Foot Two, Eyes of Blue," "Baby Face," and "The Sheik of Araby." But for real entertainment they depended on Lakewood Park, an amusement complex on the Chapel Hill Road that boasted a concrete swimming pool (Durham's first), a skating rink, a merry-go-round, a bowling alley, a pavilion, a lake, and a roller coaster that hurled its riders so high above the treetops and flung them down with such heart-stopping suddenness that only dedicated thrill-seekers patronized it often.

Established around the turn of the century, Lake-

Lakewood Park Casino. Summer Theatre. ca. 1930.

wood Park was a haven from Durham's scorching summer heat. Its first pool had been a mud-bottom pool and was the city's first public swimming facility, and a few local churches had occasionally held baptismal services there on warm Sunday afternoons, when the park was closed to the general public.

For a number of years, the Runkel Stock Company, of New Jersey, rented a house on the Chapel Hill Road, opposite the park, and staged its productions in the Casino. The plays were popular with Durham people, as was jazzman Joe King, whose orchestra provided music for dancing in the Pavilion. Tom Foster, a longtime manager of Lakewood Park, advertised it as "The Coney Island of the South," and once got a request from a northern vacationer for "a room overlooking the water."

On June 19th, Lakewood Park sponsored a marathon dance, a current craze that was sweeping the country and one Frances Foushee and her friend,

Blanche Hobgood, longed to see. Somewhat wistfully, Frances confided to her diary: "We wanted to lag out to the park where the marathon dance is beginning but we didn't have a way to get out there. So doomed to disappointment we hung around Blanche's and I spent the night."

"Lagging" was slang for driving, and lagging around Durham in an indulgent parent's car was a favorite pastime. When John Sprunt Hill allowed his daughter, Frances, to drive the family Jackson, Frances Foushee thought it was "the berries," especially when they lagged downtown to Five Points Drug Company, where curb service was provided and the "soda-jerkers" were Durham High boys.

Boys, naturally, were of vast importance, and the pages of Frances's diary are peppered with the names of Dan (Horton), Skip (Cobb), Gene (Wily), Lewis (Walker), Grogan (Beall), Pace (Fuller), Allen (Murdock), Finley (White), Boots (Green), Lyman (Wilkins), Bill (Michie), and Mercer (Guthrie). Lewis Walker, by far the most important to Frances, assumes significance on page two and maintains it to the end.

Fielding Lewis Walker III, the son of F. L. Walker Jr., an official of Liggett and Myers Tobacco Company, was so much on the mind of Frances Foushee that merely to "lag down Liberty Street," where the Walkers lived, was a major thrill. On June 11, after going for a ride with her neighborhood chum, Grayson Baldwin, Frances wrote: "Grayson of course had to lag by Liberty Street. She started blowing her horn before she passed Patsy Mason's house and didn't cease until she reached the corner . . . can you imagine why?" That night, after the gang had congregated at Grayson's house, Frances records what must have been the end of a perfect day: "Lewis and I sat out in the swing and I enjoyed myself immensely. I'm not spoofing!"

Her euphoria ended later that week, when Frances Hill took her riding in the Jackson and "We went down Liberty Street and saw the whole Walker Family sitting on the porch. . . . I felt like sinking through the seat but all I could do was sweetly wave. We went way out on Holloway road and then Frances for devilment went by Lewis's again. Wasn't that tacky? Tonight he didn't come to see me. I know he is mad."

But gloom turned to joy the next evening when Lewis came to an impromptu party at Margaret Farthing's house. "We had a wonderful time," Frances wrote before going to bed that night. "Lewis is as sweet as ever."

Sweet though he may have been, the object of Frances Foushee's affection also was careless on occasion, and a clipping from *The Durham Morning Herald* documents that fact. Pasted in her diary and headed BOY WAS SLIGHTLY WOUNDED BY RIFLE, the story relates that "Lewis Walker, son of Mr. and Mrs. F. L. Walker, sustained a light flesh wound Wednesday afternoon in one of his arms by the accidental charge of a .22-calibre rifle which he was holding. The bullet grazed the arm causing a wound while not serious causes the lad considerable pain. It is stated that the boy had been shooting sparrows in the back yard of his home. While he was standing with his arm resting on the muzzle of the gun the weapon in some manner was discharged."

Fortunately, what might have been a tragedy be-

Fielding Lewis Walker III

came no more than a bad piece of journalism, but the incident apparently elevated Lewis Walker to hero status in the eyes of his girlfriend, and as soon as he recovered from his "considerable pain," he appeared at her door with a gift. Later that night, after what must have been a moving encounter on the shadowy porch of "The Terraces," she wrote: "Lewis is the stuff. He gave me the shot with which he was shot."

It may be safe to say that Frances Foushee is the only Durham girl who ever glued a bullet in her diary, and even more remarkable is the fact that it remains there today, a singular token of affection and a tangible reminder of a first love that bloomed in the summer of '23.

# FIFTY THREE

*While they were young and tender . . . they danced.*

# The Embassy Club: Dedicated to the pleasures of ballroom dancing

In 1934, the Embassy club, a purely social organization dedicated to the pleasures of ballroom dancing, appeared on the Durham scene and very quickly became good copy for *The Durham Morning Herald* and *The Durham Sun*. The club's formal dances at the Washington Duke Hotel, its "script" dances at a tobacco warehouse on Foster Street, and its elaborately-staged costume balls in the City Amory got extensive coverage on the "society" pages of both newspapers, and thus the public's so called need-to-know was satisfied in what can only be seen, in retrospect, as infinite detail.

Unfortunately, only a handful of former members of the all-male Embassy Club were still around, in the spring of 1990, to reminisce with me about it; but it was immediately obvious that each of those dignified gentlemen enjoyed remembering his "salad days" as an unfettered man-about-town, when he had danced with beautiful girls to the music of big bands brought to Durham by his own club. And although each had his own special memories of those days, the only man who remembered how the club began was one of the two founders, Richard Allen Freeman.

Freeman and his friend Loy Thompson, both of Salisbury, North Carolina, went to the University of North Carolina together and were fortunate enough, after graduating, to be hired by two major tobacco companies in Durham. Freeman was working at the American Tobacco Company, and Thompson at Liggett and Myers, when they decided that what Durham needed "in the worst way," as far as they were concerned, was a club composed of young, unattached men like themselves, plus a few carefully selected young married couples.

Pre-Fancy Dress Embassy Club Ball cocktail party at the home of Mr. and Mrs. J. Lathrop Morehead circa 1938.
Front Row L-R: Mayor Will Carr, Annie Louise Massey, Mildred McMullen, Margaret Lewis, Mena Webb, Happy Kenan, Margenna Gates, Hanes Clement, Hatsy Wannamaker, John Moorhead, Louis Carr. Second Row L-R: Buck Harris, Douglas Morehead, Knox Massey, Tom Webb, Mary Banks McPhertson, Elizabeth Davis, Kathleen Carr, Unknown, Margaret Henry King, Harriet Ranson, Binkie Moore, Meredith Moore, Dr. E.S. Orgain, Lawrence Tomlinson, Frank Kenan, Eugene Wily, Joe Webb. Back Row L-R: E. G. McIver, Dick Lewis, June Mallard, John Lipscomb, Russell Ranson, Nat Gregory, Vann Webb, Hefty Teen, Unknown, J. Lathrop Morehead.

According to Freeman, the idea came to them in 1934, and originated in the room he and Thompson rented from Dr. F. E. Tucker, whose big white house on Durham's West Chapel Hill Street had become their home away from Salisbury. "We were just sitting around talking one night and decided that a dance club on the order of the Terpsichorean Club in Raleigh would be a good thing for Durham," Freeman told me. "So on two or three different occasions we asked different guys to eat supper with us, either at the Palms [Restaurant] or the Malbourne [Hotel], and then we talked it up. When we thought we had enough folks who wanted to join, we called a meeting in an upstairs room at the Palms, and that night we set the dues at two dollars a month and elected officers.

"The only one I remember now is Pace Fuller. He was the first president, and Loy and I were on the board of governors. We didn't know what to call ourselves, so we offered a prize for the best name, and that was decided at the next meeting, at the Malbourne. I don't know who thought up 'Embassy Club,' but that was the name everybody liked best, and the prize was a free year's membership."

Dances were financed by assessments of "about $10 or $15," Freeman said, and most of the early ones took place at the Washington Duke Hotel and were by invitation only, but on several occasions the club staged an informal dance at one of the tobacco warehouses on Foster Street, hired a big-name band, and charged admission.

"We'd get somebody like Guy Lombardo, or Don Bestor or Cab Callaway, somebody who would draw a big crowd," Freeman explained, "but we didn't try to make money for charity, or anything like that. All we wanted was to make enough on ticket sales to pay the orchestra, and we usually did. But once we came up short and were in a bad way for a while, trying to scrape up twelve bucks before the dance ended, and not having any luck. We didn't know what to do until Foxy [Dayton] Dean, who was business manager of the athletic department out at Duke University, made up the difference and saved our lives."

In spite of its shaky financial situation, however, by 1937 the Embassy Club had acquired considerable prestige and membership was eagerly sought after, even by "middle-aged folks with children." Because the dances were always well chaperoned by highly respected Durham dowagers, potentially anxious parents of local belles laid their fears of wild parties to rest and gave the affairs their seal of approval. They may have reasoned that with such ladies as Mrs. I. F. Hill, Mrs. J. C. Michie, Mrs. W. R. Kukor and Mrs. Mamie Dowd Walker sitting on the sidelines, no gentleman would dare to bring along a hip flask, so the Coca-Colas that relieved thirsty dancers would not be "spiked" and decorum would reign. As indeed it did, although a "Bring Your Own Liquor" party in a hotel suite at intermission had been a tradition since the Club's inception, and would continue until its demise.

Inevitably, romance blossomed at Embassy Club functions and in many instances led to matrimony. By 1938, when the first costume ball was held at the City Armory, newlyweds who had previously "gone steady" were: Allston and Hazel Stubbs, Egbert and Margaret Haywood, Bill and Helen Markham, Gus and Mary Mac McIver, Jack and Jean Martin, Bob and Gypsy Reeves, Mack and Mena Webb, Russell and Harriet Ranson, Frank and Happy Kenan, Gerry and Ellen Gerard, Clarence and Mary Lucy Cobb, Beverly and Carolyn Raney and Frank and Mary Reade.

That same year, "steadies" definitely headed for the altar were George Pyne and Mary Walker, D. L. Boone and Elinor Dunham, Joe Webb and Jeannette Ogsbury, Julian Marshall and Nancy Fowler, Alfred Williams and Margaret Gibbons, June Mallard and Elizabeth Davis, C. W. Hall and Inez Abernethy, Jones Pollard and Evelyn Barbee, Buck Noblin and Margaret Anne Knight, and John Moorhead and Harriet Wannamaker.

Twenty-nine of those forty-six people were still alive in 1990 to recall (if they could) what happened on the night of January 5, 1940, when the Embassy Club held its third annual fancy dress ball, transformed the armory into what both *The Durham Sun* and *The Raleigh Times* called a "Nursery Rhyme Town" in the "Realm of that Merry Old Soul—Old King Cole," and staged "the mythical wedding of Jack and Jill." The day before the ball, both the *Sun* and the *Times*, obviously bent on scooping Durham's *Morning Herald* and Raleigh's *News and Observer*, predicted it would be a "brilliant affair" and gave readers a preview of what would happen: Old King Cole would officiate at the wedding ceremony of Jack and Jill, who would be attended by Bo-Peep, Little Boy Blue, Jack Sprat, Simple Simon and the Fiddlers Three.

Embassy Club members, as wedding guests, would disguise themselves as Mother Goose characters and, on the stroke of midnight, take part in the "Dance of the Hundred Masques." At that time

the best-costumed couple would be selected by the dance committee and acclaimed the favorites of Old Mother Goose, the two papers said, adding that "competition for the honor has been keen on previous occasions, and this year's ball is expected to prove no exception."

Picking up on that story from its rival, *The Durham Sun*, on January 6, 1940 *The Durham Morning Herald* came out with a detailed account of the third annual Embassy Club Fancy Dress Ball. The six-year-old organization had become something of an institution during its short span, and with so many of its members being recognized as potential leaders in their various fields of business, law and medicine, the half-page spread, with pictures, was perhaps not unwarranted.

Despite their tender years—most were under 30 —they were, to all appearances, responsible citizens; and the fact that they had succumbed, for the third year in a row, to the universal desire to shed their identities for a few hours was generally viewed with amused indulgence by readers of both *The Herald* and *The Durham Sun*.

That year, having chosen the Mother Goose theme, in a joint and strenuous effort they had transformed the drab old armory into "the ballroom of the palace of Old King Cole." Decorations featured "the famous hill down which Jack and Jill took their epic tumble, the cow jumping over the moon, the famous shoe in which the Old Woman lived, gingerbread houses, and all the other things relating to Mother Goose rhymes." They were an immediate hit with the guests, who personified not only "the population of Nursery-Rhyme Town . . . [but] all the other characters who have appeared at previous fancy dress balls, including pirates, Napoleon, Mickey Mouse, Cleopatra and all the others."

Most of the costumes seen on the dance floor that night were well worth the fee a New York supplier charged for their rental. Alfred Williams, chairman of the costume committee, had provided a list of what was available to each member, double-checked their choices after they were approved by wives and/or girlfriends, sent the orders to New York, and distributed them when they arrived in Durham.

"Everybody came to the armory to pick up their outfits, but they had to pay first or they didn't get 'em," said Williams, who remembers that the company charged "anywhere from $2.50 to $3.50" per costume.

Inevitably, perhaps, there were duplications: one too many Little Boy Blues, Bo-Peeps, Dr. Fosters, Mad Hatters, Mother Hubbards and Bessie Brookses. There were even two Jacks and two Jills and, worse still, three Old King Coles; but neither Tom Webb nor Loula Southgate, the official bride and groom, nor Guy Mitchell, the designated monarch, seemed perturbed by their doubles.

Nor did Julian Marshall, the Baker joined in rhyme to Butcher George Pyne and Candlestick Maker Nat Gregory. Marshall did not seem to care that his relatively simple costume of chef's hat, apron, knee breeches and white stockings had also appealed to "Ace" Parker, of Duke football fame, Duke Athletic Department Treasurer Dayton Dean, and Dr. Angus McBryde, a popular Durham pediatrician.

The Embassy Club's third venture into the land of make-believe got unbelievable coverage, by today's standards, from at least three newspapers and prob-

ably more, considering the fact that members of similar groups—the Terpsichorean Club of Raleigh, the Carolina Cotillion Club of Rocky Mount, and the Bachelors, Assembly, Thalian and Spinsters clubs of Greensboro—attended.

A *Durham Morning Herald* feature story by the late Carolyn Goldberg, then society editor, allowed that "hundreds of people from Durham and throughout the state will be looking forward to the ball tonight, which is expected to be a gala event in the truest sense of the word. Dr. Isaac Manning will entertain at a cocktail party in Chapel Hill before the dance, and a number of other private affairs have been scheduled."

Pictures of the seven "sponsors" of the ball accompanied that story. Chosen by Tom Webb, president; Allston Stubbs, general chairman of the ball; R. Bruce White, Jr., chairman of arrangements; Egbert Haywood, chairman of program-theme; Alfred Williams, chairman of music, the sponsors were: Loula Southgate, Hazel Stubbs, Ruby Palmer of Littleton, Margaret Haywood, Margaret Gibbons, Lottie Lewis and Jeannette Ogsbury.

The armory doors opened at 9:30 p.m. on January 5, 1940, and at ten o'clock sharp, Dutch McMillian and His Men, who had earned a reputation "throughout the South," struck up an appropriate tune for the grand march "and revelry continued from that point on," said *The Morning Herald.* ·

Taking a prominent part in the march were Old King Cole (Guy Mitchell), his Fiddlers Three (J. C. Webb, James Mann, Dr. E. S. Orgain), Queen and Knave of Hearts (Mary Randolph of Richmond and Dr. W. A. Graham), Mr. and Mrs. Peter, Peter Pumpkin Eater (Evelyn Barbee and Jones Pollard), Snow White and Prince Charming (Mary Frances Council and E. N. Jones), Jack and Mrs. Sprat (Alice Poe of Raleigh and Gordon Smith), Hansel and Gretel (Sara Belk of Charlotte and Dr. I. H. Manning), Little Red Riding Hood and Tommy Green (Elinor Dunham and D. L. Boone), Goldilocks (Rheudelle Thompson), Greedy Nan (Mary Walker), Sleepy Head (Charles Wenrich), Three Little Kittens (Helen Noell, Lily Duke Clements, Laura Lyon), Mother Goose (Nancy Fowler), Crooked Man (Bruce White), Puss-in-Boots (Margaret Gibbons), Old Mother Hubbard (Ruby Palmer of Raleigh), Little Miss Muffet (Lottie Lewis), Margery Daw and John Stout (Mr. and Mrs. W. S. Markham, Jr.), Tom, Tom the Piper's Son (Alfred Williams), Simple Simon (W. A. Fulford, Jr.), Mary Had a Little Lamb and Little Jack Horner (Mr. and Mrs. Allston Stubbs), Mistress Mary (Kay White), Daffy Down Dilly and Georgie Porgie (Mr. and Mrs. Egbert Haywood), Bo-Peep and Little Boy Blue (Mr. and Mrs. Evan McIver), Little Tommy Tucker (Francis Beard), and Jack and Jill (Tom Webb and Loula Southgate), whose mock wedding took place when the march ended.

About sixteen of the above-mentioned revelers still live in the Triangle area, and possibly all of them suspected that America might soon go to war. But nobody knew when, or where, or how soon it would happen, so on that January night in Leap Year, 1940, they danced.

While they were still "young and tender under the apple boughs," to quote Dylan Thomas, they took a happy trip back into the never-never land of childhood, and they danced.

# FIFTY FOUR

*Like good schools and a good climate, good clubs
made any city more appealing to new business, and
attracting new business . . . was vital to progress.*

# The Cotillion Club set lofty standards

When it comes to ancestor worship, or "high society," we daresay no thinking person would ever speak of Durham, North Carolina and Charleston, South Carolina in the same breath, but the two cities do have one thing in common: both have a pioneer gentlemen's club that refuses to compromise its lofty standards of decorum while pursuing the pleasures of dancing and dining. Charleston has its St. Cecilia Society and Durham has its Cotillion Club, and although formality in manners and dress seems to have plummeted to an all-time low in much of the world, these two organizations still insist upon it at least once a year.

It was back in 1762 that a group of wealthy planters, merchants and lawyers decided that their provincial little city of Charles Town badly needed "the appurtenances of civilization" and forthwith organized the St. Cecilia Society, which continues to flourish and describes itself as America's oldest and most exclusive club. Almost 200 years later, in 1961, a similar group in Durham, planters excepted, reached a similar conclusion about their own city and formed the Cotillion Club. While the ancient and exclusive St. Cecilia may have inspired it, one of the club's earliest documents indicates that it was patterned more after the Forsyth Assembly, in Winston-Salem, than the St. Cecilia, in Charleston.

The Winston-Salem club was formed in 1956, when "an unknown source sent invitations to a selected male group to meet at Reynolda House to discuss it," and then and there the group chose a name, elected officers, and agreed on a date for its first formal dance. The white-tie affair took place at the Forsyth Country Club in April, 1957 and was "very elegant," said one member, "with a gourmet dinner and imported band of the Lester Lanin type."

About three years later, a group of Durham businessmen, including three who had been guests at the first Forsyth Assembly, agreed that an elite gentlemen's dance club might enhance Durham's image, which had long suffered by comparison to Raleigh, Wilmington, Greensboro, Winston-Salem and Charlotte in matters of culture. Like good schools and a good climate, good clubs made any city more appealing to new business, and attracting new business, as everybody knew, was vital to progress. Also, a renewed interest in ballroom dancing that had captured a number of prospective members gave momentum to the idea, and in due time it became reality.

The Cotillion Club's governing board decreed that membership would be by invitation, and that it would be restricted to not more than eighty "white, male citizens of the United States" who were over twenty-five years old, were of good character, and were members of Hope Valley Country Club. Its stated purpose was to benefit its members and their "guests and invitees (wives and out-of-town friends) by promoting dances and other social functions," and the benefiting that ensued during the next few years got considerable coverage in what was then called the "society" section of *The Durham Morning Herald* and *The Durham Sun.*

If there was any disinclination to join among the "sixty leading men" who were tapped for membership in the Cotillion Club, skillful pressure from their significant others must have dissolved it, for no one declined. Forty-six businessmen, six doctors, four lawyers, two university professors, one athletic director and one architect comprised the first roster, which listed E. M. Cameron, president; Frank Kenan, vice president; and William Cranford, secretary-treasurer.

Now forty-three years old, the Cotillion Club was conceived in the fall of 1960 and born, to considerable fanfare, on Friday the 13th in January 1961. To venture that it arrived on the Durham scene in a blaze of glory would be to resurrect an ancient cliché better left dead, perhaps, but the club's debut was by no means ordinary. Its charter members, described by *The Durham Morning Herald* as "leaders of the community," arrived at Hope Valley Country Club arrayed almost (but not quite) to a man in full evening dress and looking "absolutely gorgeous," according to one wife, who was apparently carried away by so much masculine pulchritude.

Exactly how many of these community leaders received white-tie-and-tails from their wives on Christmas Day, 1960 is not a matter of record, but those who failed to find full dress regalia under the tree either (a) took their college "tails" out of mothballs and had them altered, if possible; or (b) got them from a local rental establishment; or (c) defied the Cotillion Club's board of governors and their own disapproving wives and wore their own tuxedos, some of which were so old they had buttons, instead of zippers, on the trousers.

Although this rebellious small minority created some politely-masked consternation in the receiving line at the first "Winter Ball," it evaporated, at least temporarily, when the country club's familiar waiters appeared in the trappings of an earlier century—short crimson jackets, black knee breeches,

E. M. Cameron, President

Frank Kenan, Vice President

W. E. Cranford, Secretary/Treasurer

white stockings, silver buckled shoes and white cotton gloves. Resplendent in this regalia, they passed among the guests bearing large silver trays of exotic cocktails, sparkling wines and gourmet canapés (no bourbon-and-branch or crackers and cheese at *this* function!), and most managed to maintain the impassive expressions traditionally associated with English butlers. But a few of the old timers, confronted by grins of amazement, had the grace and good sense to grin back.

Invitations to the Cotillion Club's first gala were stamped with an impressive crest. It depicted a satyr and a dancing girl on a shield above the words "Virtus Bacchannalis Non Disputandum Est.," and announced cocktails at eight, dinner at nine, and dancing, to the music of the Meyer Davis Orchestra, until one in the morning.

And so it went, like clockwork. Promptly at nine, members and their ladies sat down to an elegant meal—and I quote from the menu—of Spanish Melon with Prosciutto, Green Turtle Soup, Fillets of Flounder Marguery, Chucker Partridge with Wild Rice, Spinach Florentine, Baked Alaska, Coffee, Liqueurs, Brandy, Salted Nuts and Mints, all served to dinner music by a special string quartet and followed by coffee and liqueurs in the French Room. There, according to next day's *Durham Morning Herald*, "an open log fire burned and . . . the table was covered with a decorative white linen cloth" and the festive red-and-white decorations were complemented by "green bankings of magnolia leaves" and "avocado candles in a five-branched candelabrum."

What the paper did not report to the public was that an amazingly efficient entertainment committee sought advice about the first dinner from the Four Seasons Restaurant in New York; arranged to have the recommended entrée, chukker partridge, flown into Raleigh-Durham airport from wherever chukker partridge could be bought; persuaded Hope Valley Country Club's governing board that the club needed new china and silver; and staged a "dry run" of the dinner, for themselves, the night before it was due to delight the palates of Cotillion Club members and their guests.

Possibly to deter them from taking all this grandeur too seriously, an anonymous wag whose identity remains unknown mailed an unsigned bulletin, typed on plain white paper, to all members of the club a few days before the first ball. Greeted with hoots of laughter by some, and stony silence by others, it read:

"TO ALL MEMBERS: By special arrangement and as an accommodation to members, we are able to offer, at a great saving to you, the Cotillion Club Do-It-Yourself Kit listed below.

"If the items in the kit were purchased separately there's no telling what they would cost. However, by lumping them together we are able to provide a special club rate at the ridiculously low price of $116.73. Actually, you will be getting them at cost. No profit is involved. In the kit you will find:

"1. Economy-size bottle of BLOOD BLUING.

"2. WHITE TIE. An expertly-knotted hangman's noose of the best quality white hemp rope.

"3. TOP HAT. Pointed to fit any size head.

"4. Box of assorted TAILS, including raccoon, squirrel and beaver. Monkey can be substituted for any one of the above if yours inadvertently was left out of the original membership package, or should a spare be desired.

"5. Finest quality burlap bag, or POKE, complete with pig.

"6. Box of PLAY MONEY. Beautifully embossed bills of large denominations.

"7. Vest pocket METRONOME.

"8. Dozen NARCISSUS BULBS. Simply gorgeous varieties.

"9. MIRROR for the wall. With a built-in Swiss music box that plays: "Am I not the fairest of them all?"

That minor effort at sabotage failed to dim the brilliance of the first Winter Ball, however, and af-ter forty successful years the Cotillion Club is still going strong, although there may have been a few changes. As of November 2000, there were one hundred names on its roster, with fifteen hopefuls on a waiting list; and members were anticipating what is now an annual affair—a cocktail party on the evening before the Carolina-Duke football game. Another cocktail party takes place in April.

In January, 2001, a new board of governors, listed as David Veasey, Bill King, Charles Atwater and Marvin Barnes, assumed responsibility for what is now called the Hope Valley Men's Cotillion at the time of the Winter Ball. For some years now, invitations to that traditionally formal affair have requested Black Tie, instead of White, a definite come-down in the eyes of a number of members and many wives. And to add insult to injury, there are still rebels, even in those ranks, gentlemen who arrive at the Club's only formal gala in business suits!

It's a far cry from the venerable St. Cecelia, but the beat, at least, goes on into a new century.

# FIFTY FIVE

*No man ever left the first tee with more enthusiasm
and greater expectations than did Mr. Hill.*

CLAUDE CURRIE

# Hillandale was Durham's first country club

No one really knows when the first American took a swing at a golf ball (some say it happened in Charleston, South Carolina, in 1786), but golf history has it that a Scotsman named John Reid built America's first course—three holes in a cow pasture in Yonkers, New York—and tried out his imported clubs there on February 22, 1888. A little later, Reid and a few friends moved around the corner to a larger field, laid out six holes, and organized the St. Andrew's Golf Club, which became the most prestigious in America. According to legend, the "clubhouse" for Reid and his golfing buddies was a large apple tree "from whose branches hung jugs of liquid refreshment," and thus they became the "Apple Tree Gang" and, possibly, the originators of what today is called the nineteenth hole.

In 1891, three years after John Reid hit his first golf ball in Yonkers, a group of Long Island men founded the Shinnecock Hills Golf Club and built the first real clubhouse. Designed by renowned architect Stanford White, the house overlooked "the first American course that actually looked like a golf course," no doubt because it had been built by a Scottish professional, Willie Dunn, who knew what he was doing. Dunn was the first of many Scots who crossed the Atlantic to design the courses, give the lessons, and sell the equipment needed to play golf, and not all were bona fide pros, like Dunn. It has been said that a Scottish accent and a passing acquaintance with the game were all it took to land a plush job with a bunch of Americans who yearned to make the royal and ancient pastime a big part of their lives.

By 1897, the game had caught on in many parts of

the United States, and for the next thirty-five years it would be regarded as one that only the well-to-do could enjoy. For that reason, it had a more or less restricted following, but it really began to burgeon around the beginning of the twentieth century, partly because "country clubs," providing social functions for the whole family's enjoyment, began to replace golf clubs for the pleasure of men only. Backed by the so-called weaker sex and touted as a healthy hobby, golf became more and more fashionable and the country club, little by little, became more and more "a home away from home" for those who could afford it.

So it was against such a backdrop that Durham took a giant step away from its image as a factory town lacking in many of the finer things of life. The year was 1911 and the times were good when John Sprunt Hill spearheaded a move to build a country club and, simultaneously, began to lay out a golf course on a large farm he owned about two miles west of the city. Supporting him in the initial stages of his effort to bring golf to the area were a number of business and professional men who were not only willing, but eager to buy stock in a club in order to play on Hill's course, once he completed it. They were J. S. Manning, W. F. Carr, C. B. Atwater, J. S. Cobb, R. L. Carr, J. M. M. Gregory, J. Crawford Biggs, C. C. Thomas, E. J. Green, W. P. Few, A. M. Webb, W. A. Erwin, W. T. Minor, J. L. Morehead, W. J. Griswold, E. B. Lyon, Dr. Joseph Graham and, last but by no means least, George Washington Watts, one of Durham's early tobacco tycoons who also happened to be Hill's father-in-law and business associate. Watts was president and Hill was vice president of the Durham Loan and Trust Company, forerunner of the present Central Carolina Bank.

George Watts, a native of Baltimore who had acquired his knowledge of golf on country club courses "from Poland Springs, Maine, to Palm Beach, Florida," may have introduced his daughter's husband to the game, and he also may have encouraged Hill to pursue it by taking him, as a guest, on golfing trips to Asheville and Pinehurst, and also up and down the eastern seaboard to various other clubs in which he held membership.

But however Hill came to know golf, he also came to love it, as have millions of Americans ever since John Reid turned a pasture into a course, and the more golf Hill played, the more he loved it.

"No man ever left the first tee with more enthusiasm and greater expectations than did Mr. Hill," said the late Claude Currie, a friend and business associate and also a devotee of golf. "His wood shots seldom completely satisfied him, nor did his irons; but he always believed in the next chance. He had more confidence in his putter than any club in his bag, and his opponents more respect for it . . . To him, golf was a gentleman's game . . . and a desire to play golf gave any man some of the aspects of a gentleman."

So because Hill took golf seriously, he became disenchanted with having to travel out of town in order to play it, and that's when he decided to build his own links in "a wild section of woods and fields, infested with distilleries, bootleggers (and) gamblers." Having played on courses both in and out of the state, he knew what he wanted, and because self-confidence was a quality he had in abundance, he was certain he could build his own, and proceeded

Certificate for Durham Country Club stock.

$50 worth of stock in the fledgling venture that was to change the pattern of social life in Durham.

This early document of incorporation, dated May 1913 and couched in language that can only be regarded as quaint, further stated that the club had been formed "for the purpose of establishing a suitable Club House and grounds for the promotion of social recreation and intercourse among the members." But the constitution and by-laws, published in 1915, put it more succinctly, and perhaps a little more delicately, by saying only that the club's "objects are to encourage outdoor sports and social recreation among its members."

The architectural firm of Linthicum and Linthicum was selected by the board of governors to design the clubhouse, which was to have a grand hall, dining room, billiard room, card room, steward's room, butler's pantry, kitchen, four toilets and a golf shop on the ground floor. Upstairs, there would be a bedroom and bath for a resident manager, locker rooms and showers for both men and women, and two porches where, presumably, players could relax after their golf games.

As is often the case, initial bids from contractors were too high, in the board's estimation, so ground-breaking was delayed while the building committee, comprising Isham Faison Hill (John Sprunt Hill's brother, and secretary of the Durham Loan and Trust Company), John F. Wily, James E. Stagg, R. H. Wright and Sumter C. Brawley, conferred about cost reductions and finally came up with a list of instructions for the architect: Use heart pine, said the building committee, instead of concrete for the floor of

to do so. Using farm labor and supervising the work from his farm office, he personally financed what was to become Hillandale Golf Course, a Mecca for lovers of the sport and an indispensable adjunct to the future Durham Country Club, (whose members would, nevertheless, have to pay Hill a greens fee).

Under the guidance of its first president, George Watts, the Durham Country Club was incorporated with an authorized capital stock of $50,000 divided into 100 shares of the par value of $50 each. The certificate of incorporation stipulated that the organization could begin business "when $250, representing five shares, shall have been subscribed," and to meet that requirement, R. H. Wright, E. B. Lyon, J. S. Hill, W. J. Griswold and E. J. Parrish each bought

Original clubhouse at Hillandale golf course.

the front porch, and eliminate the concrete terrace on the western end of the house. Also eliminate the tile drain across the front of the structure, and sink the foundation walls only two feet into the ground, instead of four. Reduce the thickness of certain walls, designated by the committee, from nine inches to four inches, and build the chimneys of brick, rather than fieldstone.

All of this, presumably, was done to satisfaction, and when the building was completed in 1912 at a cost of $12,500 (architect's fee included), its brown-shingled exterior and wide, inviting porches presented a pleasing, rustic look reminiscent of posh clubs in the mountains and sandhills of the state. It appeared to be a very fine club indeed, and local interest in it began to build rapidly.

Golf has been described as a four-letter word capable of generating "as much passion, delight and anguish as some of the more notorious four-letter words," and like those bawdy and ancient expletives, the royal and ancient game of golf has been around so long nobody knows when it actually began. Some believe it started when a bored shepherd whacked at a round pebble with his crook, accidentally knocked the rock into a rabbit burrow, and then tried to duplicate the shot. Others say it originated in Holland as "het kolven" and sometimes was played on ice. But there's no mystery or myth about when golf began in Durham. It began in 1911, after John Sprunt Hill completed the Durham Country Club and the course he chose to call "Hillandale"

The first roster of the Durham Country Club contained the names of most of the city's leading business and professional men and, more importantly, their wives. Even more importantly, it listed forty-eight lady members who either were spinsters, widows or the strong-minded mates of a few husbands who declined to ally themselves with Durham's new status symbol. A little over a decade before, no lady would have been allowed to visit a men's club, much less become a member, but Hillandale's founders had the good sense to realize that things were changing. So it is to their credit that, at a time when women were generally regarded as second-class citizens (the only people in America who couldn't vote were criminals, lunatics, idiots and women), they made the club available to the female sex, albeit with the predictable limitation: lady members could not vote in an election for club officers.

Lady members could, however, enjoy all of the remaining privileges, including golf, and a surprising number took up the game. Listed among the best players in 1915 were Mrs. E. B. Lyon, Mrs. B. N. Duke, Mrs. J. M. Lipscomb, Miss Mary Duke and Miss Sallie Glass, all taught by Alex Pirie, a Scottish pro whom John Hill hired to teach would-be golfers how to play and also to sell them bags, clubs, balls and shoes with cleats. Golf lessons from Pirie were free for ladies, but they cost gentlemen players twenty-five cents each, or four dollars a month, or six dollars a quarter, "payable direct to the Hillandale Golf Club."

According to historian and former Durham resident James Leyburn, who as a young boy caddied for his father, the local Presbyterian minister, "the quality of play on the golf links was not of high caliber, despite the efforts of the Scots professional . . . At a

tournament in 1915, for example, the winning score for eighteen holes was one hundred and fourteen." Leyburn's father, Dr. E. R. Leyburn, was minister to both George Watts and John Hill, and he and Watts had a standing game once a week. Having been an eyewitness to those matches, James Leyburn recalled that George Watts averaged around fifty-seven for nine holes, considerably over par for the course, which was thirty-five and a half.

Explaining the half stroke, former Hillandale pro Luke Veasey said the 210-yard, three-and-a-half-par hole was designated as such for good reason: the fairway curved around the reservoir of the city waterworks in such a way that the green was impossible to reach in one stroke from the tee, but it was too near to warrant two strokes. Veasey believed there was not another hole anywhere in the world incorporating a half stroke in its par. But researchers for *Ripley's Believe It or Not* informed him there was, and *Golf Digest* agreed that one did indeed exist at a course in Scotland. "But I still think it's the only hole in the world that's never been parred," said Veasey, now retired but still devoted to the interests of Hillandale and something of an authority on its past history.

A member's handbook, printed in 1915, indicates that the Durham Country Club was a real bargain by today's standards. For a $50 stock certificate, or a $25 initiation fee, an eligible Durham man could become an active member, with dues of $24 a year. Lady members paid a $10 initiation fee and yearly dues of $6, and associate members (wives and sons under the age of twenty) were liable for only $6 a year. Non-resident members (there were four in 1915) paid dues of $10 per annum, but no initiation fee. For those sums, which appear minuscule today, whole families could enjoy golf (for an extra $24 a year), meals provided by the Café Department, and Club Day every Saturday, when afternoon tea was served to the membership and no other parties were allowed. The only restaurants in Durham at the time were the New York Café on Main Street, Adcock's on Mangum Street, and the People's Quick Lunch on Parrish Street, so the privilege of dining out in an exclusive atmosphere no doubt was an added incentive for wives to put gentle pressure on their husbands to join, although how much business the kitchen did is not known.

In 1915 there were 126 members, and although the club was "out in the country," transportation was no problem because the Durham Traction Company, of which member R. H. Wright was president, provided twenty-minute service "from the center of town, the through car for the Country Club leaving on the hour, twenty minutes past, and forty minutes past." It is safe to say that neither golf nor club life would have flourished as it did in Durham had it not been for the trolley car, for only a privileged few people owned automobiles at that time.

Because no institution survives without rules, the Durham Country Club had its share, but penalties and restrictions were mercifully few. Female residents of Durham County who were not club members could be invited there by any member, but "no male resident of Durham County, who is not a member of the club, can be taken to the Club House, or invited there, except under penalty of $5 by the member acting as host." Also, any member who broke a rule or engaged in any misconduct "which

Left to right: Claude Currie, unidentified, John Sprunt Hill and W. E. Sledge on the fairways at Hillandale.

may tend to endanger the order, character or welfare of the Club" was subject to suspension, or even expulsion, by the board of governors; and no member could serve on that board unless he was a stockholder. Twenty-five shares of stock was the most any member could own, and statistics for 1913 reveal that those who owned the most were George Watts, B. N. Duke and Julian Carr, which was not surprising. They were, after all, the city's three remaining millionaires (Washington Duke had died and J. B. Duke had moved to New York), and as such they had their reputations to maintain.

By 1920, Hill had added a second nine holes to the golf course and listed among the best players at the time were George Lyon, E. B. (Buck) Lyon, W. J. Griswold, George Watts, I. F. Hill, John Sprunt Hill,

A. P. Gilbert, E. J. Green, M. A. Briggs, J. M. Lipscomb, J. H. Mahler, T. B. Fuller, the Reverend E. R. Leyburn, R. L. Bishop and H. R. Goodall. Among that group there were a few whose idiosyncrasies set them apart and caught the attention of the late Claude Carrie, who recalled at Hillandale's fiftieth-anniversary celebration: "John Lipscomb had the record for the number of balls in the lake on number one—seven, together with [his] set of clubs and bag"; and "Charlie Lawson had an Airedale dog that would take off when he made his shot and sit down by his ball." Currie also remembered, on that occasion, that John Sprunt Hill's brother, Isham Faison Hill, who was penny wise with a vengeance, "had the first wooden peg for a tee, which he preserved for years by anchoring it by a string and weight."

Hillandale's founder made a number of changes in the course before he gave it, in 1940, to the Central Carolina Bank and Trust Company "as trustee for the Durham Foundation, to be operated as a recreational facility by its authorized board," according to Currie; but before that time he maintained it "at great personal cost in time and money . . . There are no real records to show the cost of this to him, but it is easy to determine that this 150 acres of land with an eighteen-hole golf course and other improvements could not be replaced today with an expenditure of a half million dollars."

Because Claude Currie's "today" was in 1961, one wonders what Hillandale Golf Course will be worth in the year 2011, when it reaches the venerable age of 100.

Today it is a public course, and its well-stocked pro shop was evaluated best in the country for 1987, 1988, 1992 and 1997 by the Professional Golfers of America. Current pro Zack Veasey and his four assistants give about forty lessons a week during the season, and some 50,000 rounds of golf are played each year at Hillandale.

The old clubhouse was torn down in 1962, but there's a picture of it in a glass case hanging on the wall of the modern brick-and-glass structure that replaced it, and it is a poignant reminder of John Sprunt Hill's "belief in the great civic and therapeutic value of a home-town golf course for the use of his fellow townsmen."

# FIFTY SIX

## An "exclusive" new suburb in Durham
## spawned Hope Valley Country Club

The first solo non-stop flight across the Atlantic Ocean, the first "talking" motion picture, and the advent of Durham's first "high class suburban development centered about a country club and golf course" all occurred during 1927, when materialism was rampant in America and Durham, like the rest of the nation, was enjoying a spectacular economic boom, especially in real estate. Because more people were buying automobiles, life in suburbia was beginning to make sense to some of the successful members of the city's established families. As early as 1924, they began to view their established neighborhoods as too crowded, too "old-timey," and too close to the sprawling tobacco factories and cotton mills that belched their noxious fumes into the atmosphere from dawn to dark and blew their raucous whistles morning, noon and night.

As this state of mind became increasingly vocal, land developers and real-estate agents began to smell opportunity, and in 1925 they started to sniff that heady elixir in earnest, thanks to James Buchanan Duke. The tobacco tycoon's gift of forty million dollars to Trinity College that year sparked a considerable amount of talk, not only in Durham but throughout the state, and when word spread that Buck Duke's new university was not going to provide housing for its new faculty, landowners near what was to be the new Duke campus came to attention.

Durham physician L. S. Booker and the Durham-based Rand and Hessee Agency, who together owned over 600 acres of prime farmland half way between Durham and Chapel Hill, must have been pleased. And Smith Richardson, president of Greensboro's Vick Chemical Company, having acquired just under 500 acres adjoining these two tracts, no doubt was equally pleased. But the two individuals who, apparently, were most vitally interested in this recent turn of events were R. J. Mebane, an automobile salesman in Greensboro, and W. L. Sharpe, a real-estate man in the neighboring town of Burlington, and they became the catalysts for the area that today is known as Hope Valley.

Convinced that "a residential area to take care of the growth of Duke University" was a must, and that the University of North Carolina also needed housing, the two men set out to buy the three tracts of land owned by Booker, the Rand and Hesse Agency, and Smith Richardson. Because Mebane, at least, was part of an "old boy network" that included Claiborne Carr, president of both the Durham Hosiery Mill and the First National Bank of Durham, it can be presumed that their friendship facilitated matters to some extent. Carr being a known proponent of a new country club for Durham also may have helped, as did the support of Gilbert C. White and John A. Buchanan who, like Carr and others, wanted to erase Durham's image as "a working man's town."

But however the groundwork was laid, it was at least partially in place on the second day of January 1926, when White, Buchanan and Carr agreed to join forces with Mebane and Sharpe, provided they could line up 250 prospective members of a new club. These members would be given "the right and privilege of purchasing one of the lots bordering on the golf course" and a "fifty percent reduction from your standard scale of prices" if they used the lots for building their own homes. The self-appointed committee of three assured the real-estate men that it would present the idea "at a meeting during the coming week," and when the Durham Chamber of Commerce convened for its annual dinner a few days later, Gilbert White broached the question and, as expected, received a favorable response.

Mebane and Sharpe, in the meantime, had already set up shop on the ground floor of the Washington Duke Hotel building, an ideal location in the heart of the business district. Sharpe, although president of the company, remained in Burlington, but Mebane, as secretary and treasurer, had moved to Durham and was in the process of building a home in Hope Valley, a region that, as yet, had no water, no sewers, and only one road.

Even in the rawest stages of its infancy, however, Hope Valley had a phenomenal asset in the person of "Jess" Mebane, who could, it was said, "sell someone a dollar bill for five dollars and leave the buyer satisfied with the transaction." He had come to Durham fired with enthusiasm, and his goal was to create a residential section similar to Irving Park, in Greensboro, where he had formerly lived, and where Smith Richardson also was a longtime resident.

Mebane exuded the kind of charisma to which neither man, woman nor child was immune, and he was salesman par excellence for the new suburb that still existed, for the most part, in the minds of a few visionaries who wanted a posh new way of life. His obvious conviction that Hope Valley was geographically perfect, would one day be extremely beautiful, and undoubtedly would prove the ideal place in which to bring up healthy, happy children was contagious, and his advertisements reflecting that philosophy began to appear regularly in *The Durham Morning Herald.*

Repeatedly advising the populace to "Live In Hope Valley For The Whole Family's Sake," Jess Mebane put his money where his mouth was long before that phrase had been coined, and became the first to build there. He used as the nucleus for his new home an antebellum farmhouse, said to be the oldest in Durham County, and had it moved from its original location on the highway (now Hope Valley Road) to Chelsea Circle, a half-moon-shaped street bordering the golf course.

With careful renovation and the addition of two

Robert Jesse
and
Pearl Long
Mebane,
"Jess & Pearl"

large one-and-a-half story wings and three porches, it became a spacious eleven-room dwelling; and expert landscaping and formal gardening made it a showplace that attracted other early builders.

And because its owners were charming, gregarious, and blessed with a talent for hospitality, the Mebane house became an advertisement, of sorts, for the "good" life among the "beautiful" people, a life that the local chamber of commerce would begin to promote as soon as Hope Valley Country Club became a non-stock, non-profit organization.

ON FEBRUARY 18, 1926, about a month after the Durham Chamber of Commerce had endorsed the for-

mation of a new country club and appointed a committee to lay the groundwork for further action, C. M. Carr, G. C. White, J. M. Lipscomb, S. J. Nicholson, R. J. Mebane, K. P. Lewis, G. W. Hill, W. B. Guthrie, R. E. Dillard, R. L. Flowers, D. W. Horton, and J. F. Royster drove to Raleigh and presented themselves at the office of the secretary of state. There they announced their intention of incorporating the Hope Valley Country Club and stated as its reason for being the promotion of "social recreation and intercourse among its members," as well as the promotion and encouragement of both indoor and outdoor athletic games and exercises.

These were to include golf, tennis, croquet, bowl-

The house that Jess Mebane built, on Chelsea Circle in Hope Valley, is currently owned by Dr. and Mrs. William P. J. Peete.

Right: House as it looks fronting the golf course. Below: House as it appears facing Chelsea Circle.

ing, swimming, automobiling, and all other health-ful sports, games, and amusements.

A certificate of incorporation was drawn up, and the then secretary of state, W. N. Everett, set his hand and affixed his official seal on the document the following day, February 19, 1926.

The first officers of the new non-stock, non-profit organization were G. C. White, president; K. P. Lewis and C. M. Carr, vice-presidents; P. N. Constable, secretary; and T. C. Worth, treasurer; and with Jess Mebane as their guide and mentor, they began the business of transforming an idea into reality. That included signing up members (they wanted 250); borrowing money (they needed $35,000); hiring "name" architects (Donald Ross, of New York and Pinehurst, for the golf course; Milburn and Heister, of Washington, D.C., for the clubhouse); inspecting land and selecting building sites (100 acres for the course, nine for the house); and searching out the right individuals for the jobs of club manager and golf professional.

Mrs. Louise Buchanan Stubbs of Sumter, S.C., widowed sister of John A. Buchanan, was hired for the managerial position, filled it with grace and expertise, and brought with her a superb cook, Josephine Knox, whose mouthwatering low-country cuisine both titillated and satisfied the palates of appreciative club diners for a number of years.

Hope Valley's first golf "pro" also moved to Durham from Sumter, where he held a similar position at an Army officers club. Originally from Monifieth, Scotland, thirty-three-year-old Marshall Crichton remained at the club for thirty-four years, made countless friends in his adopted city, and was held in high esteem by all who knew him.

Crichton was an excellent golfer who continued to improve, winning the N.C. Open more than once and, in 1949, taking first honors at the PGA Seniors in Dunedin, Florida.

"Golf is a mental game," he often said to the uninitiated who came to him for instruction, and with each hopeful dubber who yearned to play like Bobby Jones or Glenda Collett, he was infinitely patient and consistently amiable. He became an overseer, of sorts, for the prestigious Donald Ross, who designed the 6,532-yard course that, in a few years, became "as good as any in the Carolina Golf Association," according to Durham's chamber of commerce.

Crichton remembered, many years later, that the land for the course was cleared with mule-drawn "pans," a laborious process but the only one in use at that time, at least in Durham County.

Donald Ross, who emigrated from Scotland in 1899, designed and/or renovated over 600 golf courses during his lifetime, and left his inimitable stamp on fairways, bunkers and greens in Canada and Cuba; and in the United States of America, twenty-five all told.

According to one golf historian, Ross's fairways were not very wide, his roughs were not very heavy, and his greens were "smallish," which meant that every approach to them had to be definitely pinpointed in order to be successful. The No. 2 course at Pinehurst, where he spent his later years until his death in 1948, is reputedly Ross's best effort; but to Hope Valley golfers in 1927, their own links was the best in Durham and they took to it with great enthusiasm as soon as it was playable.

On July 31, 1927, Mebane and Sharpe's ad in *The Durham Morning Herald* was, more or less, a wrap-

Louise Stubbs, Marshall Crichton, hostess and golf professional at Hope Valley Country Club.

Newly finished clubhouse at Hope Valley Country Club.

up of what had been going on in Durham for over a year. A picture of the "unique" club and the announcement that its opening the next day would be "an event of considerable civic importance," dominated one entire page.

A formal opening and dedication was planned for late summer or early fall (actually, it did not take place until the following year), and at that time a large number of "prominent people" from all over the state were to be invited to take part in a day-long celebration that would afford all of Durham and the surrounding vicinity an opportunity to see the clubhouse.

In the meantime, the ad continued, the public was invited to drive out and see the four almost completed homes in the new suburb, the 18-hole Donald Ross golf course, put in at a cost of $85,000, "with the flags flying on the greens," and the "large and pretty" swimming pool still under construction.

The clubhouse, designed by Aymar Embury, "the famous designer of club houses," had been furnished and decorated by "one of the most prominent interior decorators in the South" and would be the scene of many special luncheons, teas, bridge parties and assorted meetings.

Why Embury was mentioned, and the prominent southern firm of Milburn and Heister was overlooked has never been explained, but two local architects have supposed that famous Aymar was hired as a consultant by Milburn and Heister, who drew the plans for the clubhouse and sent Yancy Milburn, son of the founder, to oversee its construction. The new

*Hope Valley Country Club*

club, it seemed, was off to a flying start, but its progress was to be far from smooth, as it turned out.

THE FORMAL DEDICATION OF Hope Valley Country Club, featuring North Carolina Governor Angus W. McLean; Kennesaw Mountain Landis, the "high commissioner" of baseball; and W. J. Brogden, a justice of the state Supreme Court and also a Durham native, took place early in 1928, when Durham was riding high on the Coolidge-Hoover wave of prosperity that was sweeping the entire country toward financial destruction, but only a few prophets of doom would admit it.

With the exception of farmers, most people were better off, or thought they were, than they had been since before World War I, and a Big Bull Market that

simply would not quit, plus that recent and marvelous innovation called the installment plan, made it possible for many Durham citizens to buy cars, radios, refrigerators and, yes, even lots in Hope Valley. These half-acre parcels of beautiful wooded land were priced at $3,000 each, but could be had for half that amount provided the buyer agreed to build a house on his newly acquired property within the year. And the house could be financed easily, at three and a half percent, with a loan from the First National Bank of Durham, whose president, Claiborn Carr, was one of the new suburb's biggest boosters.

To be sure, a home in Hope Valley would not be cheap. It could not cost less than $8,500, the owner would have to connect it to a common sewer at his own expense, and the rate for water would be double that paid in the city, but exclusivity was not to be had for nothing. Being able to go to sleep at night secure in the knowledge that no stores nor factories nor businesses nor hospitals nor asylums nor "place[s] of public resort" would ever be built in Hope Valley; that neither signs nor billboards nor privies would ever deface its landscape; that all fences would be solidly built of brick, stone, concrete or metal; and that nobody would be allowed to keep pigs was worth something, after all.

And so was the fact that "for the purpose of achieving and at all times maintaining an attractive and artistic type of architectural beauty" all prospective homeowners would have to submit their house plans to a committee of three local architects for approval. Homes could vary in value, but by no means would anything go up in Hope Valley that was either extremely eccentric or, God forbid, "tacky," and the architectural committee selected by Mebane and Sharpe Realty Company would ensure that such never happened.

Justifying the expectations of the developers, among the first homes to be built in the new suburb were those of Duke doctors and professors W. A. Brownell, Harvey Branscomb, W. C. Davison, G. S. Eadie, Wiley Forbus, Paul Gross, William McDougall, A. S. Pearse, S. B. Shealer, D. T. Smith and H. E. Spence.

Other early builders were Durham businessmen R. J. Mebane (the first), J. H. Erwin Jr., Hubert Teer, P. N. Constable, T. E. Cheek, R. B. Fuller, H. M. Snow, W. F. Franck, Watts Norton and George Lyon. But although the steady sounds of bulldozers, hammers and saws was music to the ears of Mebane and Sharpe Realty, town dwellers were not responding to "Live In Hope Valley For The Whole Family's Sake" as rapidly as the company had hoped.

Nevertheless, club membership increased steadily, and when it reached 400 in 1929, the board of governors decided to close it. According to a member's bulletin distributed that year, approximately 1,200 men, women and children were enjoying "the extraordinary advantages" of the beautiful eighteen-hole golf course, a golf professional of outstanding reputation, two excellent sand-clay tennis courts, an exceptionally large and extremely sanitary swimming pool supervised by an expert lifeguard, a stable of fifteen saddle horses, several sylvan bridle paths, many winding trails for hikers, and a club cafe with "a wide reputation for the excellence of its food, service and artistic appointments."

And all of these "very real and valuable privilege[s]" were so reasonable, said the bulletin—they came with a $100 initiation fee and dues of $15 per quarter, a real bargain, especially in view of the fact that initiation fees at some clubs in North Carolina were as high as $2,500!

Another bargain during those early years was the Tuesday morning bridge luncheon for ladies. Contract bridge was new on the scene and becoming very popular with the club's female contingent, and even more popular was the food that followed the game—chicken salad, hot rolls, iced tea and a sumptuous dessert, all for 25 cents.

But the ultimate bargain was the annual dinner, an unbelievable gastronomic experience that, in 1931,

Gilbert C. White, left, at club with R. J. Mebane, C. B. Keen, Tom O'Brien, Murray Jones (standing)

Golfers Eric Johnson, G. C. White, W .F. Carr and Marshall Crichton

consisted of celery hearts; Canape Martadella; a choice of fried chicken, baked country ham, or braised sweetbreads under glass; rice croquettes with cheese sauce and garden peas in cream; a choice of frozen fruit salad, Biscuit Tortoni, or raspberry ice cream; and demi tasse. For that feast, members paid the sum of one dollar. (According to Hope Valley's present manager, the annual dinner will cost around $40 per person.)

The club's real drawing card, however, was golf, which by 1929 had become almost a consuming passion with many Durham citizens. A chamber of commerce brochure boosting the city that year said "the beautiful links of the suburban club are daily packed with the devotees of the alluring pastime," and listed those seen most frequently at Hope Valley as G. C.

White, R. J. Mebane, W. J. O'Brien, Lamar Weaver, E. I. Bugg, E. B. Bugg, S. C. Chambers, W. L. Foushee, C. M. Carr, W. F. Carr, T. F. Southgate, Austin Carr, L. D. Kirkland, S. J. Nicholson, R. B. Fuller, G. W. Carr, W. H. Ruffin, S. C. Brawley, W. J. O'Connor, T. W. Winston, William Lickle, Bob Montgomery, Dr. Foy Roberson and Judge W. G. Bramham.

"Those of the fair sex," the brochure continued, "are Mrs. Robert Mebane, Mrs. W. A. Blount, Mrs. Watts Hill, Mrs. Richard Thigpen, Mrs. James Cobb, Mrs. Dr. Epperson, Mrs. W. J. O'Connor, Mrs. Page Harris, Mrs. Austin Carr, Mrs. T. J. O'Brien and Mrs. J. Eric Johnson."

Of the thirty-five people on that list, only three lived in Hope Valley, a fact of such vital concern to Jess Mebane that he persuaded Smith Richardson to construct eleven homes to put up for sale, believing that the appearance of houses in the development would promote more interest in selecting Hope Valley as a place to live. The homes went up, but, unfortunately, the market went down, and on "Black Tuesday," October 29, 1929, the world witnessed what has been described as the greatest stock market catastrophe of all time. And when the Big Bull collapsed, it almost crushed Hope Valley and the club that was its heart. But like Don Marquis's famous cat, Mehitable, there was "Life in the Old Girl yet!"

IF MOST PEOPLE THOUGHT Tuesday October 29, 1929, was the blackest day in American financial history, they had another think coming, as the saying goes, for the economy grew steadily worse during the next four years.

Strangely enough however, as businesses collapsed and banks failed and bread lines grew and despairing executives jumped out of office windows, what some people thought and what they said—and that included the president of the United States and the president of Hope Valley Country Club—were entirely different things.

For instance:

Herbert Hoover said, in May 1930, "We have now passed the worst and with the continued unity of effort, we shall rapidly recover." Then he predicted that business would be normal by the fall. But before the year was out, over 1,000 banks had failed and six million people were unemployed.

Gilbert C. White said, in July of 1930, "The financial condition of the club is considered to be excellent, probably better than any other club in the State." Then he explained that because the club had been $27,000 in debt for three years and "it has become embarrassing," the board of governors was issuing $24,000 worth of six percent mortgage bonds, at $500 each, and was asking forty-eight members to buy at least one of them. "We hope that the value of those bonds as an investment in the club will impel you to purchase one of those bonds," said White in a letter to the men the board considered solvent enough to come up with $500; and it can be presumed that those gentlemen complied, and a happy issue did come out of those particular sufferings, for the club continued to function.

In spite of the fact that things appeared to be normal, the stock market crash continued to dominate conversation on the fairways, around the nineteenth hole in the men's locker room, and at the Tuesday morning bridge parties during the summer of 1930.

Then, when it became known that Mebane and Sharpe Realty Company was pulling out of Hope Valley, Inc. and the attractive and popular Mebanes were selling their home and moving to Chapel Hill, the impact of Black Tuesday was felt all over again among the eighteen families living in the little community that had started out with such promise.

What, they wondered, was going to happen to Hope Valley?

Smith Richardson, of Greensboro, president of Vick Chemical Company, the Piedmont Financial Company, and the Richardson Realty Company may well have wondered the same thing; and to salvage his $612,000 investment in the Durham suburb, he made H. W. Boone head of Hope Valley, Inc. and sent him to the Bull City to collect rents on houses and payments on lots, and also to handle maintenance and general repairs.

Collecting bills did not endear Richardson's deputy to his debtors, and Boone later said he "often had to park his car on back streets and walk through alleys so as to not be harassed by the residential pests who wanted improvements at a time when the scarcity of money made such improvement impossible."

Money was, indeed, scarce and becoming scarcer, and in 1932, when over thirteen million Americans were out of work and stocks and bonds were still plummeting, some people were staying in their Hope Valley homes only because they could not sell them. As time went on, more and more of them let their servants go, wore the same clothes season after season, and began to resign from the country club. During that "cruelest year" of the Depression, many played only miniature golf, if they played at all; and instead of going to the movies they turned on their radios and listened to the adventures of Amos and Andy, proprietors of the Fresh Air Taxicab Company, or to the crooning of Rudy Vallee, the Vagabond Lover. (Stock in RCA, incidentally, which had dropped to twenty-six in 1929, was selling at two and a half in 1932.)

Nevertheless, rock bottom was still to come, and it arrived the very day Herbert Hoover stepped down as president and Franklin Delano Roosevelt took his place.

On March 4, 1933, the American banking system failed and stunned Durham citizens, like their counterparts all over the United States, began to wonder if the country was going to survive. But Roosevelt told them, in his inaugural address a few hours later, that they had nothing to fear but fear itself, and what followed is history: ten days later, banks began to re-open, beer was declared legal after thirteen years of Prohibition, and Roosevelt began the "Fireside Chats" that boosted American morale to the point that, in what seemed like almost no time, people were talking about his "New Deal," instead of the stock market crash.

But in spite of the NRA, the WPA, the CCC, the AAA, the TVA and all the other alphabetical reforms of the New Deal, the effects of the crash on Hope Valley, Inc. were disastrous, and in August of 1935 it went into "voluntary receivership" and all of the unsold land was divided among "interested parties," i.e., Smith Richardson and Dr. L. S. Booker.

It was said that Booker sold his property at a public auction "for practically nothing," and although Richardson never regained his entire investment, he held on until 1960 and had the satisfaction of seeing sixty-one families living in the area he was largely responsible for developing and, later, saving.

As for the country club, "It was only by the strictest economies, augmented by personal endorsements of club obligations by members of the Board of Governors, that the storm was weathered," an early club bulletin states: and a former member recalls that Dr. W. C. Davison, dean of Duke University's Medical School, lent his support to the tune of forty memberships, which he bought for young Durham doctors "not to promote interest in the club, but to help the club remain intact."

A slowly improving economy, engendered by government-induced production and spending, also helped. Around 1939 the board decided it was time to forge ahead by constructing a pro shop, caddy house and grill room; remodeling locker rooms for men and boys (never mind women), improving and beautifying the golf course, and building a children's playground.

To help defray the cost, a golf privileges fee was added to the resident membership fee, and a few years later that fee itself was increased substantially, as it would continue to increase periodically throughout the coming years. Assessing members in order to make improvements also would come into vogue and, inevitably, foment dismay. At times, it would even inspire creativity, as was the case with the late William E. Stauber, a gifted and irreverent member who wrote, to the tune of "Home on the Range:"

> Oh, give me a Club
> Where it's easy to rub
> Elbows with the Proud and Profane;
> Where seldom is heard
> A discouraging word
> 'Til assessments are mentioned again.
> Hope! Hope Valley Club!
> "Rest Home" for the Proud and Profane,
> Where seldom is heard
> A discouraging word . . .
> What good would it do to complain?

The "Hope Valley Club Song" has many more verses worth sharing; and the club has many more interesting chapters in its seventy-six year history, also worth sharing but unfortunately too numerous to be contained in anything less than a book of its own.

AUTHOR'S NOTE: *Much of Hope Valley's history is contained in the fabric of its original homes and its clubhouse, all built at least seventy-five years ago. But it was the people who lived in those houses, and played at the club who were to give the community its flavor, its legends and its secrets. In this writer's memory, the most unforgettable of those were the R. J. Mebanes, Hope Valley's "first family," who lived in its first house.*

*The Shepherd-Mebane-Peete home, said to be the oldest in Durham County, had been moved from Hope Valley Road to 2814 Chelsea Circle by Jess Mebane, formerly of Greensboro, who developed Hope Valley. Extensive renovations, additions, decoration, and landscaping transformed the original farmhouse into a showplace that became the center for many wonderful parties. The charming, indefatigable Mebanes, by their own example, encouraged residents to play golf and tennis, to ride horseback, to swim, to attend weekly bridge games and monthly dances in the club ballroom, and to enjoy the good life.*

*The Mebane household was comprised of parents Jess and Pearl; their children, Robert, Anne and Esther; their widowed sister-in-law Sadie Mebane and her sons, Cummins and Gilmer (aka Cump and Gip); and Grandmother Mebane and her "spinster" daughter Annie (aka Mamoni and Partner). The six-bedroom house seemed capable of expanding to fit any number, and the dining room table, which easily seated twelve, often made room for more, including me.*

*The summer of 1929 was one of my happiest in Hope Valley, where we had already lived on Dover*

Road for two years and long since adjusted to being "out in the country" instead of on Main Street in bustling downtown Durham. My father, true to his Scottish roots, had fallen in love with golf, and my mother with her new house, so different from our rambling Victorian home in town. The Dover Road house boasted an electric stove, refrigerator, and furnace, and three gleaming white-tiled bathrooms. Such conveniences kept my mother smiling and singing much of the day, and kept my eighteen-year-old sister and my fourteen-year-old self free of household chores.

For us, life could not have been sweeter. With our new friends, the Mebane girls, we played tennis when no adults were using the courts; mounted the slowest, most predicable horses in the Hope Valley Riding Stables whenever we could scrape up a dollar for an hour's ride, and swam in the club pool. Evenings, at our house or the Mebane's, we mostly waited for boys to check by, and mostly they did. Then we danced, sometimes not too successfully, to jazz from a self-playing Magnavox. All of us, boys and girls, were practicing to be grown-ups in what is now called a "safe environment"—under watchful parental eyes.

It seems pretty tame in retrospect, but whenever I look back to the stock market crash and the Great Depression that nearly destroyed Hope Valley, I see it as one of the best of times, before one of the worst of times made us grow up too soon.

# Radio's "Amos 'n Andy" met in Durham

George Bernard Shaw once said the most unforgettable things about America were Niagara Falls, the Rocky Mountains and *Amos 'n' Andy*, but many people have long since forgotten the longest-running act in the history of broadcasting—*Amos 'n' Andy* was on the air for thirty-two years—and many more probably never even heard of it. What's relevant here, however, is that most of those who do remember Freeman Gosden and Charles Correll, whose stage names were household words in this country for more than three decades, may not know that the two men met for the first time in Durham, during the summer of 1919.

They came, separately, as new employees of the Joe Bren Productions Company, a Chicago-based firm that produced local talent shows for fraternal and charitable groups, and they shook hands on August 12, 1919, under the auspices of the Benevolent Protective Order of Elks.

Earlier that year, Durham Lodge Number 586 of the BPOE, needing money for its current benevolences, had approached the Bren company, and the end result of that initial contact was *The Jollies of 1919*, whipped into shape by stage-and-production manager Charles Correll and song-and-dance instructor Freeman Gosden, who had never seen each other until they arrived in Durham.

Correll, an ex-bricklayer who had always wanted to be an actor, and Gosden, an ex-tobacco salesman who was equally stage-struck, evidently did such a good job for the Elks in 1919 that when members of Lodge Number 586 decided to put on another fundraiser in 1921, they again called on the Bren company and Gosden and Correll paid a second visit to Durham in late August of that year. By then they were friends and obviously enjoyed the pleasant notoriety of being "show people" in a small southern town, but it is safe to say that they had no idea, in 1921, that they would one day be radio's highest-paid entertainers.

The scripts, music, costumes and scenery for *The Jollies of 1921* were furnished by the Bren company, and with the exception of Gosden, the actors were local citizens, all sorts and conditions of men and women eager to get behind the footlights and, for two nights running, be somebody else. Many were

Radio's 'Amos 'n' Andy' characters Correll, left, and Gosden.

recruited by Mary Toms, a pretty, popular and persuasive member of Durham's "younger set," who apparently had little trouble persuading friends and acquaintances that it would be fun to be in the *Jollies*.

Those who survived the tryouts and a week of intense practice were these young ladies: Mona Wilkinson, Josephine and Eleanor Erwin, Julia Carver, Virginia Green, Christine James, Elizabeth Felts, Matilda Bryant, Eloise Hannah, Mabel Duke Goodall,

Dorothy Watkins and Mary Toms; and the following young men, the majority of whom, naturally, were members of Lodge Number 568: James E. Stagg, Eugene Erwin, J. Mallory Hackney, Tom Stokes, E. K. Powe Jr., W. G. Frasier, Vernon Suitt, A. S. Noell, W. S. Markham, M. F. Murdaugh, J. C. Allen, H. E. Whitted, J. W. Spransy, Gordon Warren, Charles Crabtree, Bonnie Barbee, Oliver Lee Skinner, H. J. Hatcher, Dr. W. P. Wilson, Sam McCracken, Gene

Hughes, T. D. Bass, J. R. Bagwell, T. O. Pace, Melton McLaurin, Norman Proctor, Tom Winston, Theodore Heflin, W. L. Wilkerson, J. S. Pickett, S. J. Barbee, J. White, R. W. Honeycutt, and W. G. Wegener.

Mary Toms, the late Mrs. E. M. Cameron, remembered Freeman Gosden as "most attractive and a wonderful dancer" who also could sing, play the ukulele, and clown around as a slapstick comedian. She remembered too—and who wouldn't—that she and Gosden, playing a French maid named "Vivette" and a bellboy named "Buttons," sang a duet called "He's Me Kiddo," which got special mention in a review that later appeared in *The Durham Morning Herald.*

But better than memory was the playbill in Mary Cameron's possession, which makes it possible to imagine what took place on Monday and Tuesday evenings, September 5 and 6, at Durham's Academy of Music. Forerunner of the Durham Auditorium that houses the present-day Carolina Theater, the academy regularly showed movies and also booked a fair amount of live professional entertainment that included minstrel shows. These always featured white comedians in burnt-cork make-up, singing and dancing and cracking slightly off-color jokes, some of them aimed at prominent local citizens.

Although as an art form the minstrel show was on the wane and destined for oblivion, it was still popular at the time. It was also the best vehicle for a group of Elks Club members who, for the most part, had no theatrical talent but were sure to get a laugh from the audience simply by blacking their faces and "cutting the fool" on the academy stage.

So the first act of *The Jollies of 1921* was titled "In Minstreland" and featured Freeman Gosden and

twenty-nine well-known Durhamites, a smattering from Trinity college but the majority from the city's business and professional ranks. Individually, they represented various fields of endeavor—banking, education, medicine, merchandising, manufacturing, public safety, law enforcement and journalism—and a week of rigorous rehearsals under the tutelage of Correll and Gosden, the Chicago "pros," had convinced them that there was, indeed, no business like show business. It could take them out of their ruts, put them on a stage, and treat them to the heady sound of laughter and applause, and they were up for it.

An advertisement in the previous day's *Durham Morning Herald* touted the show as "a sure cure for the blues," with "the greatest cast ever assembled in Durham" and "the most beautiful costumes and scenery ever shown in any amateur production." The music would be "snappy," the jokes would be "clever" and, the ad warned the public, "You will be disappointed if you don't go." Determined, apparently, not to disappoint their audience were Frank Bennett and J. V. Dermott, who would sing anywhere at any time singing was called for and were billed as "Balladists." Bennett, the local fire chief, sang "A Dream of Your Smile," and Dermott, who sold and installed heating equipment, rendered "Give Me Your Love All the Time" to an assemblage that seemed prepared to love everything on the program.

They cheered when W. G. "Bill" Frasier, future owner of Durham's leading jewelry store, aped the famous minstrel, Bert Williams, in his rendition of "Somebody Else, Not Me"; and they clapped and whistled when Hugh Whitted, owner of Whitted's Sport

Shop, impersonated Al Jolson singing "Mammy." Jolson had worked in minstrel shows for four years before he became famous on Broadway.

And so it went throughout the evening. Audience enthusiasm mounted, as planned by Correll and Gosden, when the well-bred young ladies they had turned into chorus girls appeared in "the most beautiful costumes . . . ever shown in any amateur production"; and it peaked, as planned, when a handful of well-bred young men appeared "in drag" during the last scene of the last act.

As female subjects in a mythical kingdom called "Gazook," of which stockbroker E. K. Powe, Jr. was the king, Powe's queen was Gordon Warren, his royal fan bearer was Tom Stokes, and his favorite dancer, "Cleopatra," was Eugene Erwin, a seasoned performer when it came to amateur theatricals. An artist by profession and also a highly trained dancer, Erwin had no compunctions about appearing before his fellow citizens in a few gauzy veils (seven, probably),

an elaborate headdress, and plenty of makeup. His "Dance Orientale," which took place in "the Palace of the King and Queen of Gazook," inspired a *Herald* reporter to write: "The fantasy about Gazook was probably the outstanding part of the show and Eugene Erwin showed a talent that is not often seen. His dancing had real art in it and his make-up was all that could be desired for the part." The reviewer further stated that although "it wouldn't be fair or safe to pick out any one person to laud, 'He's Me Kiddo' was rich (and) we can't stop without giving special mention to the work of . . . Mary Toms."

And so it was that Freeman Gosden and Charles Correll, who would emerge as *Amos 'n' Andy* six years later, left an indelible impression in the minds of the cast of *The Jollies of 1921*. For two magic nights, each one of that small group of Durham citizens created a personal memory of show business that would remain with them always, and as everybody knows, there's no business like it.

# FIFTY EIGHT

# Durham's Rotary nearing 100th birthday

A fair amount of today's best-selling non-fiction urges us to love ourselves, to forgive ourselves, and even to "celebrate" ourselves, whatever that means, but the Durham Rotary Club apparently scorns that kind of pop psychology. At its weekly meetings it continues to remind members that their motto, "Service Above Self," still is a valid aim worth pursuing. This venerable organization, Durham's oldest existing civic club, will celebrate its one hundredth birthday in 2015, and a brief look at its beginnings will remind us that times, along with attitudes concerning the psyche, have indeed changed.

In 1915, when Durham was a small and not very pretty town of 18,000 people, it was home to a professional photographer named Waller Holladay, a rather handsome balding man with a beaky nose, light eyes, and a thoughtful expression. Inspired by a photographer friend, George Harris, a dedicated Rotarian from Washington, D.C., Holladay decided to promote a Rotary club in Durham. When polling the ranks of friendship met with some enthusiasm, he got in touch with the International Association of Rotary Clubs, in Evanston, Illinois, and stated his

intention. That august body gave him permission, on September 28, 1915, to organize a local Rotary chapter. After being schooled in the meantime by the parent organization, and also by his mentor, George Harris, Holladay set out to recruit members.

Following instructions, he made certain that those who responded favorably to his proposition were not motivated by "commercial advantages to themselves" but, instead, were willing to catch the "spirit" of Rotary. That spirit, spelled out by the club's constitution in some detail, was, in essence, a determination "to encourage and foster the ideal of service as a basic of working enterprise." Members would be expected to demonstrate, by maintaining high ethical standards not only in their personal lives, but also in their businesses and professions, that they either already had the spirit, or soon would. And of equal importance was the expectation that they would recognize "the worthiness of all useful occupation."

There was much to say about further expectations, such as "service to society" and "the advancement of international understanding, good will, and peace." These were lofty goals for small town businessmen, but Waller Holladay, imbued with the spirit he had caught from George Harris, was able to impart it to sixteen Durham men, each of them, in accordance with the rules of Rotary, representing a single business or profession. On the night of November 9, 1915, they gathered for the first time at the Malbourne Hotel on the corner of Main and Roxboro streets, sure in the knowledge that they were launching "a high class organization and that there [was] no question about it being a success and that each member [would] value his membership highly."

Not surprisingly, Waller Holladay's friend, George Harris, was on hand to represent the governor of District Four, which included Virginia, North Carolina and South Carolina, and also to stress the importance of "strict adherence to club rules and regulations," of which there were a number that would prove troublesome during the early years. Also present were twelve members of the Raleigh Rotary Club, the first and only one in the state at the time. Raleigh had agreed to sponsor Durham, and its dozen delegates had come over to assist in the initiation ceremony, the details of which, unfortunately, were not recorded for posterity.

Charter members, representing by their businesses or professions a cross section of the community, were: E. I. Bugg, hotel management; S. C. Chambers, lawyer; W. G. Frasier, jeweler; Waller Holladay, photographer; Burke Hobgood, freight transportation; D. W. Horton, retail shoes; Mahler Kramer, retail cigars and tobacco; R. L. Lindsay, public service; Orin Lloyd, retail hardware; J. H. Mahler, tobacco manufacturing; L. B. Markham, men's furnishings; T. Y. Milburn, architect; M. E. Newsom, office supplies; Holman Rawls, retail dry goods; S. W. Sparger, life insurance; N. Underwood, builder and contractor; and T. C. Worth, banker.

For some reason, the field of medicine was not represented in that original group, but by 1916 Dr. Merle T. Adkins was on the roster, as was Dr. S. D. McPherson. It can be assumed that international headquarters in Evanston gave its blessing to what appears to be a duplication but, in reality, was not, as McPherson was an eye doctor (nobody knew what an ophthalmologist was in those days) and Adkins was a general practitioner.

The powers-that-be also allowed employees of both American Tobacco Company and Liggett and Myers to belong to Rotary and got around the "absolutely no duplications" rule by suggesting that the member who worked at American be classified as "smoking tobacco" and the one at L&M be designated "tobacco, cigars and wholesale cigarette manufacturing." Clearly, rules that could not be broken could be bent a bit, on occasion, especially when it involved a Rotary Club located in the heart of Tobaccoland, USA.

Everything else about the organizational meeting went by Robert's Rules of Order, however, and those elected to office were M. E. Newsom president, Waller Holladay vice president, S. C. Chambers secretary, T. C. Worth, treasurer, and E. I. Bugg sergeant-at-arms. The first Board of Directors included Burke Hobgood, L. B. Markham, J. H. Mahler, S. W. Sparger and Mahler Kramer.

Luncheon meetings were scheduled for the first and third Tuesdays of each month, and it was decided to have a dinner meeting whenever a fifth

M. Eugene Newsom, Rotary Club's first president.

Tuesday appeared on the calendar. It was further agreed that anyone absent without good cause—and explanations had to be written to the secretary—would be fined the sum of one dollar. Nor would tardiness be tolerated. A Big Ben alarm clock would be placed on the speaker's table, and anyone who had the temerity to arrive after it went off, at 1:05 p.m., would have to pay the treasurer twenty-five cents.

Furthermore, while it was on the always-delicate subject of money, the club voted to set dues at ten dollars a quarter, with meals extra. (By 1990, meals were included in the quarterly dues, which had risen to ninety-five dollars.)

Possibly because Durham had long ago acquired a reputation among neighboring towns as an unsightly place devoted exclusively to the service of Mammon, the Rotary Club chose as its first project the beautification of an empty lot behind the city hall, which they would call Rotary Park and on which they would erect a bandstand where "suitable music would be rendered during the week and on Sundays." Thus they would show the world, and especially their judgmental neighbors to the north, east, south and west, that one of their main reasons for being was to make their town a cleaner, healthier and more beautiful place in which to live.

The idea, of course, had to be approved by Durham's governing body, the mayor and a board of aldermen, and fortunately, Rotary president Marion Eugene Newsom, whose friends called him "Gene" and whose children called him "Papa Man," was an alderman. Handsome, intelligent, extremely civic-minded and a natural-born leader, Gene Newsom was to "climb the stairs to Rotary's summit" and become its international president in 1928. So it is not surprising that, in 1916, the "honorables" that ran the city made Newsom chairman of a committee to implement the new club's first attempt to carry out its motto, "Service Above Self," by serving the city a big helping of beautification.

Eight months later, Rotary Park was a reality, a landmark the community came to regard with affection. Rotarian secretary Sidney Chambers wrote, in 1955: "The fact that it was abandoned in 1925, when the city sold the entire block where the Washington Duke Hotel now stands, and that the granite bandstand was removed to the Bennett Memorial grounds, is not important. That the Durham Rotary Club had successfully carried its first community project to completion did have far reaching results. It gave the club members a confidence that carried them with renewed enthusiasm into the even more important projects just ahead."

As it turned out, those projects took a different direction after the sinking of the *Lusitania* and the entry of the United States into World War I in the spring of 1917. The club was barely two years old, but it had already been called by *The Durham Morning Herald* "the most representative and perhaps the livest organization of men in the city." Thus it had an obligation to maintain that image during the conflict, or so it seems in retrospect, considering what those "live" men did in 1918.

Quoting briefly from club historian Sidney Chambers, that year it "appointed a War Board; supported the Thrift Stamp campaign; contributed $250 to the YMCA Blue Ridge Association for training men in YMCA war work; responded to a plea . . . for aid to Scottish sailors and soldiers; contributed to Armenian Relief Fund; and both sold and purchased Liberty Bonds."

Through the ensuing years, the Rotary Club's projects have been so numerous they boggle the mind, and all of them were brought to the public's attention during the seventy-fifth birthday celebration at the Omni Hotel on November 10, 1990. There were many speeches. Members and their wives, who have been called "Rotary Anns" since the beginning, along with ten active women members, were treated to a heady draught of nostalgia on that auspicious occasion. But getting drunk on good memories, happily, is legal. And it's also good for the soul.

# Tobacco takes Durham from hamlet to thriving city

urham was 150 years old in April 2003, and considering the fact that human beings, in increasing numbers, are living well into their nineties, 150 is not very old when you're talking about a town. But within that same time span, Durham grew faster than any other city in North Carolina, I dare say, and so much has changed during its relatively short life that it's worth noting, occasionally, just to show us how far we've come.

Officially, the town originated on April 26, 1853, when a doctor by the name of Bartlett Durham inadvertently immortalized himself by giving four acres of land that had cost him $3.80 to the North Carolina Railroad, and the railroad, in gratitude, named the new station it erected there Durhamville. By popular usage, however, the name of the little hamlet that grew up around the train station became Durham, and by what may have been sheer coincidence, it had a second beginning exactly twelve years later to the day, on April 26, 1865.

Durham's second birth, the result of what one public speaker called "a crime of petty larceny," took place when an aggregation of inebriated Union and Confederate soldiers robbed a local citizen by the name of John Green of his tobacco, which was stored in his factory near the station. Later, when the soldiers had been mustered out of their respective armies, their stories about "this mellow, fragrant leaf" went with them to other towns and cities, north and south, and "soon a prosperous market for this wonderful tobacco was established and the tonic of United States dollars began to flow to Durham in a swelling stream."

At the precise moment those carousing soldiers were filching tobacco from the hapless Green, Durham's population was 100, or thereabout, and its property value was around $15,000. It had a single tobacco factory (Green's) employing five hands, an active capital of $1,000, two small stores, a blacksmith shop, and several barrooms. And that was it. That was in the spring of 1865.

Then, in 1870, the first continental railroad opened direct coast-to-coast service and a new era began. All at once it was possible to get from New York to San Francisco for $140. The trip took seven days, but until then it had taken a month by rail and stagecoach, five months by wagon train from Missouri, and six months, by ship, around Cape Horn from the east coast. So that event began to make a difference all over the country and especially in Durham, where tobacco was waiting to be shipped and smokers were eager to get it. The cross-country railroad meant greater commerce, and that meant people in Boston could eat beef raised in Texas, people in Omaha could eat salmon caught in the Pacific and shipped in refrigerated cars, and people in Los Angeles could smoke tobacco manufactured in Durham.

It was a miracle, and it changed everything. By 1876, Durham's population jumped to 2,000 and its property value to $550,000. It had sixteen tobacco factories employing 500 hands and the active capital was $500,000. There was a hotel, six boarding houses, seven restaurants and barrooms, a newspaper, a job printing office, and thirty business operations, and all this progress was related to the manufacture and sale of tobacco. The town began attracting even more new citizens, and making money began to be the most important thing in the world. Those who had none were determined to get it, and those who already had it wanted more.

One young fellow by the name of Buck Duke, who was selling tobacco from a mule-drawn wagon, was already determined to be rich, and eventually he was. Eventually he owned ninety percent of the country's tobacco industry, and even in the depression of 1893 the American Tobacco Company, of which Duke was by then president, made a net profit of five million dollars.

Buck Duke's philosophy was tough, the way he was tough and hard and determined. "First you hit your enemies in the pocketbook, hit 'em hard," he often said, "and then you either buy 'em out or take 'em in with you." And that is exactly what Buck Duke did to almost every independent tobacco company in America, including Julian Shakespeare Carr's world-famous "Bull Factory," otherwise known as the W. T. Blackwell Company and the first one of any consequence in Durham. Carr's company was a particular plum that Buck Duke particularly wanted, and getting it must have given him particular pleasure.

While the Dukes and their partner, George Watts, and their arch rival, Julian Carr, were getting extremely rich, most average citizens of Durham were doing pretty well, too, and the exciting things that were happening elsewhere in America were affecting, and improving (in most cases), their lives.

Thomas A. Edison invented the incandescent light bulb. The bicycle and the typewriter were brand new. The elevator and something called linoleum appeared on the scene, and when a new-fangled contraption called the telephone was introduced, three thousand people across the United States subscribed to it.

Durham's first telephone exchange, backed by Julian S. Carr, George Watts and L. A. Carr, got twenty customers as soon as it was established, in 1895, at the corner of Main and Church Streets. By 1900 there were 200 local subscribers to the magneto-type phones that had to be cranked in order to signal an operator who said, once you succeeded in getting her, "Number, please?"

A lady by the name of Lydia E. Pinkham sold her first six bottles of Vegetable Compound in 1873 for five dollars, and within ten years she grossed (with the help of some Durham ladies, no doubt) $300,000 on that bitter liquid that had an eighteen percent alcohol content and was reputed to cure all kinds of "female weakness."

Other popular remedies for human ailments that were advertised in Durham's newspapers were Carter's Little Nerve Pills, Comstock's Dead Shot Worm Pellets, Mrs. Winslow's Soothing Syrup, and a nostrum called Vegetine that claimed to be a cure-all for cancer, consumption, scrofula, pimples, constipation, headache, dizziness, back pain, kidney disease and general debility.

Even in those early days, Durham mirrored the rest of the nation in styles as well as attitudes, and the nation was in the grip of Victorianism. Men wore beards or mustaches and sometimes both, and they dressed, for the most part, in dark, single-breasted suits, stiff collars and derby hats. Women were corseted and bustled, with skirts to their shoe tops and elaborate hats on their upswept hair. Men ran the country's business, voted, produced most of the art and literature, and were catered to in clubs, restaurants, saloons and barbershops, where women were not allowed.

In some ways, Durham not only was keeping up with the rest of the United States; it was forging ahead. In 1895 it was the center of the bright leaf tobacco belt in North Carolina, the first in manufacturing importance in the state, and had a population of eight thousand. The value of its real estate and personal property was $6,148,614 and second only to Wilmington, with $6,928,988.

Neither the Great Depression nor two world wars

The Durham "Renowned Around the World Sign" heralding progress, health, wealth, and success, was mounted on a three-story commercial building on Main Street. It was illuminated at night. ca. 1913.

stopped Durham's progress for long. By 1975, the population of the city and county was 149,338, property values were $1,383,458,327, retail sales were $456,140,886, and there were over 800 business, professional and industrial firms in the city. One

Durham, in 2001, was a single-city county of nearly 233,100 residents.

thing had dwindled, however: there were only seven tobacco factories, with only 4,100 people working in them, in the city that once had been known as Tobaccoland, USA. Although they still dominated the downtown scene and the smell of bright leaf tobacco still permeated the air, the handwriting was on the wall for the golden weed.

Fourteen years later, in 1989, only the Liggett Group, with its 1,146 employees, remained to remind us of Durham's origins and its former glory, and by the year 2000 it, too, was gone, one more victim of a powerful anti-smoking movement that had branded tobacco an addictive drug as well as a potentially deadly carcinogen.

Nevertheless, Durham is not only surviving, but also thriving. In this third year of the new century, we can point with pride to a combined city and county population of 218,000, approximately 5,500 businesses generating $3.3 billion in retail sales, 332 restaurants and bars (not counting "fast food" operations), fifty-nine hotels and motels, 297 churches, and four newspapers to keep us informed.

That's progress in a high degree, considering the fact that our *raison d'être*, tobacco, is currently a politically incorrect dirty word. So now we're calling ourselves The City of Medicine and, ironically enough, there's a rumor going around to the effect that current research believes "genetically altered tobacco plants could hold the key to producing a protein needed to manufacture a vaccine . . . to fight cervical cancer."

Should that happen, tobacco could come home again and, like the Prodigal Son, receive a proper welcome—singing and dancing in the streets, maybe, or a festival at the Duke Homestead . . .

It's a good thought.

# List of Photographs and Credits

# Bibliography

Andrews, R. McCants, *John Merrick: A Biographical Sketch*. Durham, 1920

Anderson, Jean B., *Durham County*. Durham: Duke University Press, 1990

Arena, J. M. and McGovern, J. P., *Davison of Duke: His Reminiscences*, Hospital Care Association.

Bassett, John Spencer and Walter Samuel Lockhart, *Old Durham Traditions*. Durham: Historical Society of Trinity College, 1906

Blomquist, Margaret M., *Recollections of Papa*. Published by the author. Durham: James Buchanan Duke Papers in the Rare Book, Manuscript and Special Collections Library, Duke University

Boyd, William K., *The Story of Durham, City of the New South*. Durham: Duke University Press, 1927

Dula, W. C., *Durham and Her People*. Durham: The Citizens Press, 1951

Durden, Robert F., *The Dukes of Durham*. Durham: Duke University Press, 1975

Durham Merchants Association. *Durham Illustrated*. Durham: The Seeman Printery, 1910

Gifford, James F., *The Evolution of a Medical Center*, Hospital Care Association.

Herndon, E. M., *The History of the Hospital Care Association, Incorporated*, Hospital Care Association

Paul, Hiram V., *History of the Town of Durham, North Carolina*. Raleigh: Edwards and Broughton & Company, 1884

Powell, William S., ed., *Dictionary of North Carolina Biography*, Vols. I, IV. Chapel Hill: University of North Carolina Press, 1979

Tilley, Nannie M., *The Bright Tobacco Industry*, 1860-1929. Chapel Hill: University of North Carolina Press, 1987

Weare, Walter B., *Black Business in the New South*. Chicago: University of Illinois Press, 1987

Webb, Mena F., *Jule Carr, General Without An Army*. Chapel Hill: University of North Carolina Press, 1987

——"The Way We Were," *Durham Sun*, May 22, 1989-December 31, 1990; *Durham Morning Herald*, March 31, 1991-May 31, 1992

Winkler, John K., *Tobacco Tycoon*. New York: Random House, 1942

Young, Betty I., *The Library of the Women's College, Duke University, 1930-1972*. Durham: The Regulator Press, 1978

——"Lillian Baker Griggs, Pioneer Librarian." *The Durham Record*, Fall 1983. 1987

# Index